# Front Line

# FRONT LINE

*Women of the New Russia*

William Millinship

Methuen

First published in Great Britain in 1993
by Methuen London
an imprint of Reed Consumer Books Ltd
Michelin House, 81 Fulham Road, London SW3 6RB
and Auckland, Melbourne, Singapore and Toronto

All photographs by William Millinship except Natalya Averina
and Alla Yemelyanova by Alexander Potapov, and those of
Yelena Djaparidze, Klavdiya Lyubeshkina and Natalya Perova
supplied by themselves

ISBN 0 413 45671 4

A CIP catalogue record for this book
is available at the British Library

Photoset in Great Britain by
Rowland Phototypesetting Ltd
Bury St Edmunds, Suffolk
Printed in England
by Clays Ltd, St Ives plc

*To the memory of my mother*

# Contents

# Foreword

The daily effort to survive in post-Communist Russia became a kind of trench warfare, with women, as usual, in the front line. Traditionally credited with immense spiritual strength and limitless resource, they inevitably took on the near-impossible tasks of feeding and clothing families in conditions of instant impoverishment, brought on by the new Government's freeing of most prices on 2 January 1992.

Prices, held down by subsidies and in some cases scarcely unchanged in decades, suddenly rocketed beyond reach and – to many Russians – beyond belief. All but a small proportion of Russians sank below the poverty line. It was at this time that I was coming to the end of my assignment in Moscow as correspondent of the *Observer*. I was looking for a way of distilling in a book what I had learnt in three extraordinary, momentous years watching a superpower trying to change its nature and face the truth about itself, but breaking up under the strain into fifteen independent republics.

I had seen a monstrous experiment come to an end at a great turning point in history. The Communist Party was decapitated. The Command Economy was on the point of collapse, but no new system had yet been put in its place. The freedoms brought by the hesitant, inconsistent reforms of Mikhail Gorbachov looked insecure, but for the time being ordinary Russians were ready, even eager, to speak their minds, perhaps because so many of them feared that a great silence might again be imposed on their land.

Some were old enough to remember pre-Revolutionary Russia and had marched for seventy years, like it or not, 'on the road to nowhere', as the bitterest slogan of the 1990s put it. They had lived through the Civil War of 1918–21, forced collectivisation, famines, real and contrived, the rush to industrialise, the terrors under Lenin and Stalin, the horrors of the Great Patriotic War against Germany in 1941–45, post-war hunger and reconstruction, the death of Stalin, Nikita Khrushchov's brief 'Thaw', the Cold War and the 'era of stagnation' under Leonid Brezhnev, the hopes raised and dashed by Gorbachov and the death of the Red Empire.

This was a moment, it seemed to me, to record the voices of people who had lived through extraordinary times. Some were at the end of their lives. Others might not for long be prepared to speak openly to a foreigner. The Soviet period was already receding into history – its cruelties and sacrifices scarcely credible. Even recent events were already taking on the inscrutable sepia tones of old photographs.

I decided to interview only women for a number of reasons. In my three years travelling around Russia and other parts of the Soviet Union, I had come to respect their energy, quick understanding, thoughtfulness, strength, sense of humour and breadth of interests. Their contribution was obviously vital to the country as workers, as well as wives and mothers. They would be the best sources of first-hand knowledge of health care, child-rearing, education. They were also, I soon discovered, willing to talk to a foreign male about sex, love and men. Perhaps they thought that, at the age of sixty-two, I was old enough to have acquired some wisdom in these subjects. I also had the feeling that they credited Westerners, in general, with advanced knowledge and experience of such matters, in which they believed Russians were backward.

I had seen for myself that Russian women had had a particularly raw deal on the Soviet road to nowhere. As the shortages of just about everything worsened during the Gorbachov years, it was women who did most of the queue-ing in empty shops, the majority of them hunting for food, clothes, vodka for their men, sweets and exercise books for their children or grandchildren. They put in time in the queues before, after and often during their working hours – for the great majority had jobs: as teachers, doctors, shop assistants, tram drivers and even in road repair gangs. In the streets you saw elderly, headscarved women plodding along with heavy plastic bags full of bread and potatoes, and young, slim women whose bodies were bent by the strain of lugging a single shopping bag. How and why did they put up with it all? There was no single, simple answer to that question, though the interviews provided clues. It was not just a matter of conditioning and resignation, for they displayed a cheerfulness, too, that was a constant, refreshing surprise.

One day in 1991 I bought a handmade rug for a British visitor in a store in central Moscow. Its price was five thou-sand roubles, at least a year's pay for the average Muscovite at the time. The shop assistant who sold it to me led me to the head of the queue at the cashier's desk. There I stood, crimson with embarrassment, while the cashier counted out five thousand roubles in ten-rouble notes, clanking out receipts from a cash till that could not count above nine roubles at a time. She kept a running total on her abacus. The process seemed interminable and I expected the queue to explode into abuse, if not violence. Instead, the women who composed it waited patiently for me to gather my yards of receipts. They smiled and joked to put me at my ease.

This sense of humour and even temper I recognised in a passage in Julia Voznesenskaya's collection of stories *The Women's Decameron*. Irishka, a secretary, has told a story about finding bananas in the course of a day's shopping and giving them away, in a gesture of superhuman generosity, at the end of it. Her companion, Emma, the theatre director, says: 'Do you think the women in the West have any concept of the joys of life? Can they understand the delight of the girl who has managed to buy a bra of her own size, or the joy of the housewife who has "shot" a kilo of smoked sausage for the holiday? Of course not! I think they have a poor life. It lacks substance.'

Galina, wife of a dissident, laughs and says: 'Yes, they don't experience our joys. I wish we didn't have to either!'

The 'joys' changed when the 'new prices' came into force in January 1992. Most of the skills needed to 'acquire' items in short supply suddenly became out of date. Now just about everything was tantalisingly available, but at prices few could afford. Yet the cheerfulness was undiminished. I met it again and again in the course of the interviews I made between January and July 1992. It was particularly evident in the three-day conversation with Kseniya Godina, who seemed to have forgotten nothing that happened to her in her eighty-two years, and who laughed at herself and the privations she had endured, as she told me her story.

It was Kseniya's sharp memory and warm character which convinced me that interviewing 'ordinary' Russian women at this time would indeed be rewarding. It also proved to be hugely enjoyable and richly educational. I knew some of the interviewees quite well already. Some were friends who had gone out of their way to help me explore and adjust to a society I knew nothing about, when I first arrived in Moscow on 19 March 1989. But I had never questioned them in detail about their lives and times. I learned something new – and found new areas of ignorance – at each encounter. I sought a variety of viewpoints and experience by meeting women of different ages, from different professional and class backgrounds and with different political convictions. Some were famous. Most were not. Friends helped me find subjects. Sometimes, one interview led to another. Some were conducted in English and one in French (with Katya, the journalist). The rest were recorded in Russian with the help of interpreters, for my grasp of that language was still not strong enough to conduct long, formal interviews.

Although I have grouped these interviews under broad subject headings, most of the conversations ranged beyond the confines of the loose grouping in which they are placed.

# Acknowledgements

Any foreign correspondent, especially early in a new post-ing, incurs debts of gratitude daily, simply because it is not possible for a sole reporter to cover every aspect of the area he or she is assigned to, without the help of people who become literally too numerous to thank individually. My debts in the Soviet Union were very heavy indeed, for I came to it with no specific qualifications, late in a career covering Western capitals. I was helped by colleagues on the *Observer*, fellow correspondents on other newspapers, Russian journalists, diplomats, officials and politicians in Russia and other Soviet republics. I owe a special long-term debt to Regula Schmid of *Le Journal de Genève*, to Pierre Bocev of *Le Figaro* and to their assistant Yevgeny Smirnov.

I was made to feel at home by many Russians who were generous in their hospitality and warm friendship. Moscow, in my experience, is difficult to come to grips with, and hard to leave. I am grateful to Donald Trelford, the Editor of the *Observer*, for sending me there at what was to be a time of high excitement and intense interest.

The book grew out of this assignment and so benefits from the help I depended on as a foreign correspondent. But there are specific debts, too. The idea of a series of inter-views came from Nora Beloff, who gave me my first part-time job on the *Observer* when she was Paris correspondent in the late 1950s. It was she who, on a trip to Moscow, met and told me about Kseniya Godina (see chapter 2) who was to spend three days taking me on a tour of Soviet history. Another *Observer* colleague, Mark Frankland, gave much-needed encouragement and practical advice both in the early stages of writing and later. Sue Jameson, Moscow correspondent of Independent Radio News and the *Evening Standard*, with whom I did a crash course in Russian in London, read the interviews in draft, and pointed out strengths and weaknesses. In London, my agent Faith Evans responded with warm enthusiasm to the idea of the book and provided essential support and guidance throughout. Her assistant, Rosie Gilbey, coaxed a manuscript out of floppy disks. My first editor, Elsbeth Lindner, gave me a strong helping hand over the obstacles in the path of a first book. Her criticism was always clear, fair and constructive. She was especially helpful in identifying gaps in the background material and in sensing the existence of valuable, unused passages in interviews. Mary O'Donovan, of Methuen, saw the book through to publication.

In Moscow, John Crowfoot helped in many ways. He introduced me to some outstanding people, interpreted during the three conversations with Yelena (Lena) Sannikova (chapter 4), and read many of the interviews in their first rough form. He saved me from errors and suggested practical improvements. So did Sergei Zakin who, with his parents, befriended me and my wife Vera from our first days in Moscow. He read the interviews in draft and made valuable comments and corrections. Others who were generous with their time and assistance, during the research and early drafting of the book, include Yelena Zolotova, Henrietta Debryakova, Marina Smirnova, Katya Ivanova, Tanya Stepanova and Valentina Vaskakova.

Canon Michael Bourdeaux kindly gave me personal insights into the workings of the Russian Orthodox Church and provided material about it from the files of Keston College at Oxford. Dr David Priestland, of Lincoln College, Oxford, read the first draft of the book and corrected many errors of fact and interpretation. John Silverlight saved me from others, when he read the proofs. For those that remain I am entirely responsible.

I owe special thanks to my family for their patience during the writing of this book, when I neglected my duties as son, brother, husband, father and grandfather. Vera joined me in Moscow and created a home there, as she had done earlier in Paris, London and Washington. She read interviews as they were written and again when the first draft was complete.

I am deeply indebted to each of the women whose conversations are recorded here. This is their book, for any value it has springs from their experiences, their characters and their comments. Only two women I approached declined to meet me. All the others gave me a warm welcome and spoke freely, even those who feared that the freedom introduced by Mikhail Gorbachov's *glasnost* policy might not last. I wish to thank the *Observer* for its kind permission to use the translation of Yevgeny Yevtushenko's verses on the red flag (p. 77) and *Glas* for allowing me to quote at length from Nina Iskrenko's poem 'The Other Woman' (pp. 268–9).

Throughout this enterprise, I have been helped and supported by Yelena Vozdvizhenskaya. Lena was secretary, assistant, chief researcher, chief interpreter and friend. She joined the Moscow staff of the *Observer* in September 1989 and we worked together for close on three years. She brought to the job a lively intelligence and practical knowledge of every aspect of Soviet life. She had travelled widely in the country and had an instinctive understanding of politics. Her interpreting was quick, accurate and unobtrusive. She developed a refined talent for spotting stories that would interest foreign news editors in the West. She organised most of the interviews here, interpreted them, arranged the transcripts, researched the background and, with unquenchable enthusiasm and good humour, continued to field queries and fill in gaps for months after I had left Moscow to write and revise the book in France and London. My debt to her is immeasurable.

# Note on the rouble

The free-falling rouble (R.) and a rate of inflation exceeding two thousand per cent in a year inflict great hardship on Russians and present a problem to anyone writing a book about Russia to be read in 1993. One cannot predict what will happen to the rouble between writing and publication. But rapidly rising prices, repeated devaluations and impoverishment of much of the population of Russia were obviously of intense concern to everyone I spoke to, as the Government in Moscow struggled to build a modern economy on the wreckage of the Communist system.

Many of the women I interviewed spoke about costs and earnings, but the value of the money changed week by week, if not day by day. Wages and pensions also went up, though more slowly. There is no simple way around this difficulty, and I have chosen to quote the figures as they were given to me at the time of each interview, between January and July 1992. Where possible, I have inserted clues to the value of the sums mentioned but felt it would be tedious to set each figure systematically in its inflationary context.

It may be more helpful to place the interviews against a backdrop showing the great arc of the falling rouble.

For decades, after the Second World War, the Soviet currency enjoyed a remarkable stability. This was artificial.

Prices were held down by massive subsidies. Western scholars did what they could to calculate a relatively true rate of inflation from official figures designed to prove there was none in the USSR. Gorbachov's economists in the mid-1980s were more open, but the rouble was still protected by unrealistic rates of exchange.

When I took up my post in Moscow in March 1989, the official rates were one rouble to the British pound and sixty-five kopeks (k.) to one US dollar. A good monthly wage in Moscow was about R.250. This had increased to about R.500 by the end of 1991, largely as the result of 'price reform' (i.e., price increases) decreed by the Soviet Government on 2 April 1991. The rouble was sinking fast against hard currencies. By the end of 1991, it was down to R.90 to the dollar.

Then came the Yeltsin shock therapy of 2 January 1992. Most prices were freed and went through the roof. In Moscow, a taxi ride suddenly cost what the month before had been a good weekly wage. Wages went up, too. In February, a senior salesman at the Zil car plant in Moscow told me he was getting R.2,500 a month, as against R.250 at the beginning of 1991. A Zil worker was earning R.1,400 and said he could not manage on that. By September 1992, the average wage in Moscow was R.5,000 a month, but it was reckoned that the basic cost of living was R.5,000 a month *per person*.

The price of bread illustrates the problem. A loaf which cost k.26 before the Yeltsin reforms cost R.6 by March 1992, R.10 to R.14 by June and R.25 to R.40 by October. The exchange value of the 'wooden rouble' continued to plummet. It was down to R.168 to the dollar by the end of August 1992, to R.260 by September and to R.300 by early October. It fell to R.450 by January 1993 and a bottle of sparkling wine for New Year parties cost R.1,000. By February one dollar bought R.600. Inflation was up to about ten per cent per week: perilously close to the threshold of hyperinflation, generally put at about fifty per cent per month.

The reformist Government did what it could to get a grip on the money supply. Some workers in state enterprises were not paid at all for months in 1992. Moscow claimed that the Mint could not print money fast enough to keep up with demand. Russians assumed that the shortage was deliberately engineered to impose a crude form of wage freeze. However, the Government did introduce new high-denomination banknotes. The highest used to have a face value of R.100. Then the R.200 note began to circulate in late 1991, and R.500, R.1,000 and R.5,000 notes soon followed. (The blue R.5,000 note was the first not to bear the head of Lenin.) The cash shortage strengthened the rouble briefly in March 1992, when the official tourist rate was R.70 to the dollar. But it soon fell to R.120. A year later the R.10,000 note appeared.

The shock therapy was painful for everyone, but women, who did most of the shopping, were hit hardest. The worst off were the single woman pensioners, like Alla Yemelyanova, whom I interviewed in March (see chapter 3). But even women who, only months before, had thought of themselves as relatively well-off also found fresh fruit and vegetables beyond their reach, as Tanya Petrenko (interviewed in June) explains in chapter 6.

The later the interview, the higher the prices and the lower the value of the rouble. This is why I name the month in which each interview was recorded.

*London, February 1993*

Chapter 1

# Women, sex and health

The Bolsheviks undertook to solve 'the woman question' after the revolution. Lenin denounced domestic slavery and his declared aim was nothing less than 'the complete emancipation of women', which would come about once they took part in 'common productive labour'. He gave only one Cabinet seat to a woman, but she was Alexandra Kollontai, the fiery feminist and revolutionary idealist who became the first Commissar (Minister) of Social Welfare. Writing in 1920, she was specific and emphatic about the 'heaven on earth' which Russian women – and men – would ultimately enjoy 'under the red flag of the social revolution'.

The old type of family had had its day, she said. It was an obstacle to the advancement of women's interests 'since it needlessly holds back the female workers from more productive and far more serious work'. The family was no longer needed because 'the task of bringing up the children . . . is passing more and more into the hands of the collectivity'.

Kollontai forecast that from the ruins of the outmoded family would rise a new kind of relationship between men and women: 'a union of affection and comradeship, a union of two equal members of the Communist society, both of them free, both of them independent, both of them workers.' There would, she said, be 'no more domestic

servitude of women. No more inequality within the family
. . . The woman in the Communist city no longer depends
on her husband but on her work. It is not her husband but
her robust arms which will support her. There will be no
more anxiety about the fate of her children. The State of the
Workers will assume responsibility for these.' In place of
the 'conjugal slavery' of the past, Communist society offered
a 'free and honest union of men and women who are lovers
and comrades'. Under the new conditions, prostitution, an
evil that sprang from 'the institution of private property',
would 'automatically disappear'.

Kollontai understood that the new relationship would
entail difficulties. In her novel *Worker Bees*, set in the period
of Lenin's New Economic Policy after 1922, she describes
the pain felt by a woman Party activist at the unfaithfulness
of her comrade husband. But in 1920, her vision of the future
ideal union appeared unblemished.

In its early years, the Bolshevik Government passed legislation of great interest to women. In October 1919, Lenin
claimed that in two years, 'one of the most backward countries in Europe' had done more 'to emancipate woman, to
make her the equal of the "strong sex", than has been done
during the past one hundred and thirty years by all the
advanced, enlightened, "democratic" republics of the world
taken together.'

On paper, Lenin had something to boast about, for in
December 1917, only six weeks after seizing power, the new
regime issued decrees radically changing the laws on marriage and divorce. Women won the right to divorce and
alimony and could choose their surname after marriage.
New laws gave them full citizenship and the vote. Their
rights at work were legally protected.

Then, in November 1920, in the midst of famine and civil
war, the Government found time to legalise abortion, which
became available in hospitals, free of charge.

Women had, no doubt, earned attention to such matters

by their efforts and sacrifices for the Revolution for decades before October 1917. They joined in and sometimes led strikes. They died outside the Winter Palace in St Petersburg on Bloody Sunday, January 1905. Women helped to organise the assassination of Tsar Alexander II in 1881, and one of them, Sofia Perovskaya, hanged for it.

But the new regime did not introduce the social legislation of the post-Revolutionary years out of gratitude to women or simply to save them from 'the individual domestic system . . . that strangles them'. The traditional family unit was an obstacle to what Lenin called 'a large-scale socialist economy'. So it had to be destroyed. Further steps in this direction were taken through legislation in 1926. By then marriages and divorce were simply a matter of registration. Divorce by mail was introduced and there was no distinction between unregistered *de facto* marriages and registered ones.

Policy changed under Stalin in the mid-Thirties. The family unit came back into favour as a stabilising element in a period of economic upheaval as the country rushed to industrialise and urbanise. The unit was now the 'Soviet family of a new type', but it was a long way from the free union advocated by Alexandra Kollontai. Briefly, in the early 1920s, Moscow and other cities witnessed the extraordinary spectacles of nude parades in favour of free love. But this kind of thing was never encouraged by Lenin and, under Stalin, a sexual puritanism took hold. In 1935, abortions of first pregnancies were banned, and a year later the ban was extended to all non-therapeutic abortions. (Abortion was made legal again in 1955.) Divorce by mail was ended, and both husband and wife were required to appear in person to register the breakdown of a marriage. Kollontai fell from favour long before then, because of her association with the Workers' Opposition faction. She was, in effect, exiled into a career as a diplomat in Norway, Mexico and Sweden from 1923 till she retired in 1940. She died in 1952, a year before Stalin, at the age of eighty.

Very few Russians know about her feminist writings, and her vision of the new Communist love-match was never realised. Women benefited greatly from the immense strides that were made in education, but their legal right to equal pay was not matched by access to well-paid careers. Today, the majority of medical doctors and teachers are women, it is true, but these are low-paid jobs.

Seats were found for many women in parliamentary bodies at all levels. But they were rubber-stamp councils which met rarely and then only to pass whatever the Party put in front of them. Women never got far in any numbers inside the Central Committee, where real power was concentrated. They remained a minority within the Party as a whole. In 1922, only eight per cent of Party members were women, and the proportion was still less than twenty-five per cent in the late 1970s. It continued to increase, but slowly, reaching just over twenty-seven per cent in 1983.

The promise of emancipation in the home was not kept, either. The State did eventually build a large network of daycare centres, nurseries and kindergartens, but their main purpose was to free women to swell the labour force, not simply to relieve them from the tyranny of household chores. Mothers complained that their children were constantly falling sick with illnesses picked up at kindergarten. Those with enough *blat* (influence, pull) got their children places in special, well-equipped and well-staffed kindergartens reserved for the offspring of the élite: Party workers and civil servants in Government Ministries and Departments. In January 1992, ordinary and most special kindergartens were suddenly required to cover their own costs. In a panic, they raised their fees beyond the reach of many families. Some mothers found that the cost of a single place was now more than they earned.

I could see the roof of one exclusive kindergarten from the window of my office in the foreigners' ghetto at 12, Bolshaya Spasskaya Street in north central Moscow. It was

Dyetsky Sad 694, a pale-green, three-storey building run for the children of the staff of a Council of Ministers committee. It had spacious, airy classrooms, lots of toys, a large staff, good food, a big playground and an indoor swimming pool. Film director Tanya Petrenko had managed to get a place there for her second son Alex, and she took me to meet the deputy headmistress, Anna Ivanovna.

'The State has abandoned us,' said Anna Ivanovna. 'We have total independence but no money.' Fees shot up to almost two hundred times their previous level – from a nominal contribution towards food costs to four times the average wage in the Moscow of December 1991. This figure was halved, when the initial panic subsided, but half the children left, and the kindergarten sought replacement infants from the local foreign community, whose parents could easily afford a hard currency fee of $40 a month.

The red flag which had floated over the Kremlin had barely been hauled down, when Dyetsky Sad 694 and its like – which Lenin saw as a 'simple, everyday means' to emancipate women – were trying to become profit-making enterprises. In the process, they were making themselves inaccessible to many Russian children and adding to the already considerable difficulties of their mothers.

Modern labour-saving devices could have eased the burden, but women's needs were never high on the list of priorities of the central planners in charge of the Soviet economy. It could hardly be otherwise in a country as militarised as the USSR. Industry was dedicated essentially to supplying the biggest army in the world, and it had no chance of meeting in full the demand for the kind of consumer goods that could reduce household drudgery: modern automatic washing machines, microwave cookers, efficient vacuum cleaners and other gadgets which the West produced in abundance. Even now, few Russian women are aware that dishwashers even exist.

Nor did the State provide enough contraceptives.

Abortion became the most commonly practised form of birth control, and so it remained in the post-Communist era. Imported condoms and pills became available, after the price increases, but they were both expensive and unfamiliar. Cotton wool was still used in place of the sanitary towels domestic industry was unable to provide, and sometimes cotton wool was in short supply.

Housing did get better during the Soviet period, despite the enormous destruction of the Great Patriotic War of 1941–45, but, generally speaking, it was an improvement from appalling to poor, from overcrowded barracks to cramped, often overcrowded individual flats in ill-maintained blocks. In St Petersburg, millions in 1992 still lived in single rooms in communal flats, sharing kitchens and bathrooms with neighbours. A woman photographer, living in a communal flat there, showed me the bedsitter which she shared with her son and his wife. It was officially estimated that about ten million families in the Russian Federation were on waiting lists for better housing.

The housing shortage was a factor in the falling birth rate, which dropped by thirty per cent in Russia between 1986 and 1991. Young married couples commonly live with parents. Lack of privacy is, of course, inhibiting, but Russians have worked out ways of coping with it, as Katya explains. But the prospect of raising children in such conditions discouraged women from having more than one child, even when they were prepared to face the grim experience of childbirth in a Russian hospital a second time.

There were other factors at work, not least the enormous Soviet losses in the Second World War. Revised estimates now put these casualties at between twenty-six and twenty-eight million dead, and the slaughter changed the population balance between males and females. Before the war, it was forty-eight per cent male and fifty-two per cent female. When the war ended, it was forty-three per cent male, fifty-seven per cent female, and it has still not returned to the pre-war balance. The unborn grandchildren of the men who died in the 1940s would now be parents themselves. There were nine million more women than men in Russia in 1992 out of a total population of a hundred and forty-eight million.

For decades after the war, many women drifted into unsatisfactory marriages in a society where an unmarried woman over thirty was considered to have virtually no chance of finding a husband. But divorce became increasingly common, especially in the post-Stalin period, when it became easier to get. In 1950, only 67,400 divorces were officially recorded in the whole of the Soviet Union. By 1965, the figure was 354,500 and this jumped to 646,000 in the following year. The Soviet average was 650,000 annually between 1966 and 1973. In some places, there was one divorce for every two marriages; in Moscow, the rate was even higher. Official 1991 figures for Russia are 1,277,000 marriages and 597,000 divorces – still close to the one to two ratio.

One result was the high number of single-parent families. The 1989 census recorded 5.3 million, and in 4.9 million of them the single parent was a woman.

An alarm was sounded in the Russian Parliament in May 1992 by Minrauza Nazmetdinova, who chaired the Parliamentary Committee for Women, Family and Children. She said that the declining birth rate was most serious in Central Russia. 'Nearly four million abortions a year are performed in Russia. And this is a conservative estimate. In Russia, fifteen per cent of couples are childless and over fifty per cent have only one child.'

In March 1992, *Moskovskaya Pravda* reported that Russia was experiencing its worst demographic crisis since 1945 and remarked: 'You hardly ever see a pregnant woman in the streets of Moscow these days.' The same newspaper, a few months earlier, published a letter from patients in a maternity ward of Hospital No. 64 in Moscow, which helped to explain the crisis.

It reads: 'We have become reconciled to the fact that we are doomed to wear the worst lingerie in the world . . . we have learned to cook meals, queue for hours to buy scarce food and bring up our children while working full time . . . to make a meal out of nothing . . . We have the strength to do all this, but, when sickness comes, even we women are helpless . . . Hospital means a bed in a corridor (the wards are full), foul-mouthed medical staff, slop for meals and filth galore.'

The letter complains that the floors in gynaecological wards are not washed for weeks, that a single filthy toilet serves for a whole floor of the hospital and that 'expectant mothers are fed things a self-respecting dog would not eat'. The letter concludes: 'One can put up with living in a pigsty, but being hospitalised in a pigsty is intolerable.'

*Glasnost* (openness) allowed the publication of material that demolished the myth of a Soviet system of free health care far superior to any other in the world. But the collapse of the Soviet regime could not bring quick improvements. If anything, the health service sank deeper into crisis. There were reports of surgeons operating with razor blades. Hospitals were short not only of modern drugs but even of bandages.

In big cities, prosperous enterprises could now buy privileged health care for their staffs by paying high annual premiums to the polyclinics of the 'Fourth Department', previously reserved for the ruling class. Many of those who were not covered by this kind of health insurance put their faith in alternative medicine. But, for most people, health care had to be bought by seeing doctors privately or by bribing underpaid hospital personnel. This was not new, but Russian friends told me in 1992 that corruption in the health service was spreading under the impact of rampant inflation. There was, of course, no way of measuring this with any accuracy. But the anecdotal evidence was strong that even basic attention of nurses usually had to be paid for. One mother told me she had to promise a 'present' to an eminent surgeon before he agreed on a date for a serious operation on her four-year-old son.

The reports of a demographic crisis were no exaggeration. More people died than were born in Russia in November and December 1991 (562,000 and 530,000 respectively) for the first time since the blood-letting of the Great Patriotic War. The trend continued, and over the whole of 1992 the birth rate fell to eleven per 1,000 head of population and the death rate rose to twelve.

The birth rate was depressed not only by the war, the housing crisis, the many difficulties of raising children and by the horrors of the maternity wards. Married women needed to work, because families could not manage on a husband's salary alone and taking time off to have children was a sacrifice. A mother could take up to three years off after the birth of a child, but the maternity allowance she received was far from a full salary, and increases decreed by the Yeltsin Government did not keep pace with inflation. The need for a second income became imperative as the 'new prices' continued to soar.

The high death rate was linked above all to a poor diet which became worse as the prices of fresh fruit and vegetables in the farmers' markets made them inaccessible to most families. Other factors were heavy drinking and smoking, accidents and the disastrous pollution of air, water and land. Planners had for decades ignored the damage to the environment caused by the Kremlin's economic policies. Propaganda trumpeted increases in output and concealed the cost to public health. *Glasnost* allowed the extent of the damage to be reported, and it was officially admitted that many cities and entire regions had become ecological disaster areas. One child in five was born with physical or mental defects. Yet calculations by Yeltsin's experts showed that cleaning up the mess would require colossal sums the country could not afford.

The gravity of the health crisis is harshly spelt out in an official report released in October 1992. It says that there are 675,600 doctors, 10,879 hospitals, 19,100 polyclinics and 1,186 dispensaries (health centres) in Russia for a population of 148,704,800. But forty-two per cent of hospitals and thirty per cent of polyclinics have no piped hot water and twelve and seven per cent, respectively, have no running water at all. Yet, in 1991, there were thirty-one million hospital admissions, representing about one fifth of the total population.

Life expectancy is given as 63.8 years for Russian males and 74.3 for females. The 1990 figure for England and Wales is 73 for men and 78.5 for women.

The report states that there are complications in forty to forty-seven per cent of births and reckons that, if things go on as they are, by the year 2015, no more than twenty per cent of babies will be born healthy in Russia. In 1991, only a quarter of Russian school-leavers were judged to be in good health. In the city of St Petersburg, the figure was an appalling four per cent.

In 1991, the report says, there were two abortions for each birth. The figure for abortions it gives for that year is 3.5 million, but this is only for those both performed and recorded in state clinics. The true figure – including those performed privately or not recorded in state clinics – could well be several times higher.

Family planning, abortion and health were the main subjects of a news conference in Moscow attended by the American feminist Merle Hoffman in October 1992, when she brought Russian women news of the latest available contraceptives and urged them to 'start taking control' of their health care. At the conference, Inga Grebesheva, President of the Russian Family Planning Association, said: 'Ms Hoffman asked me why we put up with such an awful situation. I told her that if – in the present conditions of economic crisis, stratospheric prices, unemployment and high crime rates – we went into Red Square to demonstrate about abortion and contraceptives, people would think we were sexually frustrated. No one would approve.'

Another response came from a George Kavkassidze, a young Georgian gynaecologist, who said that the gynaeco-logical lobby in Russia was hostile to contraceptives, because abortion was such a very good source of income – both officially and privately.

With facts and figures of such a deeply gloomy nature to live with, and while sheer survival became daily more diffi-cult, the pessimism of the Russians was hardly surprising. But it was not new. Soon after I settled in Moscow in 1989, friends began remarking on my 'optimism'. I took this as a polite way of alerting me to the danger of combining ignor-ance and naivety in a country where nothing is quite what it seems. They became particularly anxious in 1991 about any 'optimistic' assumption that the Communist Party was truly dead and gone. They feared a return of something like the old regime, some even seemed resigned to it. The belief in the existence and the power of 'dark forces' has deep roots and is well-nigh unshakeable.

To the optimistic Westerner, the profound pessimism of the Russians sometimes looks like the acceptance of misery and suffering as a normal, if not desirable, state of affairs. They seem to take a patriotic pride in their own proven ability over the centuries to endure conditions no others could survive. But the pessimism is lightened by a black humour that has little or no regard for good taste.

At the art/flea/antique market that opens at weekends near the Izmailovsky stadium in the eastern suburbs of Mos-cow, a vendor stands in the cold wind behind a trestle table covered with old, wind-up gramophones and calls out: 'Come and see my Panasonic.' The economic disaster, the backwardness of Russian industry and the poverty of the nation are, in a single phrase, pointed out and made light of.

Few of the women I interviewed expected life in Russia to get better soon, if ever, but the varying shades of pessimism were, in most cases, combined with an extraordinary gaiety and good humour. And many of them talked as if they had spent their lives thinking up answers to the questions this Western male was putting to them.

# Zoya

| |
|---|
| Zoya Vasilyevna Zarubina |
| Educationalist |
| Born: Moscow, 1920 |
| Father: KGB General |
| Mother: Seamstress |
| Interviewed: May 1992 |

*Zoya Zarubina was, for many Westerners in the Soviet period, the reassuring, acceptable face of the USSR. She trained diplomats, travelled abroad and was allowed to meet foreigners through Party front organisations, like the Peace Committee and the Women's Committee. She supported Gorbachov's reforms and remained a Party member to the end. She still enjoys some of the privileges of the élite she joined before she was twenty. Now, she readily talks about what went wrong under Soviet rule, about abortion and about how she kept her mouth shut, when the stepfather who brought her up, an army general, was gaoled by Stalin.*

Zoya joined the Soviet Communist Party in 1939, when she was only nineteen. Now aged seventy-two, she tells me in her fluent American English: 'I still have my card, though I left when Gorbachov dissolved the Party. I have not joined any other, but I am still a patriot.' The Party, in effect, left her.

In her long, busy life, Zoya has done the State and the Party much service, and her home bears witness to her high standing with both. It is spacious and light, on the eighth floor of a well-built, well-maintained, modern block in a quiet street behind the Foreign Ministry skyscraper. It is a short walk from the Arbat pedestrian precinct in central Moscow. A concierge, with an office off a spotless, tiled entrance hall, asks callers their business. In this city, both concierges and bright, clean entrances are rare.

Zoya was brought up by her stepfather, a Red Army general, now dead. Her natural father, like her mother, had only four years' schooling but rose to the rank of general in the KGB. During the Great Patriotic War, Zoya served as a nurse and interpreter. She speaks French, German and English and helped interrogate prisoners of war. Later, she was vetted by the KGB, before joining the Soviet translating teams at the Allied summits in Tehran, Yalta and Potsdam. 'I was hostess to Franklin D. Roosevelt at the Tehran conference and was with Winston Churchill in Yalta.'

She was an outstanding sportswoman: the Soviet pentathlon champion. She became Dean of the Moscow Diplomatic Academy, after the war, and still teaches there. She clearly belongs to the Soviet equivalent of what the British call 'the great and the good' – an exclusive circle of approved persons who are trusted to run public organisations. She was for many years on the Soviet Women's Committee [now transformed into The Union of Women of Russia] and was a member of the Peace Committee.

Despite the collapse of the USSR and the Party, she is still a tirelessly active committee woman, presenting a friendly Russian face to the world. She recently helped set up a Russian–American–Finnish 'women's support group' called the Hope-Nadyezhda International Association, which has held conferences in the US and Finland. After our talk, she does some shopping before going to a meeting of a new Anglo-Russian association at the House of Friendship, near the Kremlin.

I understand why Zoya is in such demand, for I know her to be an energetic, efficient organiser, highly intelligent and very good company. She was one of the first women I met in Moscow in 1989. The *Observer*, responding to the hopes raised by Gorbachov and his reforms, was sponsoring a schools quiz, with trips to Britain as the prizes. By the time I reached the Soviet capital, Zoya had assembled an enthusiastic team of Russian judges, who had already conducted the first stages of the competition and selected some twenty young finalists, awesomely well-informed about Britain.

Later, at a farewell party for an Irish correspondent, Zoya said to me: 'If you ever want to know about Soviet women, give me a call.' I did, and she began by warning me against stringing together the complaints 'of one frustrated woman after another' and jumping to conclusions. 'I think former-Soviet women are a sturdy lot: complex and wonderful human beings.'

They are, she says, tired, exhausted even, given the difficulties they have to contend with every day. 'But Soviet women never had an easy life. If you go back before the Revolution, very few women had a leisurely time. It's the destiny of Russian women to carry the burden, because the males are not really much help. Traditionally it was like that, and it is still. A very few – probably the younger generation – help a little but the rest just don't. A Russian man is patient and understanding when he has a female boss, but when he comes home, he just sits there and waits for everything to be given to him.

'At the start of the Revolution, the feeling among women inside the country was: at last we are free and we are not going to be second-class citizens. And many laws were passed which were of interest to women: on equal pay, equal opportunities to study, freedom to choose a profession, equal pensions, equal obligations and benefits in marriage and separation. All these things were very important.'

In return, women worked. During the 'terrible times',

such as the period of collectivisation of agriculture, they struggled to keep their children alive. During industrialisation, they left their villages for the factories. 'They needed to work, if they were not to starve.' They were neither inclined nor able just to keep house and 'enjoy their kitchens'.

'A Russian woman is not brought up that way. Probably she will appreciate it in ten or fifteen years, when we have a consumer society in the Western sense, but not now. She sees how her mother has to toil and everything has to be done. But I think that inside us we have the feeling that the family suffers because we are so damn equal that we forget about the prerequisite of a female vis-à-vis the man.'

From Zoya's own description, Russian women have equality on paper, but they have none at home, and most of them are obliged to work outside it. Zoya argues, however, that they have themselves to blame both for accepting the burdens thrust on them and for losing their feminine touch in the process. She uses the word 'equal' to signify 'concerned with equality', not to imply that sexual equality actually exists. This shorthand at times makes her argument hard to follow, though there is no doubting the passion behind it.

She is torn between criticising and defending Soviet achievements and sometimes attempts to do both at the same time.

'It hurts me when everything is put in the negative. The country has done a lot. Maybe it's not satisfactory, but it's done and it's there. Probably we could have had better and more kindergartens, more baby care centres and more contraceptives so that seven million women a year would not have to have abortions.'

The trouble, as Zoya sees it, is that a woman, brought up believing in equality of the sexes, is not psychologically prepared to handle the problems she encounters as a young wife and mother.

'If she has a wise, understanding mother or – even better – mother-in-law, that's fine. But her mother and mother-in-law will usually go to work. And so there she is with all her problems: pregnant and not very happy with her husband. Foolishly, some of them have their first abortion at this stage, before their first child is born. If she does have the baby, she finds that our industry can't supply what children need. And so frustrations accumulate – and aggressiveness, the sickness of the age.'

Zoya thinks her own experience is typical of Soviet women of her generation. Her daughter Tatyana was born two weeks after Hitler's troops invaded the USSR in 1941. Her husband was killed in action a fortnight later. She was a widow for fourteen years before she got married again, to a war veteran. 'I was working too hard to have another baby. Now I have been a widow again for seventeen years. We are used to taking upon ourselves full responsibility for keeping the family happy. We just got ourselves into that harness.'

As a result, women are so tired that they aren't able to teach children their 'duties as men and women' – equal but different.

'Very few men know how to take good care of a woman. I don't mean sex. I mean everything else: being a moral support. The capacity for love and deep feeling is very great in Russians, but it is not being developed. Suppose the mother is a widow or divorced and she works hard, at a job. She has to think about buying those pants and washing those pants and mending the shoes and getting the boy a job and so on. She forgets to teach the boy how to be a man and a loving husband and father. She is everything. This is why in my country women are sometimes an evil force. That's what life has made them. They may spill out their frustrations, but in the end the blame lies with them.

'When we started *perestroika* [restructuring], the first

national discussion we had was about health care, the second about education. And what did we women find out? That more than seventy per cent of the health staff were women? Now how the hell did we tolerate the health system we had? Why didn't we raise our voices for better care, fewer abortions or whatever? And in schools, eighty per cent of the staff were women. So how did we live with that system? Why didn't we work at it? If you talk about the degrading conditions in the service industries, then you have to remember that most of the people working in them are women.'

Here Zoya talks as if open dissent were feasible in the Soviet Union before Gorbachov came to power. She seems to be slipping back into a way of talking to foreigners about the USSR as if it were a democratic country. But her outburst does pose the question of why women did not 'raise their voices' effectively when *perestroika* made this possible. Zoya provides a partial answer: they have been too busy.

'A woman may be a very good human being. But she's tired, she's frustrated, she's aggressive and with the push, push, push and pull, pull, pull all the time, without noticing it, she is destabilising society. We need to give women a chance to return to womanhood. I remember right after the war my mother telling me to have a pedicure. When the first salons were opened, people said: "What the hell is that? What are you talking about? Pedicures? You bourgeois!"'

I bring the conversation back to the lack of family planning and Zoya's high estimate of seven million abortions a year.

'Abortion is frustrating for any woman, even for stupid little girls, knowing you are killing life. And it teaches men irresponsibility. It is quite clearly detrimental to health. So why don't women stand up and shout? Let me tell you about myself. I had eleven abortions. For fourteen years as a widow, when I was young, I lived alone. I didn't want to marry again. My chief concern was bringing up my child. We didn't know what contraceptives were. I was young and healthy and, bingo, I had to have that abortion. Isn't that terrible? Why should a woman pay all the moral and physical debts of free love – which she still does?'

She throws out another statistic to illustrate the poor relationship between men and women in Russia: forty-two per cent of marriages end in divorce in the first five years. The main reason, she believes, is that 'we do not prepare children for the responsibilities of married life'. Working mothers bring up latchkey children by telephone, ringing them from the office to ask how school was and tell them what to take from the refrigerator for lunch.

Schools are at fault, too, she says. The country was rightly proud of its achievements in the first twenty years after the Revolution. By 1936, she claims, illiteracy had been eradicated. But many male teachers died during the war 'and we femalised education'. Then in the Fifties the emphasis was put on subject teaching: maths and sciences. Preparation for adult life was forgotten. Poor pay discouraged talented people from a career in teaching. 'A bus driver gets more than a teacher. Why read all those books, if you can just sit behind a wheel and get all the money?'

In the early Seventies, ten years of schooling became the norm. 'Dammit, weren't we proud of that? But it turned out to be a big lie. Children are not all the same. Not all of them can absorb all those subjects and be good at them. What we lack most of all are tools to understand life.'

Zoya notes with approval that some parents are now willing to pay to have their children educated privately. She explains that the head of a State school (usually a woman) is too bogged down in administrative problems to pay much attention to what her pupils are actually being taught.

'She has to see repairs are done, get textbooks and new desks, recruit new teachers, find extra money, look for sponsors. So many things don't work. She has to fight tooth and nail to get three nails. She has no time to go into the content of education. And parents are not used to having strong parent–teacher associations.'

Are the attitudes of Russian males the cause or the result of women's frustrations?

'Mostly the result. The woman becomes the slave-driver in the family: Do this. Do that. Why didn't you do this? Why didn't you buy that? There's an atmosphere of animosity. Some people are born bastards, of course, but I think it's the attitude of the mother which produces the man. When we talk about the responsibility of bringing up children, we talk about the mother, not mother and father. There's not enough understanding between parents that there are two of them. The mother has been brought up by her *nyanya* [nanny] or her grandmother, so she doesn't understand what her child is missing when there is no father. She thinks she can substitute for everything. She will understand only much later, when her son tells her about his unhappy married life. But then she will probably blame it all on his wife, not on him.'

Zoya notes that there has been a drop in the number of women in politics, now that most elections are contested. She says they lost around one thousand seats in the Soviet and Republican parliaments in 1989 and later. Under the old system, when rubber-stamp soviets were formally 'elected' but in fact appointed, a substantial proportion of the seats were allocated to women. 'We had what the Americans call "affirmative action".' In the mid-Eighties just over half the seats in local soviets were held by women, but when there is a choice of candidates, Zoya says, electors tend to vote for men.

'Women are not elected because they are so damn busy, and other women don't trust them. Women are not brought up in a spirit of solidarity. That's why they didn't understand Raisa [Gorbachov]. Why did she have to tag along with him all the time? they wanted to know. What sort of profession is the profession of a wife?'

Asked about her own background, Zoya says she comes from 'a nice, devoted family of patriots. I was brought up [by mother and stepfather] to work for the cause, to work for the country, and I was perfectly happy with that. I was very committed.'

Then, in 1951, her stepfather, General Leonid Eitingon, was arrested and imprisoned for twelve years. He died in 1981 and was 'rehabilitated' in 1992.

'He was a war hero, but Stalin had his own way of dealing with him. I had to worry about our whole family of seven people: my mother, who became quite ill, my sister, her husband and son, myself, my daughter and my stepfather. It was a very difficult period of readjustment and disillusionment, as we came to a true understanding of what our society and Stalin were. But I was wise enough to understand that I had to stand by my family. So I kept my mouth shut. I went on working and kept my thoughts to myself. Besides, Stalin was one thing, my country another.

'It's my own land. It needs a lot of healing and a lot of understanding from your people. We are going through a difficult, painful process. We have to open up a lot of wounds: hatred, antagonisms, frustrations, misunderstandings, fear. We have to get all that out of our systems. Only then will the healing process really start.

'The old guard and people of my age are disillusioned and feel their lives are over. People say to us: "You and Gorbachov came in and things got even worse." Which is true, and it can't continue for ever. The middle generation say their lives have been ruined. And young people are so naive – all those wonderful, glittering toys and hard currency this and that, all those stupid things you can easily live without. They don't understand what is most important. If we don't pay attention to the youngsters, it's going to be bad.

'We are a spiritual nation. This is the strength of the Russians: spirit and patience. If the young people lose that, we shall lose one of the most important traits of Russian character. And whatever happens in this country will, one way or another, influence the history of the world.'

# Svetlana

| |
|---|
| Svetlana Savelievna Zotova |
| Gynaecologist |
| Born: Khorezm, Uzbekistan, 1950 |
| Father: Army officer |
| Mother: Gynaecologist |
| Interviewed: May 1992 |

*'Abortions are our main source of income,' says Svetlana Zotova, head of the gynaecological section of Moscow's Polyclinic No. 1. Now, like many other clinics, hospitals, kindergartens, holiday centres and other services once heavily subsidised by the State, it has to pay its way. It does this partly by offering privileged health care to enterprises which can pay an annual premium for their workers. Then abortion, in a country where this is the most common form of family planning, brings in steady high profits.*

*I ask Svetlana about health, sex and – because she grew up in Central Asia near the now dying Aral Sea – about one of the world's worst ecological disasters.*

---

In May 1992, Svetlana's clinic charges R.700 for a 'mini-abortion', performed by vacuum in the first twenty-three days of pregnancy. Svetlana, who earns R.800 a month, reckons that the average Russian woman has five abortions between the ages of twenty and forty-two. There should not be a shortage of patients.

The vacuum method was introduced in 1990, 'and I

remember it as a revolution. No metal instruments are used, and forty minutes after the operation the patient can go home. It's easier for her psychologically, too. She doesn't go through those early months of pregnancy, when she gets used to the idea of carrying a baby. We don't call it an abortion but a "regulation of the menstrual cycle". This method was invented in Russia in 1923, but someone stopped it being introduced till recently. The coil, too, was invented a long time ago, but only now is a factory starting mass production. We used to import some coils from Finland, but we can produce quite good ones ourselves.'

What caused the delay?

'I imagine there was a struggle going on somewhere in the top echelons.'

But why did women put up with it? Why wasn't there a great outcry?

'To do what?'

To influence the Government and get it to change its priorities.

'I don't think we would ever manage that: get the Government to change its policies.' She laughs. 'There's a solid wall around the Kremlin.'

The Soviet State put women's concerns low in its order of priorities, and it made its contempt for the medical profession equally evident by the low salaries it paid its doctors (the majority of whom were women). Svetlana's R.800 a month is far less than a semi-skilled factory worker would accept in Moscow in the spring of 1992. It has been like that since Stalin's day.

'We always knew that a worker got more than a doctor or teacher. When R.300 a month was good pay for a worker, a doctor would get R.150. I certainly agree that a miner and probably someone working in an oilfield should get more than me. But now we are below the poverty line. We have been promised better pay, but it's only on paper so far. The State is bankrupt.'

Also damaging to the health service, she says, is the absence of pay differentials within it. An outstanding surgeon is paid the same as a run-of-the-mill physician. 'Doctors are very different. It was once fashionable to go to medical college, but people who went for that reason were a long way from real medicine. And the nurses who come out of the special vocational colleges were often the worst pupils at school. They didn't go into medicine for the love of it, but because they had nowhere else to go. They don't care. The heartless treatment of patients comes from that.'

The heartless treatment of women in general is vividly illustrated by the neglect of family planning and the resulting imposition of birth control by abortion.

'Girls are illiterate about family planning. Probably not more than a third of my patients know what it means. And they are well-educated, upper-class women. If you drive fifty or seventy kilometres out of Moscow and ask a girl what method she is using, she won't know what you're talking about. We never had any sex education in schools. Now we do, but only on paper. There are no specialists. If it is taught in schools, then the lessons are taken by Russian language or biology teachers. And they don't know how to present the subject to boys and girls.

'My daughter Lena is in class 11 and a fifth of the seventeen-year-old girls in it are sexually experienced. One of them has already had an abortion. They have no sex education, and some of her classmates used to come and put their questions to me.

'Now we have lots of contraceptives on sale in our chemists in Moscow. They are part of the humanitarian aid we have been sent, including very good pills made by Western firms. But even the local gynaecologists who give consultations don't always know how to use the pill. And young girls wouldn't go to them anyway, for fear of being called a prostitute.'

The ready availability of contraceptives is new. Soviet

condoms are of notoriously poor quality and have never been manufactured in adequate quantities. It will take a long time to change the attitudes such shortages have fostered. In the meantime, abortion remains the most usual form of birth control.

'The impact on the health of individual women is, of course, very bad. Some become infertile. And they are prone to all kinds of infections and illnesses. The long-term effects on the nation's health are also serious. The young generations are weak and sickly. Women who do give birth don't produce healthy children. The mothers themselves are weak after repeated abortions, and almost every baby is born with two or three health defects.'

The Soviet infant mortality rate, she says, was one of the worst in the world. She refers me to a recent article in the weekly magazine *Ogonyok*, written by Professor Vyacheslav Tabolin. I look it up. It says that in 1913 the rate was a staggering 277 per thousand live births. By 1970, this was down to twenty-five per thousand, but soon afterwards it rose to twenty-eight and official figures ceased to be published for some years. It has been reckoned that forty-nine countries, including former colonies of the West, have better infant mortality figures than Russia, which ranks just below Barbados.

However, this may not be the true picture. The infant mortality rate in Russia in 1991 was 17.9 per thousand live births, according to the official report on health released in October 1992. (The figure for England in 1990 was 7.9.) However, the report itself points out that, if international criteria are used, the true Russian figure could be much higher. Soviet figures were always unreliable, if only because of the practice of counting many premature and underweight babies as miscarriages rather than as live births.

I ask Svetlana how she would describe the general state of the Russian health service.

'All tears,' she replies. 'We don't have anything. No

cotton wool or bandages. No staff to sterilise instruments. We are even short of gut for stitches.'

She does not deliver babies now, but when she did work in a maternity hospital, she was horrified by the general attitude 'to the poor women in the labour room. We were at such a primitive stage, but it was impossible for one person to change anything.'

Svetlana grew up in the Central Asian Republic of Uzbekistan and learned at an early age of the State's lack of concern for the effect of its policies on the health of individuals and on the environment they lived in.

She was born at Khorezm, on the bank of the Amu Darya, one of the two rivers that fed the huge fresh-water Aral Sea. Her mother was a gynaecologist and her father an army officer. 'I remember we used to get big sturgeon from the river, and the Sea was full of fish. It used to have fleets of fishing boats. I used to sail on them as a child. The Sea was so big, sometimes you couldn't see any shore from the boat.'

The Aral Sea began to shrink and die, when water from the Amu Darya and the Syr Darya rivers was diverted to irrigate the immense cotton fields the Kremlin had ordered into existence in Uzbekistan. In thirty years, from 1962, the Sea lost sixty per cent of its volume. It once covered 66,000 square kilometres. By the early 1990s, it was down to 40,000. The ports used by the boats Svetlana sailed on as a child were now twenty kilometres or more from the water's edge.

Svetlana and her schoolfriends were sent into the fields to pick cotton and came out with their hands and arms covered with sores caused by the defoliants, pesticides and other chemicals liberally applied to increase production. In autumn, lessons were stopped while the children separated the cotton from the balls they had picked. They never drank local water; their supplies were brought in from elsewhere.

This was a wise precaution, because the local rivers were poisoned by the chemicals washed into them from the cotton fields. As the Aral Sea shrank, its muddy bottom, thick with chemicals, dried, cracked and flaked in the sun. Winds whipped up the poisonous dust and deposited it on the surrounding countryside. This had a catastrophic effect on the health of the local people.

The monthly magazine *Novy Mir*, in 1989 quoted a local doctor as saying: 'Out of a thousand new-born babies, a hundred die before they are a year old. Deformed babies have begun to be born . . . without an anus, with shortened intestines, feeble-minded, without a limb or without a skull, just skin on the face.'

Svetlana had an Uzbek nanny and spoke only Uzbek (a Turkic language) till she went to school. She learned very early how a child was born, because her mother often took her to attend patients in labour. The birth rate in the republic was high and still is. Families with eight children and more are not uncommon. The population of Uzbekistan is expected to double to thirty-four million by the year 2005. 'They will not learn what contraception is in a hundred years,' says Svetlana.

Before the break-up of the Soviet Union, there were frequent warnings that the high birth rates in Central Asia would upset the country's demographic balance. This was already happening in the Red Army towards the end of the Soviet period, because it was taking an increasingly high proportion of its national service recruits from Central Asia. In Russia, the birth rate was and is still falling, largely because of the cost, time and ingenuity required to clothe and feed children, the poor state of health care, and the horrific experience of having a first child.

This was described for me soon after I arrived in Moscow by Sheila Kitzinger, the anthropologist and child care expert, who visited Russian maternity homes with a team of British specialists. What she saw, she said, was 'cattle-market obstetrics'. Women went into labour on narrow beds in communal rooms behind 'great big windows, as if in a shop window. The staff and visitors like us can just watch women in agony, writhing on the beds and screaming . . . Then, when they go into the second stage of labour, they move to a high delivery table, with just a little cushion under head and shoulders . . . As soon as the midwife or doctor, usually a woman, can get her hands on the baby, it is forcibly extracted. There is no question of a baby swimming out of a woman's body.'

The Russian Statistics Agency reported in 1992 that the birth rate had dropped by thirty per cent over five years. In November 1991, for the first time since the slaughters of the Second World War, the death rate exceeded the birth rate. The figures were even worse in the first quarter of 1992, when the population declined in forty-three regions of Russia.

The trade union newspaper *Trud* in July 1992 reported the experience of a single Moscow maternity hospital. It used to have between twenty and twenty-five deliveries a day. Now it had ten. In the first half of 1992, it recorded 927 births, less than half the figure for the first six months of 1991.

Svetlana's daughters Lena and Katya, who is nine, listen to the conversation. Svetlana herself sits straight-backed, wearing a black skirt and a pink striped blouse, her blonde hair pulled back and tied with a pink bow. She has small gold earrings. We drink tea from dark blue cups and, before I leave, she takes me on a tour of her flat, something that would occur to very few Muscovites. The flat has two rooms, kitchen and bathroom. But it is unusually well decorated. There are gleaming new tiles in the bathroom and rugs on floors and walls.

Svetlana is a widow. Her husband died in 1990, but in one crucial respect her life has changed radically for the better: the flat has a single family in it. She and her daughters are the only occupants. Two years earlier, it somehow housed three families. Three tables were squeezed into the tiny kitchen, and three women cooked on the same stove.

They must have been singularly nice people to survive that.

'No, there were lots of quarrels. You couldn't leave even a piece of bread in the kitchen: it would be gone by morning. Sometimes a neighbour would inspect what we were cooking in a saucepan. There used to be three different electric meters, so that we only paid for the light each family used in the kitchen, bathroom and lavatory.'

The flat is in an undistinguished block near the Leningrad railway station, but Svetlana is beyond question the most house-proud Muscovite I have ever encountered. Despite all the problems hovering over her country and her family, she looks to be a happy woman.

# Katya

| |
|---|
| Yekaterina Leonidovna Deyeva |
| Journalist |
| Born: Moscow, 1970 |
| Father: Biologist |
| Mother: Medical school lecturer |
| Interviewed: April 1992 |

*Katya has worked in newpapers for six years, starting part-time while still in school, and works almost full-time now, while also doing a diploma course in journalism at Moscow University. She is still only twenty-two and has already done a long stint as a kind of agony aunt, answering readers' letters about love and marriage. She speaks with equal candour about sex and editorial freedom.*

Katya is a writer and editor on *Moskovsky Komsomolets*, which used to be the daily paper for the capital's Communist youth movement. Now it sells under the breezy title of *MK* and has a broad readership of all ages. It is the best-selling local paper in post-Communist Moscow. Katya used to run its family-life section called 'You and Me: the Young Families Club'.

'"You and Me" had a wide range. There were interviews with sexologists and psychologists, and we had lots of letters asking for basic information, about how to use condoms, things like that. It was like teaching the ABC. We talked about family rows and how to settle them. About having children: conditions in maternity hospitals, how much it cost to have a baby. We wrote about abortions, about unmarried people living together, why they did it – and how. There were some jokes, too. I wrote an article about a council of witches and how to win the heart of your beloved.

'I was still in school and had lots of my own questions on these subjects. I had a rather conservative upbringing and I never talked to my parents about such things. I found people to advise me. Now I am a bit more grown up. I've talked to people a lot and I have some experience. I always thought something ought to be done for the fourteen- and fifteen-year-olds who ought to find the minimum they need in the paper. I never wrote about the problems of people older than me. I asked older writers to do that. When I wrote for people of my own age, I didn't speak like an aunt, but like one of them. I asked questions and answered for myself as well as for them. I talked to experts and read books on the subjects. Sometimes I used articles from foreign papers.

'When we started dealing with this sort of thing in the paper, five years ago, we never talked about "sex". I remember, in 1985, when television started live hook-ups with the US, an American asked what sex life was like in the USSR. A woman on the Russian panel was outraged and shouted: "There is no sex in the Soviet Union!" What she meant to say, I think, was that there was romantic love, not "sex" here. Afterwards, people made fun of the poor woman. But it was rather sad, because most of the country agreed with her.

'A well-known journalist called Vladimir Shahijanian wrote a book on sex called *1001 Questions About It*. In 1988, we decided to publish extracts in *MK*. We ran two pieces and there was an enormous row. We were still under the control of the Komsomol [the Young Communist League], and our editor was called in and almost lost his job. So that's why in the page for young families we didn't mention the word "sex", but wrote either about romantic love or economic problems. When we began to deal a little more with sexual questions, we got a lot of letters, especially from young people.'

How can unmarried people possibly live together when there is such a terrible housing shortage?

'They only half live together, and even then only in big cities like Moscow and Leningrad, perhaps Kiev and Sverdlovsk [Yekaterinburg]. Even now in the Urals, where I worked for a while, a woman is treated like a prostitute just for smoking. Young people are very lucky if they have their own flat. In most cases, couples live apart, with their own parents, and meet three or four times a week. They may spend days together but not nights. And it can go on like that for years. It's halfway love, rather than living together. They meet either at friends' places or at home, when their parents are out. These days students make a business out of letting their rooms in hostels for two or three hours. In summer, there are the forests and in winter there may be a well-heated cellar.

'Sex life is starting at an increasingly early age, depending on one's background. Girls in vocational schools, who left secondary school in the eighth year, start at fourteen or fifteen. Girls from more educated families start at seventeen or eighteen.'

Attitudes to marriage depend very much on family background.

'A girl from a low-income family will try to marry young, say between eighteen and twenty, because to have a husband is to have a position in life. She won't be earning much. The father and mother are both working in factories, and the father drinks. Girls from this background try to marry as soon as they can. Girls who have been to college try to marry later. They are economically independent, with pretty good salaries. Take my class at secondary school: all the girls from the poorer families – fourteen of them – are married already. Not one of the eight others who went on to higher education has married yet. They will probably wait till they have their diplomas and a job – say at twenty-four or twenty-five.'

Katya decided on a career in journalism when she was about fourteen. It was her parents' idea, although there were no journalists in the family – doctors and army officers but no reporters.

'My mother and father are both biologists. He's in charge of a laboratory at the university. My mother teaches at a school for nurses. I went into journalism as a way of learning about life, but it's like a drug: once you start you can't stop.'

Did a journalist have to be a Party member?

'You couldn't get into an institute without belonging to the Komsomol. To get into the faculty of journalism, you had to have a recommendation stamped by the Komsomol committee of your district. I had to do that. There were rules and I never broke them. I didn't touch politics. I was a Little Octobrist from seven to ten, then a Pioneer from ten to fourteen and a member of the Komsomol after that. There was a primary Komsomol organisation in every secondary-school class. Each cell had a secretary. Then there was a committee for the whole school, at the head of all the cells. The secretary of that committee attended regular meetings of the district committee of the youth movement.

'In my school committee, there were six or seven people, each responsible for a different activity. I was in charge of the wall newspaper. Someone looked after classroom studies. Someone else was responsible for political propaganda. We had meetings once a week.

'When I was fifteen, we didn't pay much attention to politics. The beginning of *perestroika* was astonishing, but people were doubtful and weren't sure what was going on.

Although the Komsomol was well organised and some things made sense, ideology and all that bored us. We didn't think it was important. People had become cynical. But eventually we understood that we could be powerful and do something. That was in my first year at university.'

I first met Katya when she was twenty. She interviewed me for *MK* on what it's like to be a foreign correspondent in Moscow. We used French as our *lingua franca*. The interview was published on one of the biggest public holidays of the Soviet period: 7 November, Revolution Day. It earned me a smart salute, then and thereafter, from one of the policemen on duty at the entrance to the foreigners' block I lived in.

Katya is blonde and dresses with style. She is a serious reporter with frank, steady eyes, and she does her homework well. She arrived to interview me with a long list of good questions, including one wild card: what did I think of the Russian soul? In the published interview, she mercifully ignored my floundering attempt to fudge an answer.

Her enthusiasm for her job is undiminished. She is no longer an agony aunt. She has a special page once a week for articles about foreigners in Moscow and Russians abroad.

'I am still at *MK* and also in the fifth year at the university faculty of journalism. Most students of journalism start working very early. I've been on full salary for three years. I started on *Komsomolskaya Pravda* [then a country-wide youth daily], when I was still at secondary school. In those days, there were some specific subjects we couldn't touch. Once, six years ago, I suggested doing something about the business activities of secondary schoolchildren, who were already doing deals and speculating a bit to earn a living.

'The idea was turned down on the grounds that it didn't fit in with the paper's political line. You couldn't criticise leaders of Komsomol. That was completely impossible. Even in 1987 or 1988 [under Gorbachov] there was someone at

*MK* from the Moscow Komsomol Committee who kept a check on the paper. He had the power to stop the presses, if there was something that deviated from the Komsomol line. There was censorship, too. Till 1989, a woman read all the articles, and she could stop production, too, if she found something she thought infringed State secrets. I don't think she ever used this power. We just altered the offending articles. But the paper could have been stopped, if the staff had resisted the changes.

'Our editor was called every week or two before the Komsomol Central Committee or the Moscow Committee to be told what line he had to follow and what should be written. Things began to change in 1986 and '87. Now our paper has a wide readership and many of our subscribers are pensioners. When it was only a youth paper, it was less strictly controlled than *Pravda* and the rest. With *perestroika*, we were able to publish articles about subjects such as prostitution and, little by little, began criticising political leaders. Older people became interested in the paper and it changed to meet the new readers' tastes. So we worked out a combination of youthful style and adult content. Our circulation went from 200,000 to 1,800,000, eighty per cent subscriptions.

'Newspapers got their independence two years ago, and their staffs were allowed to run them. Before that, papers had been under the control of the Komsomol or the Communist Party. The weekly *Literaturnaya Gazeta* was under the Writers' Union. But there are two sides to independence. On the one side, editorial freedom but, on the other, economic independence. Papers, subsidised for years, found this hard, because they didn't have any commercial structures. All that had to be built from zero.

'Now they have to buy their own paper and ink and pay the printers. The situation is especially threatening for the papers like *Komsomolskaya Pravda* which are distributed all over the country and have big circulations. It's easier for

MK to make ends meet, because we sell just in greater Moscow. We also make money from a brick plant and a sausage factory that we bought.

'Even so, there are problems. Most of our readers are subscribers and they paid their subscriptions for a year in advance in October 1991. But the prices of paper and ink are going up every day. Before, it cost, say, two kopeks to produce a copy of the paper, and the cover price was five kopeks. Now the cover price is the same, but it costs fifty kopeks a copy to produce. We decided not to ask our subscribers to pay extra in the middle of the year and to make up the losses with advertising. Our prices are high but people accept them because we have the biggest sale in Moscow. Thanks to this and to our factories, we can survive.'

Katya takes heart from signs of a change in attitudes to work these days.

'My father used to take me to his laboratory, when I was little. At six o'clock, everyone went home. No one worked in the evening or on Saturdays. But now lots of people work on Saturday for themselves. There's a taste for hard work especially among the young. You've seen those teenagers in the street washing car windscreens. Many people of my age have their own businesses: buying and selling, making plastic bags or T-shirts, or bringing out their own newspapers. They have understood that you can make money, if you work hard. People talk about businessmen who don't produce anything. But I don't blame them. When you see a gap, you fill it and make a profit.

'On the other hand, there's the tragedy of our parents. People over forty now have a mentality stuck in the old system. Most of them have lost any sense of initiative. They need someone to tell them what to do. My father is different. He is a scientist in charge of research in a laboratory subsidised by the State, but two months ago he began to do something on his own and set up the Association of

Chernobyl Veterans, since he used to work at Chernobyl [the nuclear power station in the Ukraine, which caught fire in 1986]. But most older people can't change their ways.

'As for politics, anyone the slightest bit honest wouldn't go in for it. In my opinion, our leaders lack education and general culture. They have been promoted according to the Peter Principle [beyond their level of competence].'

How are you managing personally?

'My newspaper salary is about R.3,000 [in April, 1992], R.2,500 after tax. On top of that there are freelance earnings and my student grant. I also earn hard currency as a Russian–French interpreter, but I am paid abroad for that and spend the money abroad.

'According to polls *MK* has had done, most Moscow families – eighty per cent of people – have not bought any major items in the past five years: cars, furniture, computers, TV sets, etc. Now prices have gone up ten or even fifteen times – and my salary has only trebled. A pair of jeans made in Taiwan costs R.3,000 – what I earn in a month. A kilo of good meat costs R.300, and you have to queue for that. My parents worked for twenty years but have no savings. I have R.2,000 in the savings bank. So we live from one pay-day to the next. My parents used to be able to buy nice furniture for the living room, a fridge, a television set and a fur coat for mother. That's all we have.

'It will take twenty-five years for things really to get better. My hopes are based on the people. I have travelled a lot and think that, in spite of all the repressions and the enormous destruction of the genetic base, people have kept their Russian character. It's not true that Russians are lazy. The people of my generation have a chance to do what they want. We lived in the period of stagnation [under Brezhnev] and can compare the past with the situation today.

'What worries me is the attitude of those who are fourteen and fifteen now. They are only interested in American things, all this chewing gum and baseball. They just want to pick the flowers of life. They are in a system that looks to the West, and they want to enjoy its fruits without making the slightest effort themselves.'

# Tatyana

Tatyana Yevstafievna
Agarkova

Sex shop manager

Born: Nikolayev, Ukraine,
1951

Father: Shipbuilding
engineer, Ukrainian

Mother: Shipbuilding
engineer, Russian

Interviewed: June 1992

*Tatyana manages Moscow's first sex shop and expects eventually
to run a chain of them in the city. She and her shop, which opened
in March 1992, are a dramatic sign of the sudden sexual liberation
of a country dragooned for decades into behaving as if sex were just
one more aspect of life fully controlled by the State and Party.*

The shop is on the ground floor of a building with a forecourt
set back from a quiet road off Peace Avenue, in north Moscow. It is a ten-minute walk from the Cosmos tourist hotel.
It consists of two rooms, the first essentially an enquiry
counter. There is a charge of R.20 to enter the second room,
in which imported sex aids are displayed, guarded by several muscular young men. The entrance fee and the guards
were introduced when it became clear that most customers
look, ask questions and buy nothing, while others steal what
takes their fancy.

Tatyana Agarkova is slim with light brown hair and fine features. Her eyes usually have a concerned, soulful expression, which is now and then replaced by a twinkle of amusement. She dresses with simple elegance and one would never associate her with men in grubby raincoats. But then, in Moscow the sex shop is regarded more as an exciting but still respectable symbol of a new freedom, rather than a sleazy form of commercialism. Many younger Russians are disarmingly eager to admit their ignorance about sex and look to the West for guidance, accepting the sex shop as a healthy, proper source of accumulated experience and wisdom.

Tatyana herself underlines the educational nature of the enterprise and the essentially noble purpose of the items on display, which include red and black underwear, vibrators and condoms in quaint shapes and colours. On a shelf in her small office, I note a device labelled 'Willy Exerciser' (in English). A pair of thigh-length black lace-up boots hang from a coat-stand in a corner.

Tatyana, sitting behind her desk, tells me that she read medicine at Simferopol in the Crimea and specialised at first in microbiology. Then she married a psychiatrist who was dealing with family and sexual problems. He became increasingly interested in sexology and often treated couples.

'He didn't always find it easy talking to women patients. Not every woman wants to discuss such things with a male doctor. So I began to help him. When he started writing a book about erotic problems and sexual disharmony in families, I helped him with that, too. I was an amateur, but I found it very interesting and gradually became a specialist. Sexology is one of the most complex branches of medicine. It requires wide knowledge and imagination, especially when you are working with couples. But now I have a new profession, in the shop, and it takes up all my time.'

She is on the secretariat of a sexologists' association

which, supported by another body concerned with Aids and venereal diseases, decided to set up a chain of sex shops, starting in Moscow. The association has already opened shops in Novosibirsk, Siberia, in Murmansk, northern Russia, in the car-manufacturing city of Togliatti and in the Crimea. General policy decisions on what the shops should sell are taken by a council of specialists from all the countries of the Commonwealth of Independent States (CIS). They include journalists and arts experts as well as doctors and psychiatrists. Orders are actually placed by Tatyana, who has never travelled abroad and who buys from catalogues and from sales representatives.

'At their worst, sex shops in the West are purely commercial. We decided to do something different and help people more. Our job is to raise the level of sexual culture. We know this is needed, because we've had letters from people all over the former USSR telling us about their difficulties. We sell imports mostly. They are very expensive and so are beyond the reach of ordinary people. But we intend to get the attention of local businessmen and encourage them to manufacture similar things in this country.

'There are many lonely women who need our help. Women are in the majority in the country. The tragedy of women in rural areas is that they start families with men they don't love or respect. The men may be heavy drinkers and family life unhappy. We hope our shops will give women the freedom to choose between an instrument and a stranger. One of the main vices of our socio-economic development in this country is a lack of creativeness in family and sexual life. We are trying to enrich sexual experience.'

She says that people buy what they can afford, usually condoms ('We have all sorts of non-standard shapes and flavours'), sprays and substances to increase sensitivity and prolong intercourse, and tampons ('which are difficult to buy otherwise').

This casual remark speaks volumes of the gulf that exists between the expectations of women in Russia and the West, between the notion of going into a sex shop to buy sanitary items and the assumption that such essentials will always be available on the shelves of supermarkets.

Tatyana says that women who look round the shop are interested in but do not buy erotic underwear.

'It's not just that they can't afford it, but that they don't know how to wear it and don't know if their partner will understand. We didn't know such things existed, and anyway our women have never been used to spending much on underclothes. There are some things I don't understand, either. What do you think this is for?'

She opens a plastic bag and drops onto her desk a device consisting of a series of metal rings connected by a thin strip of leather. The mystery is solved by a catalogue in English which a young male assistant brings her. The contraption is a penis decoration.

'It is hard to perceive the beauty of it,' Tatyana says with an explosive giggle, 'I don't understand what it's supposed to do. From a commercial point of view, it is difficult to justify stocking it. I don't think anyone will buy it. But we are trying to show what is available in the world.'

She does not think there will be many takers for the erotic boots either, at R.25,000 a pair – a year's salary for many people in mid-1992 – but she does understand their purpose.

'Sexologists believe a naked woman excites a man less than a partly dressed woman. But think how long it would take him to undo those laces.'

She giggles again but quickly composes her features to stress that the shop has 'serious' backers.

'The biggest problem was raising the money and getting the premises. We haven't had any trouble with the bureaucracy. The whole building was taken by the Association of Medicine and Reproduction, a private clinic, who rented us our premises on special terms, because we are useful to each other. On the ground floor they have sexologists and psychiatrists dealing with family problems, and on the second floor they treat impotence and infertility. We advertise their services and help find patients for them.'

She has no doubt that these services and her shop are desperately needed, because of the sexual repression of the Soviet years.

'A woman feels embarrassed and ashamed to reveal her own sexuality. She has been taught to be passive and wait for a man to arouse her and blames him if he doesn't. It's very serious. She demands a lot from the man but doesn't help him. The clash between the outer world and the inner life is typical of the Soviet experience.'

# Yekaterina

| |
|---|
| Yekaterina Yurievna Sobchik |
| Psychologist and director of a school of beauty for women |
| Born: Moscow, 1955 |
| Father: Ministry of Trade official |
| Mother: Head of a private institute of applied psychology |
| Interviewed: July 1992 |

*Yekaterina Sobchik took advantage of* perestroika *to start a business that would have been unthinkable before the Gorbachov era. After seventy years of a regime which 'actively desexualised' society, she is running a 'school of feminine charm' to teach women how to reclaim their femininity. This, she explains, is far more difficult than it sounds.*

Yekaterina is a beautiful woman in her prime, with a warm smile and manner. She has an easy poise and wears her Russian-made black and white satin suit as if it came from Paris. I put to her a question I often heard while in Britain on holiday from the USSR: 'You keep on telling us what a hard life Russians live, but on television we see lots of attractive women in the streets of Moscow. How do they do it?'

'When something is very difficult,' she replies, 'it's a challenge. There's an incentive. But, in fact, I see a different picture from your questioners. I see tired women, with shoulders slumped and unpleasant expressions on their faces. And I want to tell them to straighten up, smile and say life is wonderful.'

The school offers a basic forty-hour course to put that message across. In several evening sessions and two full days over a weekend, the pupils, in groups of twenty, study thirteen different subjects with specialists trained by Yekaterina, but psychology dominates, taking up sixteen of the forty hours. An advanced course is on offer, going over the same ground in greater depth.

Yekaterina graduated in psychology from Moscow University in 1978. For ten years, she worked as a psychotherapist, treating potential suicides and working with patients in groups. She knew about Western practice in the field. But she lost faith in the most popular forms of group therapy, whose results, when beneficial, she found to be short-term.

'Our patients are very different from those in the West. They are not prepared for therapy. They come for concrete advice and don't know what to expect from therapy. They are ill at ease. I found they were often disappointed with the treatment. The women were in a desperate situation: they just didn't know how to behave as women, how to build a family and keep it happy. There were all sorts of other problems, but that was the main one. I'm absolutely sure that if you can make women behave like women, fewer will be unhappy. That's how the school was born.'

It opened in 1989. Then the basic course cost R.150. Now the price is R.2,500, and it is kept down to that only by having classes of twenty, instead of fifteen, as Yekaterina would prefer. Her lessons are practical and based on psychological training and role playing. 'First basic knowledge, then practice, giving students the chance to look at themselves from the side.'

A man plays the part of a man in the lessons. Yekaterina calls him a 'plastercast' man, but he is real and helps to teach 'non-verbal communication': body language and 'the relationship of people to each other in space. It's very important for women to move properly.'

I ask her why Russian women have the problems she describes.

'It goes a long way back. The history of the Soviet period is reflected in the poor position of women. Many men were killed – were shot, or died in camps – men who were capable of real male behaviour. The most creative men suffered. As a result we have a society in which there is no "male" achievement. The success of the *nomenklatura* élite was questionable, for it promoted the men who compromised with the system. A man with male characteristics who reached the middle level had to break himself if he was to get further promotion.

'Then, at a certain moment, the need for labour led to what was called the emancipation of women, but which was very different from emancipation in the West. There, as I understand it, there is freedom of choice. If you want to be a housewife, you can. What we had was an emancipation which forced women to work. They didn't have the right *not* to work. If they didn't have a job, they were parasites. I don't know what the new Russian Constitution will say about this, but under the Soviet regime, our women had to work as much as men, usually in boring jobs. And at the same time, all the housework fell on her shoulders, too. Women are responsible creatures and try to do everything properly. The result is very strange: women's self-respect increased, but as a class, not as individuals.'

Women took on such essential family tasks as getting better accommodation.

'She has the patience to go to the authorities and queue, beg and cry for a bigger flat. But then she tries to prove that she is better than a man. She doesn't respect the man she has and has no prospect of finding anybody better. If a man with a strong character does come along, she tries to prove he is bullshitting. That's why we see the tough attitude of women towards men in Russia. Once you get women together, they start telling each other how hopeless men are. They don't realise that they can shape their men the way they want them to be. We try to teach them to cooperate with men, not compete with them.

'For seventy years, society actively desexualised women. When a beautifully dressed and made-up woman appeared in a film, you knew she was a villain. The heroine wore a dressing-gown or an apron. She had smiling eyes and a flag in her hand, cheering the news of industrial success. My parents lived in London when I was a teenager [her father sold timber to the British], and they bought me nice clothes there. But I was embarrassed to wear them in Moscow. You weren't supposed to look different.'

Things changed in the mid-Seventies, when she says there was something of a sexual revolution in Russia. Women began to understand they were supposed to look attractive, but they didn't have a happy mean. At one extreme, some women remained very reserved. At the other, there was bold sexual behaviour: women looked like prostitutes. They had no feel for what was normal.

'We teach our students how to find their own style. We show them that clothes and make-up can be sexy without being provocative. Even if a woman dresses with strict propriety, she should underline her femininity. We teach them how to be coquettish, how to flirt and when to stop. This is important for many women, because we are reviving their sexuality. Many women treat sex mechanically and get satisfaction just from the fact that it takes place. Other women place no limit on their desires and have a consumer attitude to sex. Still others are afraid of it and behave as if it's impure and unclean. They are upset if a man treats them as a sex object. They say they want to be first of all respected as a human being. In these cases, I ask them what they think the sex of that human being happens to be. Our job is to give them a chance to be physically and spiritually satisfied in love, and for that they have to learn to love their own body and that of their partner. When they are told to kiss legs and toes, they are terrified. We tell them: "Well, you can wash him first."'

Yekaterina's head goes back and she laughs loudly. She says she helps her pupils get over their fear of the body by using the technique of group touching, familiar in the West. She also persuades them to dress up as Cleopatra and recite Pushkin's lines in which the Egyptian queen asks who will pay to spend a night with her.

What kind of women take the course?

'Most are fairly intelligent. Some are girls just out of school. Some are graduates. They are not primitive. They are capable of asking themselves questions and of improving themselves. We have tried to find out what our clients are looking for by getting them to fill in a multiple-choice questionnaire. Some come just out of curiosity, but usually there is some feeling of discomfort, of inferiority. But there are surprises. Not long ago, three girls arrived from a successful company. They were rich and beautiful and we called them the Three Graces. At the end of the course, they told us they had come just for fun but had learned so much they were now going to take the advanced course.

'Some women are so beautiful that I wonder what I can possibly teach them, but I find that they have high expectations and are unhappy. It's wonderful to see women change by the end of the course.'

# Anna

Anna Yakovlevna
Logvinskaya

Psychologist

Born: Moscow, 1952

Father: Physicist

Mother: Chemist

Interviewed: June 1992

*Anna belongs to a team of some forty dedicated psychologists and psychotherapists who operate the State-run suicide hotline in Moscow, the Telefon Doveriya (Telephone of Trust), from offices near Myakovsky Square. She has worked there since the service started up ten years ago and says she is addicted to the job. Suicide was once a taboo subject in the Soviet Union. Figures were secret or unreliable. Anna says she still is not sure that published figures are accurate, but her work gives her a special insight into what is driving Muscovites to desperation, as their country moves from old certainties and disciplines to a new system and entirely different values. She feels that she really does have her finger on the pulse of a great city.*

Anna is married, without children. Her husband is Maxim Kantor, a young painter who has exhibited in the US, France and West Germany. They live in west-central Moscow. She is dark-haired and speaks quietly, looking coolly self-possessed in a white blouse and floral cotton skirt.

'The level of suicides, strangely enough, has been

declining in Moscow,' she says, 'probably because life has been *so* difficult that people have had to marshal all their strength just to survive.'

Then suddenly, in June 1992, there was a sharp increase in the number of calls. Anna welcomes this as a sign that the city is coming back to life and taking a fresh interest in itself after a period of near paralysis, like a rabbit frozen in terror in the lights of a car. Now, she feels, Muscovites are suffering and complaining 'in the normal way'.

There is, however, a new type of client: the former Communist Party official who cannot adapt to the post-Communist world and whose children blame him and his kind for the mess the country is in. One called the hotline number, 205 0550, and told Anna: 'I'd love to find a new job, but all I can do is chair Party meetings. I graduated from technical college more than thirty years ago. Now I can't even work as a draughtsman.' Whenever he applies for a job and people hear what he used to do, they make fun of him – and this is painful for a man accustomed to deference.

'When he called, he said he had a pistol in his hand, and perhaps he had. He was close to hysteria. But this can quickly pass and is not very dangerous. He had lost his footing, it's true, and it *is* very difficult to start life all over again after you are fifty. But I reminded him of the people who spent dozens of years in camps and were released when they were his age. They found the courage and energy to start again. I tried to appeal to his masculinity. Men like that, even when they are planning to die.'

She says that the ex-apparatchik is 'a specific type of personality with a passion, a lust for power that can be compared with alcoholism and drug addiction. If they lose power, they lose themselves. It's most difficult for the older officials, because they can't do anything else. Others paint themselves in new colours, launder their money and emerge as businessmen.'

There are also many calls these days from white-collar workers who cannot cope with the new world. For years all they really had to do to earn their salary was turn up for work on time; they had no real job to do. Now aged between forty and fifty, they find it difficult to change their attitudes and get new qualifications. 'They are subject to depression and a failure complex.'

There are cases, too, of 'camouflaged depression'. A woman called the day before, saying she was suffering from nostalgia: she could not get out of her head the house she used to own in the country twenty years ago. It wasn't a summer dacha, but a house she could live in all year round. After a long talk with her, Anna concluded that the woman was retreating to the happy days associated with the house in order to stop thinking about life in Moscow today. Fear of the present was hidden deep inside her and the resulting depression was dangerous.

'We talked for about an hour and I think she will call again.'

Did she say she intended to kill herself?

'Yes.'

Did you believe her?

'Yes. It's useful to a person to know he or she is ill and can be cured. If you have a toothache it's unpleasant, but you know a dentist can deal with it. When the mind is in pain, it feels irreversible. The psychotherapist's job is to explain that not only muscles get tired but the spirit too. Sometimes understanding this is a medicine in itself.'

The woman agreed to see a doctor, something that had not occurred to her before.

'We are an emergency service. We don't claim to change people; we provide first aid. A person does not usually feel desperate for very long, unless there is a serious psychiatric illness. The fact that someone calls us is a sign that he or she wants to be helped.'

Sometimes, callers say they have already taken pills, and

then the only thing to be done is to get the address, quickly. Anna had a call from a nineteen-year-old mathematics student who said she had just taken a fatal dose. 'When I heard her speech changing, I believed her.' She refused to give her address at first. 'She just wanted to say goodbye to somebody. But when she began to feel the effects of the drug, she got frightened. So did I. But she seemed more afraid of the stomach pump than of death. She was calling from a phone box. I had to persuade her not only to give me the address of her hostel but to go back to her room and wait. The doctors said that if they had reached her twenty minutes later, it would have been impossible to save her.'

The staff are divided into five groups and work round the clock in twelve-hour shifts of four or five people – not a lot, says Anna, for greater Moscow, which has a population of eleven million, taking into account the country region, visitors and refugees.

During the day shift, there are more women than men callers. 'Women are usually tired by evening.' What the Telephone of Trust team call 'night men' are often suffering from loneliness or a sense of failure at work or in family life. The night callers tend to be 'mysterious' and introspective. Anna says the night shifts are hard but professionally rewarding. 'The most dangerous time for suicides is just before dawn. When day breaks, things become easier and the dark forces retreat.'

Young callers often want to talk about their 'love dramas' as happens everywhere, but there are specific problems for young Russians associated with the current upheaval in the whole system.

'Their life used to be programmed. Society had a clear idea of how they should develop. Their parents at least sketched out their lives for them. For those of weak character, this was fine because they didn't have to choose for themselves. The strong-willed had to put up a fight for their freedom. Today, parents are themselves so demoralised that children have stopped believing in them. This does not worry the strong, but for the others such unaccustomed freedom and independence create serious problems.'

Anna says this new situation has existed for such a short time that new patterns of behaviour are not yet established. But she worries about the way young people set their features 'to look like gangsters rather than like scholars' and have little interest in education. 'They can see it's easy to make a lot of money given time and a bit of a risk. They are contemptuous of higher education.'

Young callers often talk to her about this. Their love stories are changing, too, she has noticed. 'Young girls – even those under the age of consent – say they prefer rich, grown-up men, because they are afraid of living in poverty. They aren't interested in studying or training for a profession: it's easier to be a kept woman. The laws on sex with under-age girls are not being enforced. If they really fall in love it's a tragedy, because then they have to make a choice. This is something new for us. There didn't used to be so many sugar-daddies – not so openly anyway, because such men held official positions and had to be careful.'

Many callers want to talk about drug addiction. Anna believes this became a serious problem after the Gorbachov Government launched its anti-alcohol campaign. 'Young people like intoxication and they used to drink to get it. When wine became expensive, it was cheaper and easier to use marijuana and pills.'

One call was from a woman who suspected her son was on drugs. Asked for the symptoms, she said he didn't smell of drink when he came home late. Other parents, perhaps heavy drinkers themselves, just don't worry about their children. Anna says there is little her team can do about drugs. There are not enough addiction centres and those that do exist do not guarantee confidentiality. They may even report patients to the police.

Afghan veterans pose particularly difficult problems, and

there is a special hotline for them. Anna says they are of two main types. One type are aggressive and consider themselves misunderstood heroes. They are usually divorced and drink heavily. They can't cope with family life. In many cases, they volunteered for a second tour of duty in Afghanistan to avenge dead comrades. Anna finds this type hard to talk to. The second group were conscripted into the war. They feel guilty for their part in it. Sometimes they can't sleep. One caller was haunted by memories of an incident high in the mountains, when he took part in massacring the whole population of a village in a reprisal operation. Such people, says Anna, are high-risk potential suicides, because their depression goes deep, although they are easier to talk to over the telephone.

She talks about the way Soviet society impeded normal relationships between men and women.

'The man was supposed to be loyal to society and the Party and to an abstract bright future. A private life was something alien. This is reflected in our language: *nash narod* [our people] and *nash chelovyek* [one of us]. The word for "personality" appeared only when Stalin's cult of the personality came under attack. Anyone who tried to live an individual life was considered a potential enemy. You had to march in step and try not to be different.'

Famous people never talked about their husbands, wives or families, until Mikhail and Raisa Gorbachov came along and broke that taboo.

'Ordinary people disliked them for it. How can there be a relationship between a man and a woman in a State which bans private life? The relationship inside the Soviet family was purely functional. The pressures of everyday life deprive women of their charm, and a man ceases to be a man when he can't treat his love like a princess. This is how women and men began to lose the qualities that are described in Russian literature.

'On top of all that, public opinion and the laws of the

country discouraged people from living together. Till recently, love outside marriage – even when people *were* living together – was regarded as a dangerous illness. The result is a large number of unhappy marriages. People often rush into marriage without thinking it through. But when society is pushing in the same direction, it makes things even worse.'

The Telephone of Trust staff are trying to break away from the State and become more like the Samaritans in the West. Unlike the Samaritans, the service now uses only trained specialists to man the phones. There are no lay volunteers. The staff are badly paid, like all medical workers in Russia, and people are drifting away to better-paid jobs.

'We'd like more independence,' Anna says. 'We want to be able to guarantee anonymity to callers. Remember that Russians haven't trusted their psychiatric service for many years. The whole purpose of our service is contradicted by the fact that we belong to the psychiatric establishment. We come under the Psychiatric Dispensary No. 14. But to do our job we need to be able to promise confidentiality. Half of our callers ask if there's someone else listening in to the conversation.'

There was a revolt at Telephone of Trust early in 1992, when the staff discovered that their bosses had equipment not only to monitor but to trace calls. Press and television reported the row and the case went to court. As a result, the equipment is still there, but there is an agreement not to use it.

Big Brother habits die hard.

# Yevgeniya

Yevgeniya Yevgenievna
Debryanskaya

Writer and gay rights activist

Born: Sverdlovsk, the Urals,
1953

Father: University lecturer

Mother: Defence plant
engineer

Interviewed: May and August
1992

*Yevgeniya is a lesbian. She has been deputy-editor of* Tema
*(Theme), a magazine for homosexual men and women, since it was
launched in 1990. She came out in February of that year first at
a news conference and later, in spectacular fashion when, with a
handful of supporters, she staged a demonstration in favour of
gay rights and legalised prostitution outside the Intourist Hotel in
Tver (formerly Gorky) Street. They handed out leaflets on safe sex
and threw handfuls of American condoms to a small crowd which
consisted largely of Soviet and Western reporters. They carried a
banner that read: 'One nuclear sub = five billion condoms.'*

Jokes like this save Yevgeniya and her friends from the kind
of intense earnestness one might expect from a group dedicated to such varied causes as gay rights, the abolition of
the death penalty and of the State tobacco and alcohol monopolies and to the defence of prostitutes' human rights. But

humour is inadequate protection in a society which has suppressed sexuality of all kinds for most of the past seventy years and which still makes male homosexual acts a criminal offence.

When we meet, there is a bruise under Yevgeniya's left eye, and she is afraid she will need an operation to straighten her nose. About a month earlier, close on midnight, three young men jemmied open the door of the flat she was staying in in north-west Moscow and beat her unconscious. Ostensibly, the motive was robbery, but Yevgeniya is convinced that the break-in was part of a series of attacks on known members of the gay communities in Moscow and St Petersburg. She did not recognise her attackers and cannot prove that the assaults are coordinated, but Russians have been conditioned by decades of repression to believe in conspiracies.

'I don't think the break-in was accidental,' she says.

Her sense of humour has not been beaten out of her. She still has a ready laugh. But she has aged markedly since I first met her in 1990. Her dark brown hair is turning silver, and she moves slowly, almost warily, around the small, nearly empty flat, in which the bed is a mattress on the floor.

She is wearing black slacks and green canvas shoes and has a woollen sports coat over a white T-shirt advertising, in red letters, an Aids march in the United States. She introduces me to Lena, her girlfriend (she uses the English word) who, she says, fought the attackers.

'Lena is stronger than me, and they had to fight her. They kicked her. If she had gone on resisting them, I think they would have beaten her to death. They took everything, even our underwear. And before they left they cut the telephone line and burned papers they found in our desk. The worst blow was the theft of a floppy disk I had written a book on for an American publisher, about gays in the USSR. I'll have to write it all over again. Now I feel all right and am ready to continue our struggle. But I don't want to experience all that again.'

A few days later, she and Lena reported the attack to the police, who arrested three men. 'The investigation may show who was behind them.'

Her attackers, she thought, were lower in the criminal hierarchy than the hardened gangsters believed to have robbed and beaten up fellow campaigner Roman Kalinin, the editor of *Tema*. He made himself a target when he stood as the gay rights candidate against Boris Yeltsin in the June 1991 Russian presidential election. He did it for publicity and as a joke, since, at twenty-six, he was too young to be elected.

'He was severely beaten and his health has suffered; he's not very strong. He was worried when he heard that gangsters were still after him, but twelve of them have been arrested and he hopes the others will be soon.'

The main aim of Roman and Yevgeniya's gay rights campaign is the repeal of Article 121 of the criminal code, which makes sexual intercourse between men a criminal offence. They do not object to section two of the article, under which homosexual rape is punishable by up to eight years' imprisonment, but they argue that all kinds of rape should be punished without distinction.

They have no illusions about the difficulty of their enterprise. When we first met, Yevgeniya said: 'If we had a referendum, ninety-nine per cent would vote to make the laws [against gays] even tougher. The intelligentsia sympathises, but that's only a small part of the population.' Roman quoted a poll which indicated that thirty-five per cent of Russians were in favour of having homosexuals shot.

There is no mention of lesbians in the criminal code, but Yevgeniya insists that 'repression' has been used against them. In 1990, she introduced me to Olga, then aged twenty, who said she had been put in a psychiatric hospital when she was fifteen.

'I was at a students' hostel in Leningrad,' Olga told me, 'and made friends with another girl. One day the authorities found us in bed. I was sent to a hospital, because the director of my vocational training school demanded a certificate stating whether I was sane or not.'

She spent two weeks in the hospital for seriously ill people and said she was given injections that caused severe pain. She was never told what her diagnosis was but was allowed to return to school, where she was closely watched until her friend, who was two years older, graduated and left.

Is reform of the law any nearer? I ask Yevgeniya.

'Nothing has changed yet, in spite of all our efforts. Our appeals to the USSR Supreme Soviet [the standing Soviet Parliament, now defunct] got nowhere. We can probably find a dozen deputies in the Russian Parliament who sympathise, but they aren't ready to speak out openly, not even against Article 121. As for public opinion, I think, if anything, it has hardened. Homosexuals have always appeared alien, a closed group in this country. People could accept that such people might exist in prisons and among leading figures in the arts world. But once the mass media began to talk about the subject, people saw homosexuality around them in ordinary life. To be fair, some of the articles are objective, but homosexuality is usually mentioned in pieces about Aids.'

When did she first realise she was gay?

'I always felt it, but I was brought up in a traditional, provincial family [in Sverdlovsk, Yeltsin's power base in the Urals, now renamed Yekaterinburg – where ex-Tsar Nicholas and his family were shot in 1918] and I believed I had to marry in order to have a child. That's how Slava appeared. I don't regret that.'

Slava, now an eighteen-year-old student, listens to our conversation, sitting beside Lena on the mattress and leafing through magazines. The flat is registered in his name, but he was away on the night of the burglary. That is why

Yevgeniya, who normally lives in Lena's flat, happened to be there that night. This is one reason why the two women believe they were the target of the break-in. If burglary had been the true motive, they say, the intruders would hardly have waited till midnight, when they could expect the flat to be occupied.

Yevgeniya has a second son, Artur, aged seven, but she did not marry his father. 'I did get married several times later – once to a foreigner. I was using these husbands for my own purposes. I've kept the family name of the husband who helped me to come and live in Moscow. Marrying a Muscovite is one of the easiest ways of doing this.'

Yevgeniya showed little inclination to rebel in Sverdlovsk. 'My mother was chief engineer in a secret defence plant. My father, after their divorce, went to teach at Moscow University. He was a member of the Communist Party and I was never close to him. He died in 1985.'

But she did stage one small act of rebellion – without quite meaning to – and was expelled from the Komsomol as a result. Her crime was to miss a special Lenin anniversary *subbotnik*, when Komsomol members were required to donate a day's labour free of charge to the State.

'I was going to do it, but that morning I took my dog for a walk and he got hurt. I had to take him to the vet and so missed the *subbotnik*. When the Komsomol officials asked me why, I told them the truth, but that was fatal. They expected me to betray my mother rather than miss the *subbotnik*, and all I had done was take care of my dog. They thought it was an insult. The district Komsomol committee members came to my school to hear my case, and teachers who belonged to the Party took part, too. I thought it was very funny. The speeches were ridiculous. Teachers said I was beyond the pale, a criminal. I think if they'd had their way, I would have gone to gaol.

'Being expelled from the Komsomol was like a punishment for robbery or murder. I didn't care. The most serious consequence was a hostile *kharakteristika* [final school testimonial]. This meant that I couldn't get into a higher education institute. It didn't stop me getting a job, but I didn't want one anyway, because I didn't agree with the system.'

She dropped out.

'At the end of the Sixties, the Hippies appeared. I wasn't one myself, but I liked their philosophy. I joined up with people in the arts, who considered themselves underground. We helped to distribute *samizdat* [unofficial] literature. We were very poor, but prices were low in those days, and we were happy.'

Officially, Yevgeniya has never been employed. That is to say that she has never worked for the State. But when *glasnost* made it possible to produce and sell independent papers, she helped to bring out an anti-Communist paper called *Dem Op*, short for Democratic Opposition. It sold up to ten thousand copies an issue and she and the three men who produced it made a little money. Her three colleagues left Russia in 1987 for Poland and now are all living in Vienna.

The new freedom of the Gorbachov years allowed Yevgeniya to travel abroad for the first time, too. She went to Italy in 1989 and made her first trip to the United States the following year. An American gay rights organisation invited her, and prostitutes who had read US newspaper reports about her Gorky Street demonstration welcomed her as a celebrity. She went to Los Angeles, Boston, Washington and New York and gave lectures at Princeton. She stayed in the US for three months and made a second trip in 1991.

Contact with the outside world gave encouragement to the Russian Libertarian Party, which Yevgeniya invented in the summer of 1989. 'It isn't a real party. It has never been registered. But it was a way of raising all sorts of subjects: gay rights; the sexual emancipation of society and the right of women to a free sexual choice; the legalisation of drugs;

the problem of Aids; civil rights for children; animal rights and their treatment in zoos and circuses; prostitutes' rights, and so on. We wanted to test popular reaction to an extreme radical programme. It was a trial balloon. The Soviet Press took no notice at first, but then it reacted to foreign articles about us. But it still wouldn't touch the subject of gays. So we decided to come out and to launch *Tema*.'

In October 1991, a 'coming out' conference was held in Moscow and thirty-nine people declared themselves homosexual, enough for them to apply for official registration as a group with Moscow City Council. Ten days later the application was rejected. They were promised a letter setting out the reasons for the decision, but they never received it.

Yevgeniya and her group have continued to make occasional forays into the streets of Moscow. In December 1991, they staged an unauthorised demonstration opposite the City Council building on International Aids Day. Again they handed out leaflets and condoms. 'We weren't afraid of the police but of passers-by. But there was no attack from that quarter. People were friendly and took the condoms. No one was beaten up.'

She smiles and her eyes twinkle, and I ask her how she gets on with her neighbours. Well, she says, but concedes that they did not come to her help on the night of the break-in. They did not even call the police.

Despite her courage, stamina and sense of fun, Yevgeniya declares herself a pessimist. 'The situation is unpredictable, but the signs are that things will get worse: crime will increase and Aids will spread, because there's no programme to combat it. And when there is economic chaos, people aren't interested in such things as gay rights and Aids. We shall carry on campaigning, though. If we don't, who will?'

# Ludmilla

Ludmilla Leonidovna
Timashkova

Faith healer, speech therapist,
mother of four

Born: Krasavino, Vologda
region, Central Russia, 1951

Father: Builder

Mother: Chemist

Interviewed: June 1992

*Ludmilla is a faith healer, what the Russians call an* extrasens.
*Most of her patients hear of her by word of mouth and she diagnoses
them by scrutinising their aura with her inner eye. Her husband
Vladislav is a psychiatrist with a belief in alternative medicine and
in Ludmilla's powers. In Russia, faith healing has a long tradition,
as might be expected in a vast country where, for all the Soviet
efforts and boasts, hospitals are often far away from patients and
the quality of conventional medicine is poor. Too many general
practitioners in polyclinics function essentially as machines for
issuing sick notes, Russian friends complain. Alternative medicine
and trust in herbal remedies, massage, acupuncture and so on
flourish today, as the health service collapses and modern medicines
are still hard to find. Another very remarkable fact about Ludmilla
is that she is bringing up four children in Moscow, when one at
most is the norm.*

She lives with her family in the Fili district, a western suburb, where the Fili Park – a large expanse of tamed forest – dominates an oxbow loop in the Moskva River. The flat has four rooms, a medium-sized kitchen and the usual bathroom and lavatory. By normal Moscow standards, it is a big, rambling place.

'We got it nine years ago, when our third child, Zhenya, was a year old. It seemed a palace to us then. Before, we had just two rooms, and my mother-in-law was living with us. There was a rule that all families with three children should get better accommodation within a year of the birth of the third child. But this was not always done. We were lucky.'

Ludmilla talks as she peels and chops up carrots and potatoes for a vegetable-and-nettle soup. She is a big woman with a deliberate manner. Her brown hair is long and is held by a clip. She is wearing a turquoise tracksuit with white, yellow and dark blue stripes. Her fourth child, a boy called Vasya (Vasily), was born on 14 January (St Basil's Day) 1992.

'I put on weight after he was born. Before that I didn't look as if I'd had a lot of children. As a mother of three, I had a card which theoretically allows you to go to the front of a queue. But in practice it depends on whether the other people in the queue object or not. Usually they do. They used to curse me and say they didn't believe I had three children. The card was a forgery, they said.'

Ludmilla laughs, though later she confesses that she hates standing in queues because people are so unpleasant to one another in them, just as they are in crowded Metro trains and buses. However, her great store of patience shows in her steady eyes and calm, low voice. She has a rugged sense of humour.

'It's one big problem having a large family, but we're not afraid of it, as you see, because we keep on having children. Vasya was born to teach *perestroika* a lesson, as a kind of protest against falling living standards in the country. The Government doesn't encourage people to have children – so we do.'

It is one of her very few references to politics. In this household, life revolves around the children, the daily routine largely determined by baby Vasya's waking hours.

The eldest son, Arseny, is sixteen, a first-year student in art school. Kiril, twelve, is about to go to a gymnasium, a secondary school, which specialises in biology. Zhenya, the only daughter, is ten and at the local secondary school. There is a cat called Mashka, bought as a kitten for two roubles by Kiril at the Moscow pet market. Its favourite resting place is on top of a small portable television set on the kitchen table. Their mongrel dog Byelka [squirrel] was a stray which followed them home one day. Kiril, the budding biologist, also keeps mice and tropical fish.

They often have people to stay, because Ludmilla is the only member of her extensive family who lives in Moscow. She took in one nephew, when his mother died, and he stayed for two years. Now he is grown up and works as a carpenter.

Ludmilla graduated from a theatre school and for a time performed in an amateur folk theatre at Ramenskoye, outside Moscow. When she got married, she gave that up and went to a teacher training institute part-time. She took evening classes and worked at a kindergarten during the day. She earned R.80 a month and her husband Vladislav, as a full-time medical student, had a grant of R.40 a month. Arseny was born when Ludmilla was in her first year at the institute; Kiril, when she was in her fifth year.

Ludmilla has also worked as a speech therapist, using skills learnt at theatre school. She used to do most of the shopping for the family. Now she is on maternity leave from the speech therapy job, and the males have to help with the shopping. She and Vladislav do a big shop twice a week, but there is something to be bought every day and one has to hunt around. Since the prices went up, there is more available: cheese and pasta, for instance. But food has become very expensive. They buy their vegetables at the nearest farmers' market, where beetroot costs R.50 a kilo.

Vladislav joins us in the kitchen and takes Vasya on his knee, handling him in a confident Western fashion. Russian babies are normally bound like parcels in swaddling clothes and treated for years as if they are fragile. In this household, Vasya is bounced and moves his limbs freely. His father is a handsome man with grey hair and moustache and a lithe, compact body. He talks about the holidays they are about to start.

He has found a house in a village near the Volga River, about a hundred and twenty miles from Moscow, a journey of five hours in his 1953 Pobyeda [Victory] car. They will leave the car near the Volga and cross the river by boat. On the other side, they, their children and their possessions will be carried to the village on a cart pulled by a tractor. There are no shops in the village, but he will work as a general practitioner and his potential holiday patients – delighted at the prospect of having a doctor at hand for a few weeks – have promised to supply the family with eggs and meat. Bread is delivered by tractor from a bakery in the nearest town.

There is a large *sovkhoz* (State farm) in the area surrounded by big villages, but these have been abandoned by the young workers who prefer to live in blocks of flats on the farm itself. The villages are kept going by retired people and by Muscovites who have bought up old houses as holiday homes in the depths of the country. There, the air is clean and the forests have berries, elk and deer – and are rich in herbs for natural remedies.

In Moscow, Vasya sleeps on the balcony of the flat in the summer and Ludmilla takes him to Fili Park in his pram, when the the weather is fine. At home, she sings to him and tells him fairy stories. His sister and the younger brother come home to lunch between 1 pm and 2 pm. Vladislav and Arseny are back in time for supper. In the evening, Ludmilla helps the children with their homework and reads to them.

During the day, she fits in a daily load of washing and an occasional patient. She examines me. She sits in a chair in the kitchen with her back to the window and I stand in front of her for what seems an age and is probably about fifteen minutes. She keeps her eyes on me for the whole of that time, moving them from one part of my body to another, giving each her silent, full attention. At the end, she pronounces me reasonably fit.

She discovered her gifts in the 1970s, when her husband became interested in extrasensory powers and took her to an 'underground' laboratory on Kirov Street. She says that such experiments at the time were not exactly forbidden, but they were not allowed either. At the laboratory, a professor examined her aura and she revealed that she could also see such things. She found that she could measure a person's energy by looking at him or her. Her husband helped her develop her gift and she cured him of an eye complaint.

When she treats patients, she places her hands close to, but not on, them. The essential part of a consultation is the diagnosis, arrived at by the silent contemplation of the patient's body. She says that she studies seven main and two subsidiary 'chakras', energy centres.

'The upper chakra is closed when a person is asleep. When a patient is awake and in good health, you can see a huge current of energy going along the spine and up into space, broad as a river and multi-coloured. You judge the state of health by this current. This chakra goes deep into space and an *extrasens* can see how far it goes.'

It was this ability to see chakras which Ludmilla discovered at the laboratory in Kirov Street. She watched the way faith-healers examined patients there and tried their method herself on Vladislav. She found she could see his energy current and began looking in the same way at people in the streets and in the Metro.

'From childhood I have had an image of Christ inside me and I have always spoken to Him when I am troubled. He always helped me. Now, when I examine sick people and see what is wrong with them, I ask Christ whether I have the right to help them. I ask His permission.'

Ludmilla also uses Buddhist terms to describe her methods and says that her main aim, when curing patients, is to fill them with 'prajna' – wisdom and understanding.

'I don't give anything of myself. I just give back to them what they have lost or don't know how to use. I purify their energy and open it for them.'

She says that the Russian Ministry of Health has been conducting experiments to check the powers of faith healers. Sometimes conventional doctors refer patients to them and then re-examine them after treatment. Vladislav occasionally asks his wife to look at one of his patients, when he is not absolutely sure of a diagnosis, but they do not work as a team.

Ludmilla comes from a family with a long line of clergymen. She is a believer, herself – though not what she considers a 'real' believer – and traces her healing skills back to mystical experiences as a young girl. She uses common sense in diagnosis, too.

'One patient came to me with a swollen womb. I saw her and said that she didn't like her husband and was trying to avoid sexual contact with him. That's where her trouble came from. It's very difficult to treat such people. She would rather die than leave her husband and children. There are many such cases. Things are difficult for women here. And in workers' families it's even worse, because many husbands drink and beat their wives. A Russian woman is a horse pulling a cart. But she is very kind-hearted and humane.

'Every person has his own purpose, and if he is to fulfil

his destiny, he can do it in any country and under any conditions. In the West, women are better provided economically, but I don't think they suffer any less than we do. We have to put up with a worsening situation. The best way to be ourselves is to help other people.'

Chapter 2

# The Communist Legacy

The failure of the Soviet experiment was rammed home to Muscovites daily by empty boasts preserved in bricks, stone and concrete. The grandiose Exhibition of the Economic Achievements of the USSR, in north Moscow (known by its Russian initials VDNKh, although it was renamed the All-Russia Exhibition Centre), was mocked by evidence all around of economic disaster. Russia, the biggest country in the world, could not feed itself. And on the territory of the world's biggest producer of oil, the small minority of citizens lucky enough to own a car had to queue for hours to get petrol.

I had only to look out of my office window to be reminded of the soaring ambitions of the Soviet leaders and the reality of their legacy. Immediately below was a playground shared by the children and pets of the foreign diplomats and journalists allocated accommodation in the foreign ghetto block I lived and worked in. Beyond the playground was the back of a crumbling polyclinic. Then, towering above that, was a stone-faced modern office block with brown mirror windows.

'Block' is a weak word for this grand structure which is half a mile long and fills one side of Masha Poryvayeva Street (formerly Novokirovsky Avenue), a broad thoroughfare which Leonid Brezhnev's town planners built on the wreckage of what used to be a quiet, beautiful part of old

Moscow. Their plan was to drive the avenue into the heart of the city to Dzerzhinsky (now Lubyanka) Square.

The project was abandoned and the great office building is still unfinished and only partly occupied by sections of State-owned banks. Parts of the building are closed up with corrugated sheeting and there are bare patches of brickwork waiting for stone facing that may never come. It was one of the massively expensive, uncompleted white elephants which Mikhail Gorbachov so often complained about but could not stop. At the back of it was a strip of waste ground littered with broken bricks, twisted steel rods, a half-buried electric motor and the burnt-out carcases of two cars. Dyetsky Sad 694, the kindergarten, shut out this squalor with a high concrete wall.

From the kindergarten, a short, narrow road between two blocks of flats leads back to Bolshaya Spasskaya Street and joins it opposite a bread shop. For weeks, in early spring 1992, the road outside the shop boasted what must have been one of the biggest, deepest potholes in a city renowned for them. After a while, some public-spirited citizen dropped the casing of an old gas cooker into it, as a warning to drivers. A lorry crushed the cooker, and a new hazard-warning signal was inserted: a length of stove-pipe, which rose from the hole like a broken mast. Then, one day, a road-mending team arrived, removed the flattened cooker and the piping, filled in the hole and patched the surface of the road.

The ambition and squalor so evident in my district of Moscow were a mild reflection of what the Soviet system bequeathed to Russia, as a whole, and to the republics which broke away from the USSR. In the summer of 1992, the Russian Ministry of Ecology and Natural Resources delivered a detailed report on the appalling state of the Russian environment to the Earth Summit in Rio de Janeiro. It put the blame for the mess on the growth-at-any-price policies of the Soviet period.

The report includes a map of the 'ecological troublespots in the Russian Federation', with shaded areas where the situation is 'extremely dangerous'. These include the Moscow region, the Murmansk section of the Kola peninsula in northern Russia, Kalmykia in the south, the industrial centres of the Urals, the Middle Volga, the oil, gas and coal fields of Siberia, the Norilsk industrial area in northern Siberia and Lake Baikal in the south. The report says that there is an 'extremely unfavourable environmental situation' in forty-three Russian cities, 'where a high pollution level produces an adverse impact on the health of the residents.'

No fewer than twenty-five Russian ministries had a hand in another report on the Russian environment made public in October 1992. This reveals that almost a sixth of the total area of the Russian Federation is so contaminated by toxic wastes that it is 'ecologically unsafe'. In other words, territory totalling close on one million square miles has become unfit for human habitation. Another grim fact added to so many others is that in eighty-four towns and cities – including Moscow – air pollution is more than ten times the permissible level.

The poisoning of the air, water and land catalogued in this report makes depressing reading, but President Yeltsin's own ecological adviser, Dr Alexei Yablokov, is convinced that the greatest danger of all comes from radiation. In his office in the Kremlin, this white-haired, passionate scourge of polluters, tells me that the Chernobyl nuclear power station disaster in the Ukraine in 1986 is only 'one thousandth of the problem', although a map on one of the walls of his office shows sixteen regions of Russia contaminated by fallout from Chernobyl.

The town of Bryansk is in one of them and a few days earlier, a Russian friend, a young mother, had told me she and her husband were thinking of buying a dacha there, so that their two children could play in the fresh air during the holidays and at weekends. What worried her was that the people living in the village they were interested in near Bryansk were receiving a payment from the State of a few roubles a month.

I ask Dr Yablokov if this is fallout compensation. 'We call it *grobovye dyengi* – coffin money,' he replies and takes me to another map, of Moscow, which is covered with dozens of little yellow, blue and red circles, each indicating an abnormal level of radiation. 'The red spots are really dangerous,' Yablokov explains. 'You can walk through such places, but if you spend a few hours in them, it is not good for your health.' He talks about radiation pollution caused by nuclear power stations and the military–industrial complex, like the plutonium plant at Krasnoyarsk 26, a 'closed', secret town, which for some forty years disgorged cooling water from two of its reactors straight into the mighty river Yenisey, which flows north across Siberia to the Arctic Ocean. There are stretches of the river, says Yablokov, with levels of radioactivity 'like the worst places around Chernobyl'.

The Rio report and Yablokov himself find some comfort in new anti-pollution laws and heightened public awareness of what is at stake. However, Yablokov and his colleagues have calculated that to clean up the pollution inherited from the Soviet period would require Russia to spend, over twenty years, the equivalent of twice its Gross National Product in 1991, and this at a time when both production and the value of the rouble are falling steeply.

High inflation gave new point to the old phrase attributed to the Soviet workers: 'They pretend to pay us, we pretend to work.' The new Soviet man, 'homo sovieticus', has not developed into a Stakhanovite hero-worker but is rather, as Soviet wives often point out, 'good at idling'. One of Gorbachov's unrealised ambitions was to change the attitudes to work of the labour force. In a speech to the Central Committee, in 1989, he claimed that this was in fact happening: 'A new type of working man is taking shape,' he declared, while complaining at the same time that many 'have forgotten how to work. They have got used to the fact that they are paid just for turning up to work.' Gorbachov advocated an incentive pay structure with higher salaries for those who worked harder and better. This was not what homo sovieticus had been brought up to expect. He was, in the main, used to overmanning and a broad equality in poverty.

The reforms of 1992 came as a severe shock to this system. Suddenly a vast gap opened up between the haves and the great majority of have-nots. Equality had never been real, of course. The privileges enjoyed, fairly discreetly, by the *nomenklatura* had ensured that the Party élite were comfortably off. Individuals also became rich from the corruption which flourished under Brezhnev. But in the late 1980s, very few Russians owned a Western car. If one saw a Mercedes with private Russian plates in Moscow, it was a fair guess that the woman driving it was the popular singer Alla Pugachova. Now, it is common to see shiny new German, French, Swedish and Japanese cars shooting away from traffic lights, leaving home-produced Volgas, Ladas and Moskviches for dead. In a country unable to repay its foreign debts, the traffic police were driving BMWs.

In the summer of 1992, Moscow staged its first international motor show since 1913, and James Walker, representative of a firm distributing American cars in Russia, was reported as saying that about three per cent of Muscovites (300,000 people) could afford to spend $30,000 on a car.

The new climate was alien. The way forward, Russian reformers and foreign experts agreed, lay through privatisation in a country where the State owned almost everything. Yeltsin launched a form of privatisation designed to give a slice of the giant pie to everyone. But there was a deep distrust of the idea. When State assets were sold off, some argued, they would wind up in the hands of foreign speculators, home-grown gangsters or the old Party élite. There was also the suspicion that, if ordinary people did acquire property, they would not be allowed to keep it for long.

The suspicions and the uneasiness were understandable. For the idea of private property as the basis of a new economy and society was at odds not only with the ideology preached for seven decades by an all-powerful political machine. It was also alien to the experience of most Russians for centuries. A favourite exercise of Western diplomats, journalists and academics, seeking to demonstrate the continuity of this experience, is to quote the writings of a French traveller and then to reveal that he is not a visitor to the USSR but the Marquis de Custine, who went to Russia in 1839. His book is indeed full of observations about a tyrannical State, systematic secrecy, deep distrust of foreigners, the denial of freedom, censorship and 'the political enslavement of the Orthodox Church', which can be taken as perceptively referring to Soviet Russia. Custine explodes with joy at regained freedom on his arrival in Berlin *en route* for France in October 1839 and concludes his book with the bleak remark that 'whoever has seen Russia will find himself content to live anywhere else'.

Another Western writer describes Russia as a 'tyrannical state . . . without true knowledge of God, without written law, without common justice.' Those observations appear in *Of the Russe Commonwealth* by Giles Fletcher who, in 1588–89, was ambassador of Queen Elizabeth I of England. Scholars have found similar comments in the writings of diplomats in Russia through the centuries.

Looking at pre-Revolutionary Russia through these eyes helps the visiting Westerner to understand why the country feels so foreign, even when it looks and sounds quite European – and to be wary of trying to predict how its people will behave. For it is too pat to answer a question such as 'Why do Russian women put up with it all?' simply by noting that Russians have been putting up with the intolerable for centuries. This does not take account of the many occasions when they have violently run out of patience.

The women I interviewed often surprised me with their reactions to their experiences in Soviet Russia, whether it was the irrepressible cheerfulness of Kseniya, as she told me the story of her long, hard life, or Kira's calm, stubborn worship of Joseph Stalin. Even Kira's extreme position is not totally divorced from a prevailing mood of uncertainty in which there is a melancholy sense of loss – loss of purpose, of idealism, of community. Women, I found, often spoke about the break-up of the USSR with regret, if only because they were horrified at the bloodshed that accompanied it and because they were afraid for the twenty-five million Russians living, like hostages, in now independent republics of the former USSR.

A young Russian friend told me that his mother, now a convinced Yeltsin reformer, had been a Stalinist in her youth and had even been part of the crowd that tried to attend his funeral in 1953, with the loss of some two hundred lives in the crush.

An autobiographical film based on this event was completed in 1991 by the poet Yevgeny Yevtushenko. He was often dismissed as a licensed *enfant terrible* of the Soviet system but was consistent in his contempt for Stalin's crimes and his opposition, sometimes feeble, sometimes brave, to attempts to cover them up. His voice may be suspect, but he no doubt touched many Russian hearts with his farewell to the red flag:

> I did not take the Winter Palace,
> I did not storm the Reichstag,
> I'm not one of your old Commies,
> But I stroke the flag and cry.

# Kseniya

Kseniya Pavlovna Godina

Glass-maker

Born: St Petersburg, 1910

Father: Printer

Mother: Housewife

Interviewed: March 1992

*A conversation with Kseniya is an extraordinarily lively introduction to the political and social history and geography of Russia under the Soviet regime. She lived through the whole of the Soviet period, and her memories of Petrograd in 1917 and many other parts of Russia in the Twenties and Thirties are pin-sharp. She travelled widely as a child and teenager, when her family was on the move for seven years in search of food and better living conditions. As a young woman, Kseniya believed in Communism, but she lost faith in the Party and eventually in Lenin himself.*

Kseniya grew up in St Petersburg (named Petrograd in 1914) and was seven at the time of the Revolution. It was a hungry childhood – in the First World War and especially during the Civil War that followed – and typically her child's eye view of 1917 was dominated, not by memories of the Winter Palace or the Smolny Institute ablaze with light, described by John Reed in *Ten Days That Shook The World*, but of the day she was robbed of food and the family's ration cards.

'I did most of the shopping for food. I kept the money

and ration cards in a knitted bag. One day, I remember buying meat and bread in Maly Avenue. The queues weren't very long – the shops still had stocks then. I was very trusting as a child, and I still am. I believe every word I'm told. Opposite the food store was a toy shop with dolls in the window. As I was going home, a boy of about fifteen came up to me and said he would buy me a doll if I would do him a favour and go and get his sister for him. He said he couldn't go himself, because he had quarrelled with his parents. He led me to a building across the square and told me I'd find his sister on the fourth floor. He gave me the number of the flat and the family's name and said he would look after my heavy bags for me.

'I found the flat, but there was no one there of the name he'd given me. I went back downstairs but couldn't find him. I cried. I was in despair and a crowd gathered around me. The people took me to the head of the workers' committee which issued ration cards. He lived in our block and knew us. The people told him what had happened and he said I was from an honest family, so he gave me new cards.'

It was a sad little story but, as Kseniya tells it, her eyes sparkle with fun. She seems permanently in high spirits. She is tiny, with grey hair and glasses, and shows two teeth capped with steel, when she laughs. She says she has always been teetotal, has never walked if she could run and has only recently given up skiing.

Her mother Anna was a Lutheran; she went into service as a maid with a German family in St Petersburg when she was nine. Kseniya's father, Pavel, was an atheist, but he went to church at Christmas and Easter and took Kseniya with him. He took her to the opera, too. At home, he carried his children around singing arias to them. 'He didn't have a good voice, but he was very musical.'

Her mother told her about Bloody Sunday, 9 January 1905 (22 January, according to the new calendar), when troops fired into a crowd of workers marching to the Winter Palace to present a petition to the Tsar. Anna saw carts pulled through the streets piled with bodies. The massacre was a shock to the city. Pavel joined the Russian Social Democratic Labour Party and was a member of the Workers' Soviet which, for a while, came close to controlling the imperial capital. He was active in the revolutionary underground, but his children knew nothing about that at the time.

He later supported the Menshevik wing of Social Democracy in Russia, which was eventually defeated by Lenin's Bolsheviks. He never joined the Communist Party after the Revolution. As a printer, he belonged to a workers' aristocracy. There was Swedish blood in him and he earned a hundred roubles a month. He considered himself well-to-do, 'though we didn't have any gold, jewellery or investments – they spent their money on us. My father didn't have his nose in the air.'

Kseniya's mother had a child every two years ('no abortions, no medical care'): twelve babies in all but only six survived. Anna's mother had been what the peasants called a *shpitonka*, an illegitimate child of rich parents sent to the country to be brought up.

When Kseniya was four, her nine-year-old sister Tanya died of pneumonia in their home on Vasilievsky Island. She remembers her mother telling her: 'Be quiet, Tanya's dying' and wondered how keeping quiet could stop anyone dying. After Tanya's death, they moved to a different building in the same area. It was a four-storey block built for war veterans.

'There were long corridors on all the floors, like an hotel. All the flats had just one room. There were two kitchens on each floor and everyone cooked on a huge stove. Every room was heated by a Dutch stove.'

Her parents were strict and deeply reserved. 'I never knew how they met. And I never kissed them, though we loved one another. I feel the same about my children. They are the dearest thing in the world. We didn't show our feelings to our parents, but if I came home and my mother wasn't there I missed her terribly. She was like the woman in Nikolai Nekrasov's famous poem "who could stop a galloping horse and enter a burning building". My mother would share her last piece of food with a stranger. Even in the most difficult times, when there was almost a famine, she never turned people away.'

The worst years were during the Civil War of 1918–21, 'when there was real hunger and we expected to die every day. The bread ration was fifty grammes (less than two ounces) per person per day, and there were longer and longer queues even for that.'

At the end of 1918, Pavel decided to take his wife and six children (including a baby born in October that year) away from Petrograd to go in search of food. He had a friend in Saratov on the Volga, who occasionally sent him big loaves of brown bread. So they set off for Saratov on a journey that was to last seven years, taking them across Russia via Moscow to the north Caucasus and back. Before they left Petrograd, Kseniya watched a little girl standing in front of an ikon, saying: 'God, please give me some bread' and stamping her foot.

Early on their travels, they met Cossacks who were on their way to fight the revolutionaries in Petrograd (the soldiers gave the children a melon). In Saratov, they stayed with their father's friend for a while. The house had no lavatory and the children had to walk barefoot into the snow outside and crouch there. 'Our stomachs were so weak that we couldn't digest the lentils, potatoes and bread we were given, so we excreted food for the dogs, Palma and Tomka.'

Then life became hard in Saratov, too, as the town filled with refugees. 'My mother used to walk forty kilometres to exchange spare clothes for bread and milk in the countryside.' The baby born in 1918 died of dysentery at eleven months, and in the spring of 1920 they left the town on foot. 'The sun was shining and the snow had melted. We carried everything ourselves. We walked through the fields. I was carrying a suitcase with porcelain in it. But I could never walk quietly. I jumped on some logs and knocked the case against one. The cups began to clink and my mother realised something was wrong. My brother called me an elephant in a china shop and the nickname stuck.'

Kseniya is sure she became a girl by mistake. 'I was intended to be a boy. I never liked make-up and wasn't interested in clothes. I climbed every tree and jumped every fence. I caught frogs and mice and climbed mountains. I was never afraid of men, until four years ago, when my daughter was attacked in Moscow.

'I was never keen on caressing and kissing. Even after I had been married for several years I couldn't kiss my husband goodbye. I first fell in love with a schoolfriend, when I was seventeen. We couldn't touch each other even with our elbows. We didn't even take each other by the hand, except when we were skating. Now teenagers kiss each other on the escalator in the Metro. There's not sixty or eighty years between us but a thousand.'

After leaving Saratov, Kseniya's family stopped at the first village they came to, but her father couldn't get work and they seemed to be getting closer to the famine they had left Petrograd to escape. So they went on to another village where they lodged with the widow of a peasant, 'a real kulak, who worked hard from early morning till late at night.' (A *kulak* was a 'rich' peasant of the type who were dispossessed and exiled or starved to death during the forced collectivisation of the early 1930s.)

Pavel and Anna moved on again, this time to Samara (later named Kuibyshev, now Samara again) further down the Volga. From there they travelled by ship and train to a village near Mineralnye Vody, in the north Caucasus, but found people there were dying of hunger and cholera. They were warned not to buy meat, because it was human flesh. Her parents found work in Pyatigorsk, capital of the region, and they settled there. Her father was a trade union clerk; her mother worked as waitress and laundress.

By the time the family got back to Petrograd, by then re-named Leningrad, in 1925, Lenin himself was dead, but his New Economic Policy – NEP – had filled the shops. 'Everything was on sale. There were buns I hadn't seen since tsarist times. They had the same smell and taste.'

For six months, they all stayed with Kseniya's aunt and her husband in a single room. Some of the children slept on a table. Then Pavel found a room in a communal flat and they were glad to get it.

Kseniya finished school in 1928 and, at the second attempt, passed the examination to the Leningrad Technical Institute. It had been famous before the Revolution. Now it was named after the Workers' and Peasants' Soviet of 1905. The fact that her father had been a member of that Soviet helped her to get a place. She was one of only three students in her year who came straight from school. People with work experience were preferred.

Among them was Zinovy Godin, a handsome young man with a mop of black hair 'and a gentle temperament', who had gone to work in a glass factory when he was fifteen. At the institute, he was specialising in glass and ceramics. Kseniya found this interesting, too, and they went on work practice together to a china factory in the medieval city of Novgorod.

Zinovy, who is a Jew, was born in 1907 in Grodno. (This was then part of Poland. In 1918, the Germans occupied it under the Treaty of Brest-Litovsk. Later it belonged to the Soviet Republic of Byelorussia, now the independent state of Belarus.) He was one of seven children. His father was a baker.

'The family survived the Polish occupation and the German occupation but suffered terribly from anti-Semitism under the Poles and Germans. When he was sixteen, Zinovy joined the Komsomol with great enthusiasm. He liked the slogans about internationalism (respect for all the nationalities in the multi-national USSR) and equality. It was a new world of dignity for a persecuted Jewish boy from a small village who at last became a human being. This is why so many Jews took part in the Revolution. When he was twenty, he joined the Communist Party, and he was loyal to it.'

Kseniya was also a keen Komsomol member. 'I wasn't a leader – I wasn't vain enough – but I hoped for a happy future. I really believed and took everything I was told for the truth.'

In their two years at the institute, she and Zinovy went on three work-experience courses together and became very close. One day, strolling along Nevsky Avenue in Leningrad, they passed her local wedding palace. They went in to put their names down for a wedding but, since they both had their internal passports with them, decided on an impulse to get married right away. 'No Mendelssohn, no wedding breakfast. My parents were upset. They thought I was too young at twenty-one. That was on 15 December 1931. In 1991, we celebrated our diamond anniversary.'

Her husband, she says, was always proud of being part of the Soviet system, although he knew at first hand about the treatment of the peasants during the period of forced collectivisation from 1929 to 1932. When they were on work practice at the White Bull glass factory at Cheryepoviets in northern Russia, he was one of six students who were given guns and sent off into the country to help with 'dekulakisation' – rounding up kulaks who were to be sent into exile.

The early 1930s were hard, and the artificial famine imposed on the Ukraine affected food supplies to Leningrad. Pavel got extra rations once a month as a veteran revolutionary.

'People were bought with privileges; they were hungry

and couldn't refuse. There was real hunger in Leningrad and Novgorod.

'My husband knew that Stalin was a tyrant and that many people perished because of him. He worked for a time with military people at a chemical research institute. He witnessed the "leadership reshuffle" (the purges) in 1937–38. He knew that those who were repressed couldn't be enemies of the people.'

In 1938, when they had settled in Moscow, one of Zinovy's former colleagues called on them and asked them to shelter him. He was thirty-five, a Jew and former plant director. He told them he was being persecuted at work. 'We had to refuse. We had a baby in a one-room, ten-square-metre flat and had already refused to put up Zinovy's younger brother.'

Nevertheless, when the Germans invaded in 1941, she invited her family to stay with her. They chose to remain in Leningrad and were there throughout the siege. Pavel died in March 1942. Anna lived to be ninety-eight.

'My husband still believed in Communist ideals, although Stalin had corrupted them. To him Lenin seemed without sin and I believed in Lenin, too.'

When Gorbachov came to power and launched his policies of *perestroika* and *glasnost*, there was a split in the family over the critical re-examination of Soviet history. Zinovy, the loyal Communist, was on one side, Kseniya, her children and grandchildren, on the other.

Kseniya lost her faith in Lenin when the Soviet mass media pointed to similarities between his and Stalin's policies. 'I realised that Lenin's image was falsified. There was nothing left. My own experience was not enough. Now we have more information about what had happened. The critics of the Soviet system are right. What happened under Stalin did not happen just because he willed it so, but because of serious mistakes in ideology after the Revolution: the one-party system, the suppression of all criticism.

Totalitarianism was created under Lenin and developed under Stalin. Stalin continued along the road chosen by Lenin. He needed Lenin like a banner to cover his actions. But it is only now that I have begun to criticise Lenin. I used to believe in the way he was presented to us, as the most humane of men. The NEP was based on good ideas. Lenin was much cleverer than Stalin. Inflation was defeated and the shops were filled. In 1925, when the family came back to Leningrad, the country was on the right road. Every year since then, it has got worse.'

Her husband, too, has lost his Communist beliefs. 'He has trouble with his eyes and I read to him. Now when he listens to articles criticising Lenin, he doesn't argue any more. But he criticises democratic changes, too. He has lost all faith in everyone.'

But she does not believe the Communist system is quite dead yet.

'All the structures that existed before *perestroika* are still there. He [Gorbachov] hasn't destroyed them. They are hidden but they are still functioning. I can see that myself.'

She lives for her four families: herself and her husband, her two daughters and their husbands, and her married granddaughter and her family.

'I am afraid that when the children are my age, life on this planet will be bad. There will be an ecological disaster and it will start in a country like ours. I am more worried by the ecology than by politicians.

'People are cutting the branch they are sitting on. They don't understand they are killing themselves with their machines. We often used to be able to forecast the weather using old sayings. Now the forecasts are upset by the Greenhouse Effect.'

Kseniya is old enough to remember Russia before Stalin industrialised it, and she travelled widely in those days of pure air and clean water. She is therefore personally able to measure the extent of the damage done to the environment by planners who took its infinite forgiveness for granted.

She has evidently communicated her deep concern about this aspect of the Soviet legacy to her granddaughter Lyuba (see chapter 6) who is studying to become an ecologist.

# Liza

| |
|---|
| Yelizaveta Sergeyevna Shevchuk |
| Factory worker |
| Born: Karabanovo, Vladimir region of Russia, 1909 |
| Parents: Farm workers |
| Interviewed: May 1992 |

*Liza is a much decorated* udarnitsa *(shock worker), the title Stalin borrowed from army élite 'shock troops'. It was handed out to millions of workers, men and women, together with a red udarnik certificate, like a Party card, and a badge bearing a portrait of Lenin. Udarniks and udarnitsas got their award after twenty-five years in the same factory or for completing their Five-Year Plan targets ahead of time. Liza certainly earned her title. She retired in December 1990, at the age of eighty-one, after working for more than sixty years at the same Moscow defence plant, making parts for tanks and aircraft. In a country whose economy was geared to supplying a massive military machine, her job placed her at the top of the workers' hierarchy. Now, the world which honoured her has gone. The factory she devoted her life to is on the brink of bankruptcy. Her son is a broker and thus part of the strange new world of market economics, whose vocabulary she cannot pronounce.*

Liza is far from optimistic about the future of Russia, but she betrays not a hint of bitterness at having so little to show for her exceptionally long working life. She is proud of her worker's medals and, as she surveys the wreckage of the

Communist experiment, she finds no fault with Stalin. She is not typical of her class or sex. Soviet women, though they theoretically have full equality with men at the workplace, in practice tend to get jobs in low-paid industries and professions: teaching, shops, hospitals, light industry. Liza was one of those who laboured beside men, lifted the same heavy loads and drew the same pay, proof that the regime meant what it said about sexual equality.

She does not look big enough. She is stocky but barely five feet tall. Her white hair is tied in a bun, and she wears an open-neck knit top over her blue skirt. When she grins, you see that the lines in her face have been formed by laughter, not frowns. She tells her story in a low, nasal voice.

She has lived in Moscow since she was five. When she was born, her parents worked for a landowner in Karabanovo, north-east of Moscow. Her father earned extra money delivering newspapers. At the beginning of the First World War in 1914, the family moved to the ground floor of a two-storey wooden house at Ostankino, now the site of the Russian Television Centre and tower, near the former VDNKh (the Exhibition of the Economic Achievements of the USSR). Then Ostankino was in the countryside, outside the city limits.

They lived in the same house till the outbreak of war in 1941. By then it was dilapidated beyond repair and they were given a communal flat at Medvedkovo, now north Moscow. Like others of her generation, Liza's childhood memories are dominated by the terrible hunger of the Civil War years, 1918–21.

'There was no food at all. Children ate grass. My elder brother was in the army and got bread made from oats, and he used to bring some home. It had an awful taste. I never ate oats again. We had some help from an aunt who still lived in the country. In 1921 and 1922, she sent us ears of wheat. My mother ground them into flour and baked bread.'

After secondary school, Liza went to a vocational college to train as a salesgirl but did not complete the course. Her father died in 1930 and she had to start earning.

'I went to the labour exchange, which still existed then, and got a job at a factory named after a rich German who had cooperated with the Soviet authorities and put up the money for the plant. It didn't have a proper building at first, just a shed. After my normal shift, I used to carry bricks for the builders. They had training courses at the factory, and eventually I became an electrician.'

She reckons she has Lenin's widow, Nadezhda Krupskaya, to thank for that. The two met by chance at a concert in Liza's factory on International Women's Day (8 March) in the early 1930s.

'She chatted to me and called me "daughter". I was just a messenger-girl in those days and she said she'd do her best to get me a trade. A month later, I was transferred to a workshop.'

Stalin, too, visited the plant.

'I never saw anything wrong with him. He brought prices down after the war and rebuilt the economy.'

During the Second World War, most of her fellow workers were not women, as she expected, but men in reserved occupations and so excused military service. The reason for this, she says, was that few women were strong enough to lift heavy tank parts. She says she was.

She earned the same pay as the men, sometimes more 'when special orders required the skilled, delicate fingers of women'. She is doing relatively well in retirement, too. She has a pension of R.1,500 a month, in May 1992. It does not go far at the 'new prices', but it is well above the minimum pension and twice the salary of a woman doctor in charge of a polyclinic department.

As a defence industry worker during the war, Liza got the same rations as servicemen at the Front and collected eight decorations from a grateful State, including the Medal for Labour Prowess and the Veteran of the Labour Front award. She is proud of the fact that she was sent on detachment to Kiev to help set up a new factory.

It was there that she met her husband.

She helped at a military hospital in her spare time and wrote letters at the dictation of a wounded sergeant called Vladimir. After the war, he sought her out in Moscow and they married. She was happy till one day about seven months after the wedding, when she got a letter from a woman who said she was also married to Vladimir. He promptly left Liza, who was pregnant, and later wrote to explain that he had bigamously married her simply to have the right to Moscow residence. His letter reached her just after she had given birth to a son, also called Vladimir.

'I fainted in hospital and the doctors thought I was dead. I was taken to a chapel which was serving as a mortuary. I woke up there three days later. It was very cold. I saw hospital workers bringing a corpse in. I couldn't speak, so I waved to them. They ran off and found a doctor. I was put in a special ward and had hot water bottles put around me. A few days later, I was shown my baby for the first time. Another mother had been feeding him as well as her own baby. I was in that hospital for a month and a half, instead of the normal ten to twelve days. After that I didn't want to try marriage again.'

Two weeks after coming out of hospital, Liza was back at work, but the cost of a child-minder for her son took her whole salary. She did odd jobs to make ends meet, cleaning, gardening and laundering.

Though a model worker, Liza, in one major respect, would not conform to the Communist system.

'I was brought up as a believer and I go to church on big occasions. I do believe in God and so was never a Pioneer or a member of the Komsomol. Once they invited me to join the Communist Party and called me in. I told them I wasn't suitable and, besides, I was a believer. I had some trouble after that. People found fault with my work. But eventually they left me alone. They needed me and that's what saved me.'

When her mother died in 1945, Liza was determined to have a religious service for her. She put the coffin on a sledge and pulled it alone to the nearest 'working' church. When she got there, the priest told her she was too late and should come back next day. She could not leave the body overnight, he said, because the church was infested with rats which would eat it. The following day she hauled the coffin back to church and from there to the cemetery, three kilometres away.

Liza remains cheerful, her eyes shining, even when she is recounting macabre tales of hardship, and yet she views both present and future with profound pessimism.

'Because of Gorbachov's *perestroika*, life has got worse. Maybe we didn't understand him properly. There are accidents all round us. The shops became empty and the price reform depresses people. I don't expect anything good for my grandchildren [two boys from her son's first marriage]. The environment is very polluted. The air in Moscow is bad. I don't see much future for the young people. They start their sex life very early and lose interest in it. They are burning their lives up. They don't like working. I don't know how they will manage.

'They are all going in for business. Strong young men with broad shoulders are selling beer. They'd do better helping the peasants with the harvest. The girls smoke and drink. There are many rapists because of all those video halls. It was never like that before. Now it's dangerous to go out after 9 p.m.'

She lives with her son and his second wife near Izmailovo, an eastern suburb. He trained as a printer, before national service, and later was a typographer in Moscow's Printing House No. 1, which made books – 'a good speciality'. Now he is a broker in some kind of exchange, she isn't sure which, earning R.2,000 a month.

This is a sign of the changing times, and Liza has difficulty getting her tongue around the still unfamiliar vocabulary of the market economy. She stumbles over the word *birzha* (exchange).

Another sign of the times is the sorry plight of the factory she devoted her life to. She decided to retire, she says, because, by 1990, orders from the State for tank and aeroplane parts were drying up. The plant was going bankrupt. In the spring of 1992, there was no money to pay the staff wages and no one was interested in taking the place over, because it was run down and badly in need of repair.

Even in good condition, factories like this, operating an obsolete technology, are unlikely ever to attract private capital. For a long time, Gorbachov placed hopes for economic salvation in the conversion of the hi-tech military–industrial complex to civil production. He did not have the time or money to do this on a big enough scale to make a difference.

Liza ended her long working life just in time, and she concedes as much.

'Those who are still on the staff envy us pensioners; at least we are getting some money.'

Liza died of cancer in January 1993.

# Kira

Kira Alexeyevna
Korniyenkova

Teacher of handicapped
children

Born: Moscow, 1936

Father: Agronomist,
specialising in fruit and
vegetables

Mother: Agricultural chemist,
retrained as metallurgist

Interviewed: April 1992

*Kira is a Stalinist and an active member of the neo-Communist
Yedinstvo (Unity) party led by the Pasionaria of Soviet hardliners,
Nina Andreyeva. Kira's devotion to a dead dictator, in an extreme
form reflects the feelings of the many Russians who forgive Stalin
his terrible crimes and long for another such* vozhd, *a strong leader
who knows where he is going and will stop at nothing to get there.
What Kira has to say demonstrates the strength of Communist
indoctrination. This is not the wild nostalgia of a sentimental
woman. There is an intensity of the religious bigot about her
defence of her monstrous hero. She surrounds herself with 'proofs'
of her faith. When challenged to produce evidence for a statement,
she brings out notebooks to display chapter and verse. What she
does prove is that the myths and lies which Stalin fed his people
have still not lost their potency.*

Kira made her first major public appearance in a film. In an early sequence, the head of a toppled statue protrudes from a bank of autumn leaves. There is the huge, luxuriant moustache and other unmistakeable features of Joseph Stalin; Kira is shown brushing leaves from the grey lips.

Later in the film – *Stalin is with us*, made in 1989 by Tofik Shakhverdiyev – Kira speaks into camera:

'I am a convinced and open Stalinist . . . There was *glasnost* [openness] under Stalin. They arrested people openly, exiled them openly and executed them openly. Today [under Mikhail Gorbachov], we have a lopsided *glasnost*. I feel ashamed to be living at a time when the country has renounced its history . . . I should prefer to be in a terrible labour camp, if I only knew that my country was building socialism.'

Shakhverdiyev made his film as a warning that a sizeable part of the Soviet population remained ardently Stalinist – despite decades of anti-Stalinist denunciations and the detailed exposure of the terrible sufferings and deaths he inflicted on millions of men, women and children. No Russian can be unaware that Stalinists exist, but they used to speak in code, at least in public. Their key word was the 'blackening' of the country's history.

In the film, they speak out openly. Since it was made, they have marched across Moscow and demonstrated outside the Kremlin and Moscow's television tower. Kira claims that Yedinstvo has about ten thousand members in Moscow alone, a figure that sounds reasonably accurate. To them should be added an unknown, but undoubtedly large, number of passive sympathisers. Elderly people commonly let drop remarks about how much better things were in Stalin's day.

Kira has held to her beliefs throughout the tumultuous Gorbachov years. On May Day 1992, she paraded with remnants of the Communist old guard who marched into Red Square to old Party songs, carrying red flags. She held a portrait of Stalin. After the parade, the marchers, the majority middle-aged or older, wandered about the square looking lost and aimless, half-listening to speeches by Communist diehards.

Kira does not feel lost. She says she has become 'politically active', giving up much of her time to work on the executive committee of the All-Union Society of Yedinstvo for Leninism and Communist Ideals. The party was founded by Nina Andreyeva, a Leningrad chemistry teacher, whose Stalinist beliefs caused a great stir when they were published in the form of a long letter in the conservative newspaper *Sovietskaya Rossiya* in 1988.

The political commitment has required sacrifices, Kira says. For twelve years she was head of a Moscow school for mentally handicapped children ('they all had alchoholic parents'), but she found she could not both run the school and engage in party politics. So she went on pension and took a job as classroom teacher, specialising in vocational training – teaching children how to bind books.

She has also had to cut down on the travelling she used to enjoy, regularly earning a 'Hiker of the USSR' award (for walking fifty miles and camping two nights in the open). She cannot afford the fares now she has to live on a small pension and a teacher's salary of R.1,846 a month.

Kira lives in a third-floor flat in a typically drab block in north-west Moscow, two rooms filled with plants, books and pictures, some of which are portraits of Stalin. A gold-coloured statuette of him, goblet in hand, proposing a toast 'to victory', stands on the television set, next to an old, black upright piano.

Kira has grey hair and wears an embroidered blouse. Her eyes behind her glasses are mild and she smiles as she defends Stalin, her hands clasped. She opens a cage to let her two small parrots fly around the room as we talk. She has just bought Dasha. It is a new mate for Yasha, the male, aged eight, and they whirr and chatter over our heads, occasionally clinging to a rug on a wall, patches of bright green against the dark reds.

'When I die, I want my ashes scattered around Stalin's grave, so that we shall be together,' says Kira. She never met him, but she was a friend of his Foreign Minister Vyacheslav Molotov during the last seventeen years of Molotov's life.

'Stalin,' she says, 'was a shrewd, far-sighted, subtle politician. Winston Churchill said Russia was lucky to have a genius running the country in wartime. Nina Andreyeva quoted this in her letter, but *Pravda* said Churchill never said it. This man confirmed to me that he did. [She produces a photograph of the British journalist and MP, Winston Churchill, Jnr., grandson of the wartime British leader.] Under Stalin, there was a real people's democracy. I don't believe socialism has failed to prove itself. Socialism was betrayed.'

She identifies the villain as Nikita Khrushchov, Communist leader in the late Fifties and early Sixties. She attacks, in obsessive detail, Khrushchov's notorious meddling in farm policy, contrasting it with what she presents as the ever-wise course Stalin steered. She has notes and documents to back up what she claims. But the detail she commands serves to conceal the immense cost in human lives and suffering of the forced collectivisation of agriculture in the early Thirties, when the best peasant farmers perished or were exiled.

'When Khrushchov used to say Communism would be built by 1980, it was no bluff: we were just a step away from it. But having proclaimed this, he began to ruin agriculture and industry. He did away with tractor stations [which owned and maintained agricultural machinery] in the countryside. That's why collective farms went bankrupt. Farm directors now say that machines are very expensive, but before they didn't have to worry. That was a matter for the State. They could hire tractors from the tractor stations.'

According to Kira's account, Khrushchov, and not Stalin's

rush to industrialise at all costs, is to blame for the devastation of so much of the Soviet environment.

'Khrushchov took peasants' private plots of land from them, and they went to work in cities. Organic fertilisers were lost and the earth was spoiled with chemicals which poisoned the rivers. Fish disappeared.'

When Gorbachov tries to improve the economy, she says, he has to borrow ideas from Stalin, on cooperatives, for instance.

'But Stalin gave co-ops tax allowances. Gorbachov imposed a progressive tax and the co-ops passed the cost on to the customers. Under Stalin, there were industrial cooperatives [producing consumer goods]. Now they are mostly middlemen and speculators. Before, speculating was punished by up to ten years in prison: for instance for buying clothes abroad and re-selling them in the USSR.

'Stalin's idea was to cut costs. To do this we needed the best technology and advanced equipment. The staff of our hi-tech industries worked – not smoked – under Stalin. Everything was done according to a strict, scientific plan. And in 1947 prices were reduced.'

(Here Kira's memory fails her. The Stalin price reductions came in 1951–53.)

'When planning became based on profits, people lost interest in introducing new technology. Low-priced goods disappeared. A soap factory with 2,500 machines produced soap at ten kopeks a bar. If ordered to increase profits, it modified the bar and put the price up to one rouble. Then it could make its profit while reducing production. This led to shortages.'

This is an accurate summary of one way in which prices went up and shelves became empty, but she gives no hint that the Soviet economy was geared to supplying the world's biggest standing army and that Soviet consumers came low on the list of the Kremlin's priorities. Instead there is a recitation of familiar Soviet boasts.

'It is not true that socialism lost the war against capitalism. This country developed industry and agriculture quickly and won the war against fascism. After the war, the economy was rebuilt in fifteen years. We reached pre-war levels of production in five years. We put the first sputnik and the first man into space. It is not serious to say that such a country could lose an economic battle.'

Kira's facts, where true – for example, that Yuri Gagarin was the first man in space – are unencumbered by information about the cost in resources. There is no hint that there might have been a fatal flaw in Communist economic theory. When it suits her argument, Kira leaves generalities and reverts to detail. She swoops on recent complaints about cash shortages and non-payment of wages.

'It used to be considered a crime if wages weren't paid on time. During the war, a factory was being evacuated to the east and found it didn't have the cash to pay its workers. Stalin was told about it and the same night a plane-load of money was sent to the new factory site. Now you hear of people who haven't been paid for three months. I don't know how they manage. My mother had a pension of R.120 a month and it was enough. People didn't need savings. They could always afford to buy the food they saw in the shops. I can't stop working now, because I couldn't survive. I want the old times back, when you could live on a pension and not worry about falling ill.'

Again the man to blame is Khrushchov, who denounced Stalin's crimes.

'We lost our battle not seven years ago [when Gorbachov became Communist Party boss], but in 1956 at the Twentieth Party Congress, when Khrushchov was allowed to undermine the country's socialist ideology. For the first time there was a split in our monolithic society: the first big break into Stalinists and anti-Stalinists. That is how enmity began in our society.

'Before 1917, Russian workers were almost illiterate and

knew nothing about the social protection the State could give, and yet they made three revolutions [1905 and February and October 1917]. We could find faults in the system, because people always want to live better. But we should never throw away socialist achievements. Now it is deliberate policy to treat people like fools. This has worked to such an extent that people have begun to speak against socialism, that is, against their own social interests.

'*Glasnost* is a game played with only one set of goalposts. All the Soviet newspapers have been politically reoriented, except for *Pravda*, *Sovietskaya Rossiya* and the magazine *Molodaya Gvardiya* [which speak for the Right]. We have no radio or television, so we can't influence the masses. The common people get only one-sided information. They still trust the mass media, because it used to tell them the truth [i.e., fed them the official Party line], and so they came to believe that the system of social security designed for their own protection was bad.

'Marx said that existence determines consciousness. So the worse off the bulk of the population become, the sooner they will realise someone is deceiving them and the sooner their eyes will be opened. They are beginning to unite again. Why, they are asking, are monopolies good in capitalist countries but bad in ours? *Perestroika* can't answer that question. People of my age and older can compare life now with what it used to be like. They want the previous standard of living brought back. Students in senior schools have a new interest in Marx, Engels, Lenin and especially Stalin. A few years ago, most members of our movement were old. Now we have many young ones.'

Her belief that neo-Communism is taking hold in schools is at odds with what schoolchildren say, and the young supporters of Yedinstvo, if they exist, do not show themselves at public demonstrations. Kira nevertheless proclaims confidence in ultimate victory.

'We shall win. History doesn't roll backwards and going

over to capitalism means going backwards. It was always normal for Russian peasants to work collectively. They knew it was better to sweep with a big brush than with one twig, and if the harvest failed they would be helped out. On private farms no one helps you. And collective farms mean high technology and the best seeds.'

Kira was born in Moscow in 1936, but could claim to have grown up in a farming environment, because her parents were both 'agricultural engineers'. There is knowledge behind her diatribe against Khrushchov, who did indeed tamper unhelpfully with agricultural policies. But there is fantasy in her vision of Soviet history and of the truthful Soviet Press. She says: 'The first song I remember was: "We have been born to make a fairy tale come true."'

She looks back through a rosy mist to the Great Patriotic War, when she was evacuated to Central Russia and stayed with her grandmother. She has her own version of the Stalinist myth of the Soviet empire as a joyous community from which ethnic and racial conflict were excluded.

'People lived in friendship and led cheerful lives. There were six Jewish girls in my class, but I never thought about what nationality they were. There was a Korean girl and others with non-Russian names. But I was interested only in what sort of friends they were. We were like one family.'

She visited the ruins of Stalingrad after the war, when camels were being used to clear up the streets. 'Many Stalingraders refused to leave. They stayed on in mud huts, waiting for their city to be rebuilt. They were very proud of their victory and the beauty of the city they were rebuilding.'

Now, she says, children at her school come back hungry after a weekend at home. There are reports of children suffering from scurvy, caused by vitamin deficiency.

'I haven't seen it, but colleagues tell me of children faint with hunger, something our country hasn't witnessed for a long time.'

At a pause in the long comparison between the golden

past and the tarnished present, I ask whether she sees anything negative in Stalin's performance.

'Every politician makes mistakes. He made very few. There's a lot of fuss now about the Crimean Tartars, resettled in 1944 [forcibly exiled from the Crimea], but they welcomed Hitler and set up their own republic to support him.'

She accuses the Tartars of terrible atrocities against partisans, and I ask her where she found such material. She leaves the room and returns with two notebooks. In one, she points to the figures in notes she had made on an article in *Izvestia* of 25 July 1987. She is pleased to have a chance to show how thoroughly she does her homework.

What about Stalin's habit of gaoling the close relatives of his top officials: Molotov's wife Polina, for instance? Here she produces an explanation that reeks of Stalinist 'anti-Zionism'.

'Polina herself never blamed Stalin for her arrest. She said someone slandered her. Stalin used to have lunch with the Molotovs. The official reason for her arrest was that Stalin had been told Polina was plotting to poison him. The real reason, I believe, was that Polina was a Jew and joined a circle of wives of Soviet officials organised by Golda Meir, the first Israeli ambassador in Moscow in the late Forties. Polina, at that time, was Minister of Fisheries. Gold and diamonds were disappearing abroad through that circle. Stalin was told of Polina's membership of the circle and he warned Molotov that his wife should end the association. After a second warning, she was arrested. Twenty-four hours later Golda Meir was expelled from the country.'

Kira herself raises one of the most controversial acts of repression during Stalin's purges of the late Thirties: the execution of Marshal Tukhachevsky, regarded by many Russians as a military genius who was sorely missed during the war. He was a brilliant officer during the civil war and was credited with creating the modern Red Army. Did he plot against Stalin to put a stop to the terror, or did Stalin himself invent the story of a planned coup? Kira was in no doubt. 'Tukhachevsky was always an enemy of the people.'

Stalin and he stood together to take the salute atop the Lenin mausoleum in Red Square on 1 May 1937. A few days later, the marshal was demoted. On 12 June it was announced that he and his fellow conspirators had been executed. These were just a few of the many thousands of 'enemies' shot or sent to the camps of the Gulag at that time, on flimsy, trumped-up or non-existent evidence.

Kira leaves the room again and brings back a copy of the War History Magazine – an ultra-conservative Communist publication – and points triumphantly to what is said to be a copy of Tukhachevsky's signed confession, dated 26 May 1937.

Kira lives in a closed world filled with dogma and 'facts' that cannot be challenged. But she is worth listening to at length, for she is not alone. She adopts the same unruffled manner as her leader Nina Andreyeva herself, whom I also listened to one sunny day in July 1990 in the grounds of the Summer Palace, near her home outside Leningrad. Both women repeat old claims of Communist achievements and blame failures on the 'betrayers' of Stalinist aims and policies. They remain carefully even-tempered and never speak about what those policies cost.

When Andreyeva's letter, entitled 'I Cannot Give Up Principles', was published by *Sovietskaya Rossiya* on 13 March 1988, Mikhail Gorbachov was about to leave on a trip to Yugoslavia, and the Politburo's leading diehard, Yegor Ligachov, was in charge in the Kremlin while he was away. The defence of Stalin and the attack on *perestroika* reforms seemed to signal a conservative assault on Gorbachov, and it was three weeks before a long, vigorous rebuttal of Andreyeva's arguments appeared in *Pravda*. Gorbachov won that round, but the threat from the Right hung over him till the failed coup attempt in the summer of 1991.

Andreyeva and her supporters clearly had powerful protectors within the Communist Party. Now that the Party has been decapitated, do they or Yedinstvo really matter? I think the answer is yes, at least in the sense that they could provide an instrument to focus popular discontent if the Yeltsin reforms fail.

People struggling to survive as inflation drives them deeper and deeper into poverty are unlikely to go into the details of Stalin's agricultural policies. They are more likely to accept as true what their elderly friends and true Stalinists tell them: that life was better and full of hope in the old days.

Talking about his documentary film in 1989, Tofik Shakhverdiyev warned that it was impossible to make Stalinists change their minds. His film ends with a powerful image of the human ability to believe the opposite of the truth. He inserts shots of a hypnotist's stage performance at which a girl is presented with a sheet of white paper. 'What colour is that?' she is asked. 'Black,' she replies.

# Alla

Alla Leonidovna Potapova

Freelance interpreter, former
tourist guide

Born: Moscow, 1957

Father: Teacher of military
history

Mother: Housewife

Interviewed: July 1992

*Alla worked for ten years as a guide with Sputnik, the tourist
agency run by the Moscow Komsomol organisation. For thousands
of Western tourists, she was the first representative of a
Communist State they ever got to know. She showed them the
Kremlin and the Lenin museum, answered their questions about
Russia, past and present, and mothered them. Now she reveals how
guides were trained to answer with official formulae learned by
rote, and to file reports on their groups.*

Alla joined Sputnik in 1978, while she was still studying
English at the Maurice Thorez language school in Moscow
and did a six-month training course for guides. She was
attracted by the notion of being paid to travel around her
own country. Till then, she had been only to Riga, the capital
of Latvia, where she had relatives. She also wanted to practise her English on native speakers, because everything she
had learned in ten years of English at a special school and
college had come from textbooks and Russian teachers.

'Sputnik's official title was the Bureau of International Youth Tourism of the Moscow City Komsomol. Every Sunday, we had lectures on propaganda at the Lenin Museum. We were the people through whom foreign tourists would learn about the beautiful society we were building. We were taught how to answer provocative questions about Stalin and about how prosperous the country really was. We were told to say this and that and not just what we thought ourselves. We had to learn answers by heart, and they were more important than historical dates or facts about the Bolshoi. If my English was bad but I was a good propagandist, then I was a good guide. I have five certificates that say I was a good propagandist. We had to pass exams on this, and there were people in my bus checking what I was saying to my groups. We were told that some of the tourists were working for the Soviet authorities, too. We were afraid to speak our minds.

'This is when I first began to think that something was wrong with our society. But at the time I honestly believed we lived in a good country. I wasn't suffering in any way personally, and I hadn't had any collisions with the system. So when foreigners put difficult questions to me, I thought they were prejudiced. The tourists liked it when I answered them as a patriot and Communist. They thought I was speaking from the heart. Later, when I began agreeing with them and criticising the regime myself, they didn't like it. They seemed to find it alarming, so I was never very open with them.'

Guides were badly paid: just three roubles for what could be a twenty-four-hour day outside Moscow, when they were on call day and night. But the job was considered glamorous and guides a privileged class, licensed to have contact with foreigners, something forbidden to ordinary Soviet citizens. The guides had to sign documents swearing that they would not have unofficial meetings with the tourists. If anyone asked for a guide's personal address, she was supposed to give Sputnik's address or make an excuse, such as saying she was just about to move. But in Alla's experience these rules were not strictly enforced.

'We were also thought to be privileged because we got souvenirs from tourists. They knew about scarcities in our country, and when I began the job I had piles of souvenirs: tights, scent, cosmetics, chewing gum, cigarettes, things like that, which I used as tips to nurses, when I had to go to the dentist or hospital. As I became more experienced, I got fewer presents. I think it may be that I obviously took them for granted. I also think that the presents were the tourists' form of propaganda, showing how well-off they were, and they could see that it no longer worked with me.'

She at first preferred working with Americans and, like other guides, found the British difficult.

'They hate people who speak bad English, but they never tell you. They just keep silent and sit on a different table from you. You have to learn British manners, too, like what to say when you meet in the morning. They are all small things, but if you don't know them, you fail and they just ignore you. Later, when I was a senior guide, I used to choose British groups. They have a good sense of humour. They have something to talk about and they can be very sarcastic, which I like. They are less straightforward than Americans, and I learnt a lot from them.'

She believes, however, that all foreigners were hostile towards Russians and tended to look down on them. Their greatest compliment to a guide was to say: 'You're so nice, you're just like one of us.'

'To them, we were all Communists, all Reds. They thought they were coming to meet the enemy, and some of them felt like heroes just being here. They expected to be followed by the KGB and said goodbye to all their friends before they left home. Some behaved as if Russians were like Mexicans and Puerto Ricans in the US. I felt I had to prove that, although I was Russian, I was human. I used to put on an act of myself as a human being. I was more friendly and smiled more than usual. I exaggerated feelings, as you do in the theatre according to the Stanislavsky method. Sometimes, at the end of the day, I had wrinkles round my mouth from smiling. I did everything for my groups. I told them when to put their coats on. When they were unwell, I tried to help them. They weren't used to our climate, so I came to know everything about diarrhoea and colds. I mothered them.'

But when they left the Soviet Union, she was required to answer a nine-page, mainly political questionnaire on the group. Which tourists had been to the USSR before? What were they trying to find out? What questions did they ask? Did they know any Russians? What languages did they speak? What other countries had they been to? Did they spread anti-Soviet propaganda?

That done, she had to take a blank sheet of paper and write down her personal impressions about individuals. Did anyone act suspiciously? If so, how? Did anyone miss any part of the programme? Alla says she personally avoided mentioning particular people, knowing that if she did, she would be summoned to the KGB and asked for endless details. To save trouble, she always reported that no one had missed any excursions and that they all struck her as pro-Soviet. She threw in some innocuous information to make the report look convincing: for instance, the fact that one American tourist asked why Leningrad wasn't called Stalingrad any more. Some guides put in reports like hers. Others were true Communist believers or wanted to appear as such and were more meticulous.

'I was there not to guide but to watch. If I had said I couldn't spy on people, I would have been out. My political outlook changed gradually over three or four years. Tourists smuggled a lot of literature about the Soviet Union through the customs, and I read their books. Then the foreigners themselves were lively, relaxed and free, and this surprised

me at first. There was a dramatic difference between them
and us. Talking to them, I learnt that the stories about everyone being exploited in the capitalist world and being on
strike non-stop were rubbish. I understood that the propaganda about the West was untrue, to put it mildly. After
all, there were unemployed people in some groups, who
could afford to travel. I had been brought up to believe that
in the West people died in the streets for lack of medical
attention. When I was in school, we used to collect humanitarian aid to send in parcels to the poor British working
class.'

Alla disobeyed the rules against meeting foreigners outside working hours. Some she even invited to her home.

'I felt a heroine, but nothing happened to me. I was taking
a risk when I simply spoke to a foreigner on the phone, but
the system didn't work properly. Soviet people are idle, and
the spies who were paid to watch me weren't doing their
job. Sputnik still exists, but things are different now. There
are no rules against personal contacts. Everything is commercial; all Sputnik is interested in is money.'

Alla must have been a popular guide. Sputnik thought
she was good and once named her their best guide. She met
her husband Sasha on that occasion, when he photographed
her for his newspaper. She is intelligent, vivacious and
good-looking. She has dark hair and dresses with care. She
records the interview in fluent English, wearing a mauve
top and light-green cotton slacks. She has big white earrings
and gives the impression of being permanently in a good
mood, although her four-year-old son Kiril has just come
out of hospital after another in a series of serious operations
on his chest.

Life is not easy and I ask Alla what is the single most
difficult thing she has to do.

'Hope that life will get better. You can't live without
hopes, but I don't have many. I am not optimistic. I can't
see any party or person who will take the country anywhere

and who will be any different from former rulers. I believe that an individual can mean a lot in history: no Lenin, no Revolution. I don't see anyone who will get the country developing in a normal way. Everything so far has been abnormal. Even if someone has a normal idea, it is likely in the end to have ugly results.'

Chapter 3

# Terror and the Camps

Edvard Burikhin, my guide to the mass graves found outside the city of Voronezh in Central Russia, slid aside the lid of a large wooden box containing the remains of twenty victims of Stalin's terror. From a jumble of bones and fragments of clothing, he lifted a small skull. 'Judging by its size, it's a woman's,' he said. He pointed to a round hole in the back of it.

The woman, whose name is unknown, was one of four hundred and sixty-four prisoners who were shot by the NKVD, forerunner of the KGB, in the early months of 1938 and were being reburied close to where they died in what is now a pine forest at a place called Sosnovka. Across the road from the forest is a string of youth holiday camps.

In the early 1990s, the KGB was trying to improve its image: it was cooperating with the Memorial organisation, founded by Andrei Sakharov to rehabilitate and preserve the memory of those who suffered and died in the camps of the Gulag. The KGB provided accurate information, for the first time, about long lists of people who decades before had vanished, after their arrest. KGB archives were used to locate mass graves, which men and women volunteers like Edvard Burikhin opened up.

He is middle-aged. His own father was shot in April 1938 – probably at Sosnovka, he thinks – after being found guilty of belonging to a Trotskyist group and sentenced to death by a 'troika' court of three NKVD officers, after a fifteen-minute 'trial'. But most of the volunteers who lived for weeks in tents under the pine trees were young, many of them students. They dug into the sandy soil to recover the bones, shoes, rotted pieces of clothing, rusted handcuffs and, now and then, a priest's crucifix, and placed them in the big coffins for reburial. Before that, the remains were examined to determine the age, sex and race of the victims. Tests showed that the majority were aged about thirty when they died, almost all of them killed by a heavy-calibre bullet from a Nagan revolver, the standard weapon issued to officers of the NKVD.

The Voronezh branch of Memorial assumes that the prisoners were brought to their place of execution from the camps known to have existed in the area: Boguchar, Novo-khopiorsk, Borisogliebsk, Bobrov, Ostrogorsk and Sosnovka itself.

The religious service for the four hundred and sixty-four was attended by representatives of the army, the KGB, the local Communist Party and of the Voronezh City Council. The remains of another two hundred and thirty victims were re-buried later, after their post-mortem examinations were completed.

There are no details on the gravestones. Grey marble plaques say simply: 'Here lie the remains of 109 [or 61, or 58 or 22] human beings.' They are not identified and may never be. Memorial at Voronezh, at the time, had the names of eighteen thousand rehabilitated Gulag victims but did not know which, if any, of them were buried at Sosnovka. The total number of people put to death during the Soviet period is also unknown, but there can be little doubt that it runs into tens of millions.

Thousands more bodies, local people suspect, have yet to be uncovered at Sosnovka, but the Voronezh area was only a small part of the Gulag, the vast network of death and labour camps which Alexander Solzhenitsyn calls 'our sew-age disposal system' and Nikita Khrushchov, in his memoirs, refers to as the 'meat-mincer'. The islands of the 'Gulag Archipelago', as Solzhenitsyn called it, were spread far and wide over the Soviet Union, with groups of them in the north of European Russia, on the shores of the White Sea; centred on Norilsk within the Arctic Circle in northern Siberia; in central and eastern Siberia; in the Far East around Magadan in the Kolyma region.

There is no space here even to summarise what is now known of the waves of terror and 'the deliberate killing-off of the cream of the Russian people', as Solzhenitsyn put it in an article in a Soviet newspaper in 1990. To grasp the scale of it, one must still listen to the great, angry, sardonic voice of Solzhenitzyn himself, read Irina Ratushinskaya's more recent books, study the pioneering works of Robert Conquest and read Vasily Grossman's short novel *Forever Flowing*.

This book, completed just before Grossman died in 1963, was published in the Soviet Union in the monthly journal *Octyabr* in 1989. Without *glasnost*, it would never have been made available to the Soviet readership. It contained an out-spoken attack on Lenin, which clashed with Gorbachov's own loyal defence of the founder of the Soviet State. But the importance of this book does not lie only in its political statement. It also must be read for two passages of brilliant but harrowing description: one of what Conquest calls the 'terror-famine' in the Ukraine in the early 1930s, the other of the degradation endured in the camps by the wives of 'enemies of the people'.

The arbitrary nature of the punishment inflicted on mil-lions is still hard to believe. But many of the women I inter-viewed told me about relatives who had been arrested. Some of them had been in the camps themselves. Alla Yemel-yanova was swept into the Gulag as a child, because her father – who was taken prisoner of war by the Germans in

1941 – was later shot as a traitor to the Soviet motherland. Her mother was arrested as the wife of a traitor, and she, in turn, took Alla into the camp.

Galina Karamysheva reminds us of Stalin's policy of rounding up and exiling whole peoples and, with them, any individuals who accidentally got in the way of the machine that scooped them up.

Yelena Djaparidze and Valentina Tikhanova both show how dangerous it was for the families of Bolshevik heroes to come too close to the Kremlin and to Stalin in person. But their experiences took them in different directions. Valentina works for Memorial; Yelena, who was one of the women engineers who truly believed in the new society Stalin was hurrying to construct, is still proud of her part in building the huge – and hugely polluting – industrial city of Magnitogorsk.

# Galina

| |
|---|
| Gezam Maskhutovna Karamysheva |
| Gulag survivor; accountant |
| Born: Nalchik, North Caucasus, 1923 |
| Father: Farmer, Bulgarian |
| Mother: Housewife and farmworker, Georgian |
| Interviewed: April and September 1992 |

*Towards the end of the Great Patriotic War, ethnic groups and whole peoples, suspected of collaborating with the Germans in occupied areas of the USSR, were rounded up and exiled in Central Asia and Siberia. This happened to the Tartars of the Crimea and the Chechen, Ingush and Balkars of the North Caucasus. They followed a route already taken by the Soviet German communities on the Volga, who were moved to the east en masse in 1941. Often the exiles were turned loose, in open country with few if any possessions, and left to survive as best they could. Many children and old people died. When individuals, innocent even by the insane logic of the time, were arrested in error, there was no appeal. One such mistake cost Galina five years in a labour camp and seven years' exile within the Arctic Circle.*

Galina was born in 1923, five years after the Revolution, in Nalchik, then the capital of the Kabardino-Balkaria Autonomous Republic, which the Germans occupied from 25 October 1942 to 4 January 1943. She lived among Balkars, who speak a Turkic language, but her family were of Bulgarian origin on her father's side. In Russian, the names of the two nationalities are very similar. Balkars are *Balkartsy*; Bulgars, *Bolgartsy*. The Balkars were suspected of collaborating with the Germans and the Kremlin ordered them to be exiled to Central Asia. Galina (Gezam is her Bulgarian name) and her family were mistaken for Balkars. While she was being questioned soon after her arrest in March 1944, she asked what the charges against her were and was told: 'Your nationality is enough.'

Her family had already suffered in other ways. Her grandfather had emigrated from Bulgaria to Kabardino-Balkaria, which borders on the Republic of Georgia, married a Georgian girl and prospered as a peasant farmer. Galina says he founded a village and built windmills. His four sons also became farmers. One was Galina's father, whom she describes as 'well-to-do', a perilous condition at a time when the Bolsheviks were searching for class enemies in the countryside.

These were labelled 'kulaks' and were targeted for officially encouraged enmity and jealousy from poorer farmers. Then, in the terrible years 1929 to 1933, the State delivered its triple attack on the peasants: forced collectivisation, dekulakisation and man-made famines. A *kulak* ('fist' in Russian) was the word for a peasant moneylender, but the Party used it loosely, according to political convenience. The word came to be applied to any 'rich' farmer. And the definition of 'rich' was equally imprecise and variable. Robert Conquest notes in his *The Harvest of Sorrow* that 'the most prosperous peasants in 1927 had two or three cows and up to ten hectares [twenty-five acres] of sowing area, for an average family of seven people.'

Galina's father and his three brothers tried to avoid the dangers they saw coming from Bolshevik hostility to successful peasant farmers, and all four joined an agricultural cooperative. But Galina's father was killed in 1924, when she was only a year old. She does not know who killed him or why, but suspects that it was because 'people could not forgive him for having been rich'. Her mother told Galina and her sister that he had died trying to defend a young girl from kidnappers, but Galina thinks this story was invented in the hope of ensuring that the two girls would not grow up 'opposed to the authorities'.

Galina was still only five when Stalin launched his assault on the peasants in 1929, an assault during which millions of families were dispossessed and exiled or sent to the camps. The famines of 1932–33, in which millions died, were created by the Kremlin's decision to set impossibly high quotas for grain deliveries to the State. The suffering was especially severe in the Ukraine where, Conquest estimates, five million died of hunger. But the North Caucasus was also hard hit, losing an estimated million dead.

Galina does not remember precise dates, but at about this time the family lost her grandfather's windmills and had to barter valuables for food. She remembers her mother exchanging a silver bowl for sugar at a Torgsin store, one of the State-run shops which sold food for hard currency, jewellery, gold or silver. All their china was sold in the same way. Her sister, Radimkhan, who was five years her senior, asked why the family treasures had to be given away, and her mother replied: 'We shall starve otherwise.'

Their living standards improved in the early 1930s, however, when her mother found a job on a collective farm and Radimkhan joined the Komsomol and worked part-time as a teacher, while still at school.

Both sisters were at the Nalchik teachers training college when war broke out and the Germans occupied the town. After it was liberated by the Red Army, they resumed their studies, but then, on 5 March 1944, Galina recalls, 'the worst began'.

Now close on seventy, Galina has white hair and careful manners. She lives in a western suburb of Moscow, near the outer ring road, in a modern-style communal flat. This is a normal individual family flat but shared by strangers. Galina's co-tenant is a single man. She has a sparsely-furnished bedsitter, and they share bathroom and kitchen.

She comes to see me on a cold, overcast day in April, wearing a brown coat over a dark-blue skirt and blouse. She wears glasses and a trim hat and has about her the tidy, reserved respectability women of her generation carry to chapel on Sundays in the valleys of South Wales. She tells a harrowing story in a quiet, even voice, without bitterness but with a deep sadness.

'On 5 March, all the non-Russian students at the college were sent home. The seniors said it was a mistake and we would soon all be back. But for days before, we had seen lots of army lorries with canvas covers coming into town. My mother was pleased to see us, and we didn't explain why we were home early. I went out to visit my father's grave. When I got back, there was a young man we didn't know in the house, who said we were summoned to the Komsomol committee. He took us there, but didn't go in. Inside, a man of about forty-five, who didn't look at us, told us to follow him. We asked him where. He answered: 'We are going to consider why you weren't allowed to continue your studies.' He led us out of the back door, where we saw a lorry and two policemen. He told us to get in and the policemen came in with us. "You are very trusting," Radimkhan said, and I'll remember that remark for the rest of my life.'

The lorry took them to Nalchik KGB headquarters, where they were told they were under arrest but not told why. They waited together in a room for about four hours and then were separated.

'I was put in a cell with five other women. There were no beds or chairs and I had no bedclothes with me. The cell was very small, the size of a small bathroom. We had a bucket for a lavatory. The smell made me vomit. After two days without anything to eat, I was questioned by a man called Simko about myself, my family, neighbours, friends and other people. I asked him what I was accused of, and he said: "Your nationality is enough." He kept me for two hours, then took me to a cell, where there were fifteen to twenty men. He pushed me in.

'There were a few wooden benches in the middle of the room and most of the people were sitting on them. I stood close to the door. Then an elderly man said: "Daughter, don't be afraid of us. We are not the animals they want us to be." He made room for me on a bench. The men said they were all political prisoners and warned me: "They will try to provoke you. You are young and beautiful, and they will put you in other cells with men." They told me about the interrogators' tricks, how they would ask about everyone I knew and would use every word against them. They told me I would be beaten and forced to sign things. "Be patient," they said, "and try to stand it all." I was in the room for several hours and we were watched through the peephole in the door. Then I was taken back to the first cell.'

Simko questioned her ten times about other people, but she now says she genuinely did not know anything about them of interest to him. He said: 'Do you understand that you will be sent into exile? Do you accept that?' She said she did not accept it.

'On 8 March, Simko called me to his room and opened the window so that I could hear Balkars crying and shouting as they were taken away. They had been brought into Nalchik from the villages, then put on lorries.'

Galina and Radimkhan remained under arrest in Nalchik till May, when they were put on a train with eight Balkars.

It was years before they learnt that their mother and ten-year-old brother Abdullakh (born after their father died) had been exiled to Central Asia.

The sisters travelled some 2,500 miles by train to Krasnoyarsk in Siberia. The journey took three months, including a month spent at Georgievsk, on the way, helping with the beetroot harvest. Another train had just arrived in Krasnoyarsk, bringing women prisoners from the Baltic republics. Prisoners from both trains were taken to a bath-house to wash. Here Galina met a woman called Olga, who spoke Russian badly and said she was a relative of Alexander Benois, the Russian émigré painter of French descent. She saw that Galina had only the clothes she was wearing and promised to lend her some of her own if they continued travelling together.

At Krasnoyarsk, Olga, the two sisters and several other women were locked in cells below deck on a barge, which took them down the Yenisey River to Dudinka in northern Siberia, a painfully slow journey of about a thousand miles which lasted twenty days. The prisoners spent the whole time below deck. They had no lavatory, and the food was bad. Galina and several other women fell ill with high fevers, but Olga warned them not to complain because they would be taken off the barge and separated from the group.

When they reached Dudinka, factory recruiting officers selected the prisoners they wanted. Galina was put on a goods train which took two days to reach Norilsk, one of the main 'islands' of the 'Gulag Archipelago'. The camps there were inside the Arctic Circle and it was very cold, often minus forty degrees Celsius. It was July when she reached Norilsk, and it was only then that she learnt that the war was over.

'Most of the people already there had been arrested in the Thirties, had completed their sentences and were in exile. Most of them were highly intelligent and kind, and they helped us as much as they could. They were the only good thing at Norilsk. Conditions were hellish. It started snowing in September and went on till May. I had a photo taken at a May Day parade wearing a fur hat with the ear-flaps down. But the snow was never white. When it fell, it was always black because of the smoke from all the factories.

'We slept on bunks, two hundred to a barrack. We got up at 6 a.m. and were given something between porridge and soup to eat, before soldiers marched us off to work. My sister Radimkhan, Olga and I worked in a cobalt factory. Then I spent a year on a factory building site, where we were guarded by soldiers with dogs. In winter we were given felt boots, a *bushlat* [padded overcoat] and trousers. The barracks were heated. Otherwise we wouldn't have been able to work. I wasn't allowed to write or receive letters, and so didn't know what had happened to my mother and brother.'

From the building site, Galina was moved to a chemical plant for six months. Then she had an accident. While repairing a roof, she poured boiling pitch over her feet. When she came out of hospital, she was given light duties in a factory personnel office with half a dozen other people, and remained there till she completed her camp sentence on 5 March 1949, the fifth anniversary of her arrest.

She was taken to see the camp commandant, who told her that she would have to spend the rest of her life within thirty miles of Norilsk. If she ever broke the rules, she would go to prison for twenty-five years without trial. She kept her office job but was now paid for it, and the director of the plant arranged for her to do a correspondence course in economics and accountancy. The same man found the address of Galina's mother in Central Asia, and the family were able to exchange letters for the first time since their arrest.

Galina fell in love with another prisoner, Alexander Kara-myshev, and had a daughter by him, Bella, born in 1949. He completed his sentence in 1950. The son of a former tsarist guard who had been exiled to Siberia, Alexander had studied for a time at the Tomsk theatre school, but was one day overheard criticising the uniform of the Red Army, which he thought was not handsome enough. 'He was sentenced to five years just for that,' says Galina.

His sentence, however, did not include a period of exile and so he was able to leave Norilsk after five years. He went in search of Galina's mother, found her and returned to Norilsk to propose. Galina hesitated. She was afraid that, coming from a family of exiles, she would be a burden to Alexander. When he convinced her he was determined to go ahead, the authorities tried to discourage the marriage. At the register office, Galina was told she could not take Alexander's family name, because she had no internal passport, only a certificate stating that she had completed her camp sentence. They were both summoned to the KGB office, where Alexander was warned that if he married Galina, he would spend the rest of his life in Norilsk. Back at the register office, a woman clerk tried to humiliate the couple and asked Alexander contemptuously: 'Couldn't you find anyone else? She'll soon lose her youth and beauty. Then what will you do?' He replied: 'Her good nature will remain.'

They lived in Norilsk until 1961. Khrushchov was in power and his Thaw eased the plight of exiles. They moved to Nalchik with Bella and Sergei, their son, born in 1954. Galina has two grandchildren, Zhenya and Sasha, Sergei's children. Bella has settled in Nalchik with her Leningrader husband, who lived through the wartime siege and does not want to live in his home town again.

To Galina's great regret, Bella has not been able to have children, and she believes this was the result of the appalling conditions in the camps where Bella lived till she was seven. She was weak and sickly as baby and child. Galina says that many women in the camp became infertile. Others had stillborn babies. Galina herself had to have treatment for infertility before Sergei was conceived, and spent eight months in hospital waiting for his birth. She was advised to have an abortion but refused and finally had a big healthy baby of over nine pounds. Sergei is now an aeronautical engineer and lives near Moscow with his wife, daughter and son. Galina sees them from time to time.

Radimkhan also married an ex-prisoner in Norilsk and left there with three children to go back to Nalchik. Under Brezhnev, she recovered the Party membership she had lost at the time of her arrest and remained a Communist till the Party collapsed in 1991. Galina and her husband moved to Moscow in 1969, where Alexander died three years later. Galina never remarried.

'I have had a difficult life, but I always believed in a happy future. My family brought me up with that faith, though I didn't believe in Communist promises: one thing in the newspapers, another in real life. It's not fashionable now, but my happiness was in bringing up good children. As a woman, I did my duty. It's probably not much, but it's something. In my family, we think a person should work hard and be honest, but now . . .' She opens her hands in a gesture of helplessness.

'Now it's very hard for honest people to survive. Sometimes I have regretted teaching my children to be honest but then thought it best to leave them as they are. They are both reliable. If Bella makes a promise, she will keep it, no matter what it costs her. Sometimes I want to be with my husband, but I should like to see my grandson start school, when he's six. He's five now. I also want people to stop hurting one another and to see common sense win.'

Galina never appeared in court to face any charges against her. An interrogator simply informed her that a 'troika' had sentenced her to five years in the camp.

In January 1991, she received a certificate from the supreme court of the Kabardino-Balkaria Autonomous Republic stating that her case had been reconsidered in 1956 and that she had been rehabilitated. There was no document referring to her period in exile. The authorities said they had no evidence of exile.

Galina is no longer sure that her arrest was simply a mistake. She was allowed to see her own KGB file while in Nalchik in the summer of 1992. It is slim and took only a few minutes to read. But in it she found denunciations by three of her fellow students, who quoted her as criticising Stalin's policy of deporting ethnic minorities. Two of the students were Russians and are now dead. The third is still alive. She is a Balkar.

# Alla

Alla Yakovlevna
Yemelyanova

Gulag survivor

Born: Smolensk, 1936

Father: Peasant and trainee
textile worker

Mother: Peasant, nurse,
miner

Interviewed: March 1992

*Alla does not have Galina's self-control. She was a child in the
Gulag and, as we talk, she weeps for her lost childhood. Her family
was punished because her father was found guilty of betraying his
motherland. In 1965, twenty-two years after his execution, his
sentence of death was quashed for lack of evidence. Before she dies,
Alla wants to discover why he was charged and shot.*

'I don't think about the future,' says Alla. 'I'm alone, I have
no children and no health.' She breathes with difficulty, and
tears run down her cheeks as she serves tea at a table in her
small flat on Lomonosov Avenue, south-west Moscow. She
is heavily built with a broad, puffy face and grey hair and
is wearing a green floral dress. The room is cosy, furnished
in dark colours. There is a picture on a wall of a girl with a
flower, and a portrait of Pushkin. The Russian edition of
Boris Yeltsin's autobiography *Against the Grain* is among the
books on the shelves. There is an old-fashioned Mayak radio

set. The flat is in a block a short walk from the Cheryomushkinsky farmers' market, where the prices are among the highest in Moscow. Too high for Alla who, in the spring of 1992, is living on a pension of R.470 a month. The day we meet, a single rose costs R.75 at the market, yet people with bundles of banknotes are queuing to buy them.

'Probably sometime, things will get better,' Alla says, 'but not for us. We shall never see it.'

Her parents were of peasant stock, but after collectivisation they left the land and went to live in the ancient city of Smolensk, where Alla was born in 1936. Her father got a job as a trainee worker in a textile factory. Her mother worked as a nurse. Her father was called up to do his military service just three weeks before Hitler's forces attacked the Soviet Union in 1941. Smolensk, some two hundred and fifty miles west of Moscow, stood on a hill in the path of the invading army.

Alla says her father was one of the six hundred thousand Soviet soldiers captured in the early weeks of the war. The true POW figure was almost certainly higher. The military historian Dmitri Volkogonov reckons that three million Soviet servicemen were taken prisoner by the German armies in the first six months of the war.

When Smolensk came under air attack, Alla's mother decided to take her and her elder sister Polina back to the village they used to live in. Alla was just five, but she remembers the cries of the refugees as they came under fire at night on the road out of Smolensk. Her mother and Polina were both wounded but they reached their village. It changed hands several times in the fighting that went on all round them. Then Germans took it and occupied it for about a year.

There was no food in the prisoner-of-war camps, and the Germans allowed the local people to feed the Russian POWs, some of whom were set free. They came out half-dead of hunger. One of them was Alla's father. When the men recovered, the Germans tried to persuade them to collaborate. One group of about twenty POWs in the village decided to ignore the German offer and, instead, to join the Russian partisans fighting a guerrilla war against the invaders in the area. The men left the village one night, and Alla's father went with them. She did not see or hear from him again.

'When the Germans realised the men had gone, they dealt very harshly with the families who had looked after them. When Russian soldiers recaptured the village, things were even worse. The women were blamed for everything. My mother was told she was the wife of a traitor to the motherland.'

The NKVD followed closely behind the Red Army divisions which liberated occupied territory as the Germans retreated, and arrested anyone suspected of desertion or collaborating with the enemy. More than half a million servicemen were questioned and tens of thousands were found guilty of treachery. Alla's father was among them. Many years later, she received an official letter from Smolensk dated 25 October 1989, and she shows it to me. It reads:

> We have considered your appeal to the Military Court of the Leningrad Military Region and it has been investigated by the KGB department of the Smolensk Region. We have to inform you that your father Yakov Yemelyanov, born 1905, was serving in the army and was arrested on 16 January 1943 by the special department of the NKVD of the Fourth Army. He was accused of crimes under Article 58 paragraph 1b. He was sentenced on 20 April and shot on 27 April.

The letter does not say where.

Alla has not been told precisely what charges were brought against her father. She has been told only that the case was reviewed by the Leningrad Military Region on 25 December 1965 and the sentence quashed for lack of evidence. The letter concludes: 'We unfortunately have no photographs or documents belonging to your father.'

But in 1943 Alla's mother was branded as the wife of a traitor. Before the war ended, she was arrested for that reason alone and sent to Novosibirsk in Siberia, leaving her children behind. Alla does not remember clearly what happened to her then, but Polina, who is eight years older, has told her that the sisters first went to stay with poor relatives in the Smolensk area. In 1944 or early 1945, both girls were placed in an orphanage. Polina did not stay long and went to a vocational school to learn a trade.

In 1946, Alla's mother, who was exceptionally strong and hard-working, persuaded the camp authorities to let her return to Smolensk to look for her children. She found Alla in the orphanage and took her back to Novosibirsk.

'My mother shouldn't have taken me, but she was already insane. In the camp, several families lived in one room. We were cold and hungry. I felt as if it was happening to someone else. I saw myself watching myself. The children went to school and the mothers worked in the fields.'

Alla and her mother were released from the camp in 1949 and went to live with Polina, then working in the countryside outside Moscow. She was the only close relative they could turn to, but when they reported their arrival to the local police, they were given twenty-four hours to move on. As former camp inmates, they weren't allowed to stay in or near a big city. They headed for a mining village then being built in the Smolensk area by former camp prisoners who, like themselves, had nowhere else to go. Polina, now also identified as a member of a traitor's family, followed them.

Alla's mother got a job underground at the mine and Polina worked in the personnel office. When she was fifteen, Alla went down the pit too.

'I operated an engine that pumped water out of the mine. It wasn't a hard job, but the conditions were bad and I suffered from rheumatism. The living conditions were as bad as in Siberia. All the time, we were appealing to the authorities to clear our names, since we weren't guilty of anything. My mother was poorly paid and was very sick, and because my father was judged a traitor, she got no widow's pension. But every time we appealed, the reply was that my father had been correctly judged and sentenced. Often we got no written answer; we'd just be called in to the local army office for an oral reply. Once a soldier saw my mother crying and said to her: "How can you dare to weep for a traitor?"'

Alla left the mine and trained as a nurse and for many years worked in Moscow, as head of the medical room at the House of Unions, in the building which had housed the former club of the tsarist nobility near the Bolshoi Theatre. It was here that the USSR hosted an international conference on civil rights in 1991.

Alla married a Muscovite, but he was a heavy drinker; the marriage ended without children. Her mother, who was once so strong that she was nicknamed 'the Lorry', became mentally ill, then had a stroke and was an invalid for ten years before she died in 1975. Polina, who is also childless, now lives in Odessa.

Alla herself retired through ill-health in 1989, at the age of fifty-three, and is waiting to go into hospital for a second heart operation.

Her bitterness wells out of her.

'The nightmare will continue. More and more people are getting poorer. Some were well-to-do before and enjoyed the good times. We didn't. My childhood ended when the war broke out.'

The one thing that does not worry her is managing on a small pension.

'I'm used to living in poverty and that helps.'

# Valentina

Valentina Alexeyevna
Tikhanova

Fine Arts expert

Born: Moscow, 1922

Father: Publisher

Mother: Housewife

Interviewed: May 1992

*Valentina Tikhanova was brought up by her stepfather, Vladimir
Antonov-Ovseyenko, an early Bolshevik and friend of Leon Trotsky,
who died in 1938 in Stalin's Great Terror. His place in Soviet
history is secure. On the night of 25 October 1917 (7 November by
the Western calendar), troops supporting Lenin's Bolsheviks
occupied key positions in the city of Petrograd and surrounded the
Winter Palace, where the Provisional Government, headed by
Alexander Kerensky, was in session. In the early hours of the next
day, a small group of sailors found the room where the Government
was meeting. They were led by Antonov-Ovseyenko, who is credited
with the historic line: 'In the name of the Military and
Revolutionary Committee of the Petrograd Soviet, I declare the
Provisional Government deposed.' He arrested all the ministers,
except Kerensky, who escaped. This was the coup that was to be
glorified as the October Revolution. Antonov-Ovseyenko became
a military commissar (minister) in Lenin's cabinet and was a senior
officer in the Red forces at the start of the Civil War.*

Valentina Tikhanova, at the age of fifteen, started awake during the night of 12 October 1937. She now thinks what woke her was the slamming of the front door of her parents' Moscow flat, in a seven-storey block reserved for government officials, near what is now the US Embassy. She saw a light on in the corridor outside her room. She put on a dressing-gown and went to see what was happening. All the lights were on and the doors of the study were wide open. There were no signs of a struggle or a search: all the books were still on their shelves. But there were three men in civilian clothes in the room. She didn't speak to them. But one of them was talking on the telephone, and she heard him say: 'Everything's fine; we've finished.'

Her stepfather was not there and she understood he had already been taken away without a chance to say goodbye. After the Revolution he had become a senior diplomat and lived abroad for many years, as Soviet ambassador to Lithuania, during its brief spell of independence after the First World War, as ambassador to Warsaw and to Prague, then as Consul General in Barcelona. Only twelve days before his arrest, he had been appointed Minister of Justice of the Russian Federation.

Valentina lives alone – except for a little dog named Kora – in a tiny, sunny flat, which looks across central Moscow to the Foreign Ministry, one of the seven gothic skyscrapers Stalin bequeathed to the city. She is seventy and her handsome face is lined. She is wearing a blue check dress and has a way of cocking her head and staring upwards as she thinks back to her childhood and youth. She tells her story in a matter-of-fact tone, without self-pity, even when she remarks: 'I lived with fear all the time until 1953 [when Stalin died]. That's probably why I never became an active dissident.'

There is a fine drawing of her stepfather on one wall of the room we are talking in. The long fair locks above a sensitive face suggest a poet rather than a politician. Photographs of him show a short man with thick spectacles and a little moustache like Stalin's Foreign Minister, Vyacheslav Molotov. But the artist was probably nearer the truth. For there was manifestly a strong unconventional, romantic streak in Antonov-Ovseyenko. While ambassador to Prague, he fell in love with the wife of a visiting Soviet publisher – Valentina's mother Sophia – and took her to live with him. They married just before they were arrested. She was picked up the same night as her husband but in the Caucasus, where she was being treated for a heart ailment.

It was not until January 1989 that Valentina received official confirmation that both her parents had been sentenced to death and shot in February 1938. This came in a letter from the USSR Supreme Court, which she shows me. It says her stepfather was sentenced to death on 8 February on charges of working with Trotsky, of 'armed assault on the Soviet regime' and of spying for foreign intelligence while abroad. He was shot two days later 'very likely in Moscow'.

Her mother was found guilty of knowing about her husband's anti-Soviet and spying activities and of personal connections with Polish agents. 'We have no information about where the sentences were carried out,' the letter says, 'but under the rules of the time, those sentenced were executed immediately, and the places of burial were never registered.' The letter says that both parents were later rehabilitated, and it advises her to seek any further details from the KGB. It ends: 'Sincere condolences' and is signed A. Nikonov, Head of the Secretariat of the Military Collegium of the Supreme Court.

Throughout the war years, Valentina continued to hope that her parents were alive somewhere in the Gulag. She received occasional reports that they had indeed been sighted in camps. She says that she never attempted to conceal her relationship with Antonov-Ovseyenko, but his late marriage to her mother may have saved her from some of the treatment normally reserved for sons and daughters of enemies of the people. She was never officially adopted by her stepfather, and her internal Soviet passport still gave her the surname of her natural father. Antonov-Ovseyenko's son Anton, by his first wife, was arrested in 1940 and spent almost thirteen years in the camps, apparently just for being his father's son.

Immediately after her parents' arrest, however, Valentina was treated just like other 'children of the repressed'. She was taken to the Danilov Monastery in Moscow, then being used as a clearing house for children before they were despatched to special orphanages around the country. It was also the main remand home for juvenile offenders and the assembly point for waifs and strays. Since 1988, it has been the Russian Orthodox Vatican.

When Valentina left her parents' home for the last time, she noticed that most of the front doors of the flats on their floor of the privileged block were sealed, a sign that their occupants, too, had been taken away. At the monastery, she was finger-printed and photographed full face and profile with a number 'like a prisoner'. She was sent to Orphanage No. 1 at Dnepropetrovsk in the Ukraine.

'It wasn't a labour camp, though it did have features of the Gulag. There was a police sentry-box at the entrance and we were only let out when we went to the local school. There were about three hundred of us. Very few had proper shoes; some didn't have any. So when it was wet or cold, they couldn't go to school. I kept a diary. Part of it was stolen, but I made a note that the food was so bad that we all lost weight. We had a tutor, who is still alive, who used to shout at us. But she has since written to me saying that we children from élite families were "like sunshine", and unlike any of the locals.

'There were all kinds of activities, hobby and theatre groups and choirs, to distract us and stop us thinking. But I remember one terrible day when all the younger, pre-school children were taken away to other orphanages. Brothers and sisters were separated and were crying. I spent four years there, and every day I expected my parents to meet me in a car after school. Most of the children in the orphanage got letters from their mothers. I never did.

'We all joined the Komsomol. We believed that enemies of the people did exist: people weren't arrested for nothing. But none of us thought our own parents were guilty of anything. I don't remember a portrait of Stalin in the orphanage [but one of Lenin is visible in a photograph Valentina shows me]. In the local school, there was a good attitude towards us. We never felt any stigma.

'But morals were very strict. When I was sixteen, I was friendly with a boy in the orphanage – he later became an army officer and now lives in St Petersburg. We used to walk to school together and sat next to each other. The head persecuted us and we couldn't understand why. I was twenty before I dared to kiss a boy.

'On 24 June 1941, two days after the war started, I ran away back to Moscow. My grandmother lived there, and that is where I thought my parents would look for me. It was difficult – the roads were crowded with refugees – but I found my grandmother's flat and stayed with her.'

Valentina did well at school and studied German in a foreign languages institute. Having had a German governess as a child, she already spoke the language well. She also had a degree in fine arts from Moscow University, studying part of the time in Tashkent, Uzbekistan, where the faculty was evacuated during the war. With other students, she remembers, she helped to dig trenches around Moscow, as the German forces advanced on the capital.

For several years after the war, she worked at the Pushkin Museum of Fine Arts in Moscow, looking after a collection of masterpieces from Dresden, brought back from Germany by the Red Army. 'There were seven hundred and eighty paintings, mostly Italian Renaissance – Titians and Tintorettos – but Rembrandts too. There were just two halls for the exhibition; the rest of the works were in the reserves. Very few had the right to see the exhibition: actors, artists, writers. I saw Khrushchov around. Maya Plisetskaya, the ballerina, came as a student and Mikhail Botvinik, the chess player.'

The collection was returned, in the early Fifties, to Dresden, in what was then Communist East Germany, but Moscow long continued to deny that it held other looted works of art.

Valentina lost her job at the Pushkin Museum in 1951, just before the opening of an exhibition she had organised of Stalin's birthday presents. ('I was trusted with master-pieces of art but not with Stalin's boots.') She was out of work for a year, largely because of her parents' history – and it was a difficult time, because the husband she had just married was a student with only a grant to live on.

Then she did get a job that suited her, with the Soviet Artist publishing house, and she stayed there till she retired in 1980. She specialised in art depicting animals because, she says, it was non-political.

She joined Memorial, almost as soon as it was founded in 1988, with the great Andrei Sakharov as chairman, to ensure that the victims of the repressions are not forgotten. 'At Memorial, I have discovered what work means. People ring up day and night.' One job was to go to KGB head-quarters every fortnight or so to collect – from a pleasant-looking young man with a smile – a new list of some fifty people shot in Moscow long ago so that Memorial could have their names published in a Moscow evening paper.

'We were given the name of each person, the month and year of birth, nationality, whether or not a Party member, place of work, home address at time of arrest, date of arrest, what kind of warrant issued, what the charges were, dates of execution and of rehabilitation. We could see how absurd everything was in those terrible times.'

Valentina's aim in life now is collecting works of art,

amateur and professional, produced by inmates of the Gulag. 'It's a little-known side of life in the camps. They produced embroidery for export and there were workshops which turned out banners with slogans about our happy Communist future.'

She organised an exhibition of work by Gulag artists, which has been shown in Moscow, Vienna and most recently in Warsaw. 'Memorial is considered a non-political organisation, but it is, of course, purely political. This became evident during the coup [of August 1991]. Our young members spent nights protecting the White House [home of the Russian Parliament], and it was a girl from Memorial who persuaded an army tank to go over to the White House side. I stopped water-cannon being used against demonstrators in Manège Square.'

Valentina believed in Communism 'like everyone else and for a long time. Now, I don't want history to go backwards. I don't want a return to the Soviet system for anything. I used to travel abroad, and I know full well how poor we are. Life, of course, is difficult now, but no one is starving to death.

'I think our future has to be in a normal international democratic system. But Russia is such a mixture that we can't take recipes from the West just as they are. There are different national characteristics. In Austria, there are no pigeons or sparrows, because people are not allowed to feed the birds. In Moscow, bread costs six roubles a small loaf [as against only twenty-six kopeks a few months earlier], but we still feed the birds.

'There is a higher logic dictating our way out. We are not so stupid as not to take advantage of it.'

# Yelena

| |
|---|
| Yelena Alexeyevna Djaparidze |
| Electrical engineer |
| Born: Baku, Azerbaijan, 1907 |
| Father: Teacher and Bolshevik revolutionary |
| Mother: Housewife |
| Interviewed: May 1992 |

*Yelena Djaparidze is eighty-five. She was alive before the Soviet Union was created, and she has outlived it. She is a link to pre-Revolutionary times, to Stalin's crash programme of industrialisation and also to the confused but heady period that followed the October Revolution and the Soviet–German peace treaty of Brest–Litovsk, in March 1918. The Russians were out of the war, but the blood-letting continued on the Western Front, and British, German and Turkish agents played a new version of the Great Game south of the Caucasus and in Central Asia. The British justified their move into the Caucasus by suggesting that Turkish troops might take Baku, the capital of Azerbaijan, cross the Caspian Sea and sweep across Central Asia to Afghanistan to threaten India. Yelena's father, Prokofy Djaparidze, was an early Bolshevik revolutionary and martyr. He was one of twenty-six Baku commissars shot in September 1918 (on British orders, Moscow said). Monuments were erected in their honour and streets were named after them. This parentage placed Yelena among the Revolutionary nobility. To her, Stalin was a grown-up her family happened to know. Her sister was arrested but Yelena herself was and remains a true Communist believer.*

Yelena Djaparidze shows me a photograph of herself taken on the vast building site at Magnitogorsk in 1932. She is smiling broadly, a worker's cap pushed casually to the back of her head, its brim pointing upwards. She is aged twenty-five and is an electrical engineer. She is flanked by two solemn-looking young men, one the Communist Party secretary at the plant they are building, the other a trade union leader. The picture's message is that young people have responsible jobs at the cutting edge of Government policy and that women are doing key work. The message is underlined by a certificate, dated 1932, testifying that Comrade Djaparidze is an *udarnitsa*, a woman 'shock worker' who has fulfilled her part of the First Five-Year Plan 'not in five but in four years'. The certificate is decorated with drawings of industrial and agricultural workers in action and with portraits of Lenin and a youthful Stalin.

We meet in Yelena's spacious flat in the 'House on the Embankment'. This is what Muscovites call a sinister, battleship-grey complex that stands beside the Moskva River, not far from the British Embassy. There is a fine view of the Kremlin from the room where we talk.

The complex was opened in 1930 to house senior officials and families of the Communist élite. When Stalin purged the 'enemies of the people' during the Great Terror of the 1930s, it was most often in this place that his secret police, the NKVD, came to knock on doors at night and take away suspects. The building's popular name is the title of a story by Yuri Trifonov, which was dramatised and is still in the repertory of the Taganka Theatre.

The housing the officials enjoyed was palatial by the standards of the Thirties, when families in major Soviet cities were commonly crammed into barracks or bedsitters in communal flats. The higher the flat in the eleven-storey house on the embankment, the bigger and better it was and the more illustrious its tenants. The block is still luxurious beyond the dreams of ordinary Russians. On the tenth floor,

Yelena has four big rooms with ceilings at least twelve feet high. Even today's Muscovites, bringing up families in tiny flats, would marvel at the great distance here between the kitchen and dining room, and indeed at the thought of having a separate dining room at all.

Yelena and her family moved in to the building when it was opened. Yelena, her mother and her elder sister Lyutsia (from *revolyutsia*, revolution) all knew Joseph Stalin. They were very much part of the Soviet élite, and their accommodation reflected this.

Yelena tells her story sitting at her dining table facing a wall lined, floor to ceiling, with glass-fronted bookcases. These contain a set of the Great Soviet Encyclopaedia, which she consults now and then. She is small and slim with dark, Georgian eyes. Her hair is dyed red and has a black band around it. She is wearing a white roll-neck sweater under a black dress. Her father has clearly been the central figure in her life. She shows me a photograph of him, a handsome young man with a wide, curved moustache and trim beard, wearing a tunic buttoned to the neck.

'My father was born on 3 January [16 January by the new-style calendar] 1880 in the Kutaisi region of Georgia. His father, a landowner but a poor one, died young. He had married twice and my father was born of the second marriage. There were five children from the first.

'Father went to a local church school for the children of the gentry. At that time, the rich collected money to educate the children of poor landowners, so he later went to a better school, where he was taught not only academic subjects but handicrafts too. When he was living in exile, he worked as a cobbler, he told me in a letter, and I realised he had learnt the trade at school.

'Then he went to teachers' training college in Tiflis [Tbilisi], where his education was paid for by the State. He got to know progressive young people and read a lot. There was a Revolutionary society centred on the library where he borrowed his books. Riots against conservative teachers led to his expulsion from college, and he was told to leave Tiflis. He moved to Kutaisi. It was the second biggest town in Georgia, and it was as prominent for its revolutionary activities as Tiflis itself.

'He joined amateur music and theatre groups. His wife fell in love with him, when he was performing in a Shakespeare tragedy. Two years later, in 1904, he was sent to Baku, after the Russian Social Democratic Party was founded. He was very talented and showed this in Baku. He was a cheerful man in love with life and got on well with people of all sorts, workers and businessmen. He was a very good conspirator.

'He decided to learn Azeri to be able to communicate with the most oppressed people. This was typical of the most prominent Bolsheviks. My father enjoyed great authority among the workers of Baku. Very soon there was a strike, the first to be organised by oil workers, and father was chairman of the strike committee. The strike was a success: pay and hours were improved.

'Father was sent as a delegate to the Third Congress of the Party in 1905 in London and there met Lenin for the first time. After the Congress, he went back to Baku. My sister Lyutsia was born the same year. My grandfather made my parents have their wedding blessed in church. I was born in 1907 and wasn't baptised then. But my grandmother was a believer and she had me christened while I was staying with her and became ill.'

When Yelena was three, her father was arrested and sent into exile at Rostov-on-Don. There he was arrested again and exiled for three years to the Vologda region, some four hundred miles north of Moscow. Her mother and Lyutsia went with him, and Yelena stayed with her grandmother in Georgia. She did not see her parents and sister again until 1914, when she went to meet them in Tiflis.

'I didn't recognise them. My sister was wearing a yellow

dress and a hat decorated with artificial cherries. I ran
towards them and fell at my father's feet. I could speak
only Georgian and my sister, Russian. Father became the
Bolshevik leader in Tiflis and officially wasn't allowed to
work. He gave private lessons. He helped my mother with
the housework and tried to educate his daughters. The
police followed him and he had to live underground.

'When my sister caught typhus, he spent the last money
he had hiring a horse and cab to take her to hospital. I
remember my mother at the table thinking how to make
money to buy food. My father found some coins in the lining
of a coat and bought sugar and bread.

'On 20 July 1915, my father went into exile again, this
time to a camp at Kamenka in the Yenisey region [of Siberia].
My mother sewed a rucksack for him and put money in a
seam. My grandmother gave him a bible with banknotes
inside the cover. We saw him off at the station and my
mother asked the police to let us kiss him, but they refused.
We could only talk to him from the platform.

'He wrote to my mother, from exile, asking for a hundred
nuts and a pair of glasses. We girls cried because we thought
his eyesight was going and he must have scurvy. But mother
reassured us, explaining that "glasses" was code for a passport and "nuts" meant roubles. It was a message that he
was planning to escape. He wrote: "Send me the same book
as before." So he got another bible with roubles in it. He
escaped and went to Petrograd. The Party told him to go to
the southern war front at Trebizond in Turkey [then occupied by the Russians].

'He came to Tiflis on short visits. We had a flat with a
maid and were supposed to call him "uncle" in front of her,
but we kept forgetting. He checked my school exercise books
and was upset to see how messy they were. So he gave me
a notebook with a letter at the top of each page for me to
copy and showed me how to hold the pen. He was a born
teacher.'

After the February Revolution in 1917, the Party ordered him to Baku, and the family followed in October. It was a dangerous place to be. In 1918, Turkish and British troops intervened. On 31 July 1918, the Baku Bolshevik Soviet (Council) was overthrown, and a counter-revolutionary government took over. In early August, British troops entered Baku but left in mid-September, when the Turks were at the city gates. The counter-revolutionary government fled. Bolsheviks released the commissars, who had been placed under arrest, and put them on a ship bound north for Astrakhan in southern Russia, then in Bolshevik hands.

But the ship's captain – on British orders, according to the Soviet version of events – sailed east to Krasnovodsk, on the other side of the Caspian in what is now the independent Central Asian Republic of Turkmenistan. There the local authorities arrested the commissars. On 20 September, they were put on a train and taken along the Trans-Caspian Railway to a spot about two hundred miles from Krasnovodsk. They were taken from the train and shot.

Yelena produces a cutting from *Izvestia* dated 30 March 1990. The paper's London correspondent reports that a book, giving a British version of the commissars' deaths, has just been published posthumously with the title *The Spy Who Disappeared*. The author, Reginald Teague-Jones, was a British Army officer active in Trans-Caspia and Trans-Caucasus at the end of the First World War. The Soviet authorities in the 1920s had pinned the blame for the deaths of the commissars on him, and he was denounced by Trotsky himself. This remained Moscow's official line on a tragic incident. Every Soviet schoolchild was taught how the Western interventionists had a band of heroes cold-bloodedly done to death. The *Izvestia* report recalls that a *Times* obituary of Teague-Jones revealed in 1988 that he had lived to the age of ninety-nine under the name of Ronald Sinclair.

Yelena asks me to find a copy of the book for her. In it, Teague-Jones says that the commissars were shot, not by the British, but by the anti-Bolshevik Executive Committee of Trans-Caspia.

'All Bolsheviks are now painted as a bloodthirsty lot,' Yelena says. 'But the Baku commissars were our idealists and they did not agree with violence. Lenin and Stalin were different – they believed you had to be merciless with enemies.'

She last saw her father when she was evacuated from Baku, just before the Turks entered it. Yelena travelled with her mother and sister to Astrakhan, but her mother returned to Baku, leaving her children in Astrakhan, when she heard of her husband's arrest. She was on the ship that took the twenty-six to Krasnovodsk, and she too was arrested there. She was later freed in an exchange of prisoners and began looking for her daughters. She wrote to Stalin, asking him for help. He had been the Bolshevik leader in Baku before the war and knew Prokofy Djaparidze well.

A telegram was sent from the Kremlin, and the girls were put on a train, with two soldiers to look after them on the ten-day journey to Moscow. 'We had potatoes and herring to eat.'

In the capital they stayed at first with the widow and children of Stepan Shaumian, another of the dead commissars, but at the time it was not known what had happened to them.

'People were very kind and we had lots of presents. Then, early one day, I was sent out to buy bread and decided to buy a newspaper. I opened it and saw an article by Stalin about the Baku commissars and the barbaric events in the Caucasus. My mother had learned of father's death, while she was in prison, and almost died of grief.'

When she got out of gaol, she made her way slowly to Moscow, where Yelena remembers her arriving in the summer of 1919.

'I was washing up when I saw a woman in black come in and recognised my mother. I dropped a plate. Mother met Lenin's wife Nadezhda Krupskaya, who gave her a job in adult education. But she fell seriously ill and thought she was going to die. We were living in the National Hotel [one of the finest in the capital and requisitioned to house top officials and their families]. Then the hotel was called the First House of Soviets. We were visited there by Stalin and Sergo Ordjonikidze, another Georgian veteran of Baku.

'It was my first meeting with Stalin. The two men were in greatcoats and had hats shaped like helmets. They told us not to worry; the doctors were coming and our mother would be all right. A doctor and nurse were sent and mother recovered. From that time, we looked on Stalin and Sergo as our protectors.'

Yelena and her mother went to live in Tbilisi for two years, but her sister remained in Moscow to read social science at the university. Ordjonikidze suggested she stay with Stalin and she did.

'When my mother and I came to Moscow, we had permanent passes to the Kremlin. Once when I was visiting Stalin's family – I was fifteen – he asked me what I wanted to be. "An engineer," I said, "I'm interested in electronics." Stalin said: "We have far more problems with farming. We need agriculturalists. Think it over." But I didn't listen to him. I went to an electrical technical school in Leningrad.

'I never thought about Stalin as a great leader. He was just a grown-up we knew and whose family we knew. He didn't put on any airs. In 1924 or 1925, just after Lenin died, I asked him some questions about political disputes in the Party, which I couldn't understand. He said: "Did you read *Pravda* yesterday? There's a big article by me in it. Take the paper to another room, read it and we'll discuss it." When I came back, he explained all Trotsky's mistakes.

'Once when I was having dinner with Stalin's family, he turned to me and said: "It's after eleven. Does your mother know where you are? Go and telephone her and say you are here." I told him we didn't have a telephone, so he dialled the editor-in-chief of *Izvestia*, who lived across the hall from our flat [in the National Hotel] and he passed on the message that Lena was with Stalin. He did ordinary things like that. But relations were warmer and closer with Sergo. Stalin was reserved compared with him. He was always working. But he read a lot and was fond of Chekhov, my sister told me.'

Did you know about the arrests at the house on the embankment?

'I not only knew about them, I experienced them, because my sister was arrested. It happened when I was on a trip to Daghestan, working on a power station. I got a telegram from my brother-in-law saying "return immediately". I went straight back to Moscow. I thought someone was ill. When I got home I found everyone in mourning. It was a second tragedy for my mother. She was in a bad state. She went to see Sergo, but he had no information. My mother saw the head of the NKVD, but he was no help.'

Lyutsia was arrested in 1936 and found guilty of counter-revolutionary activities and the illegal possession of fire-arms. She was sentenced to five years in labour camps. Someone had denounced her, for the flat was searched and three revolvers were found.

'One had belonged to Stepan Shaumian and was a present to us from his son. The second was mother's and the third was a little one that belonged to Lyutsia. It is true that we did not have licences for them, so the charge was accurate. Mother wrote letters and tried to get in touch with the investigator in charge of the case. She was told no one could help because Stalin himself had written a note on the documents: "Five years is enough."

'When the war broke out, a decree said that prisoners would have to stay in the camps till the war was over. But we got Lyutsia out in 1943. She was a great optimist and fond of life. Her character must have saved her. Of course, she came out looking thin and pale. She couldn't forgive Stalin. She never said anything bad about him but asked how he could have refused to see Mother. I defended Stalin and said that he hadn't even been able to save his own son Yakov.'

(Yakov, by Stalin's first wife Yekaterina Svanidze, died in a German prisoner-of-war camp, after his father had refused to exchange a German officer for him.)

Yelena still seems to be trying to reconcile the shock of her sister's arrest with the Bolshevik faith inherited from her father.

'There were all sorts of enemies around Stalin, enemies of socialism. Communism was a sacred thing in his life. He had to protect the State. I think you should be merciless with enemies. But you can always exile people to desert islands. You shouldn't kill them in this great country. If you approve of terror, then you approve of the execution of the twenty-six commissars. It [Stalin's Terror] was unnecessary and it had grave consequences. It created more enemies. But it is not true to say there were *no* enemies.'

What is your evidence for this?

'What is happening now.'

With this cryptic remark, Yelena declares her opposition to Russia's post-Communist reforms. She becomes increasingly animated as she talks about her early days as an engineer.

'All my life, I have tried with my friends to build a new, happy society. When we were young, we studied as hard as we could so as to be able to start working as soon as possible and be useful to our country. After graduating, I could have gone into research. Instead, I chose to go to the construction site of Magnitogorsk, the metallurgical city [in the Urals]. Iron ore was found there, so they decided to build an industrial centre, one of the biggest in the world – and we built it very quickly, thousands of us. We weren't slaves. We felt we were creators. Magnitogorsk started in 1929 and in February 1932 the first cast iron was produced. I worked there for four years from 1931 – when I was twenty-three – to 1935. We used modern technology to build quickly, but sometimes we were short of equipment. Then we had talented engineers who found ways round the difficulties, sometimes using methods invented in ancient times.'

Yelena concedes that the way forced collectivisation of the peasants was conducted in the early Thirties was 'not necessary. But the kulaks would not give us bread. They were difficult times to set up our own industry. Before 1917, this was an illiterate country. My sister used to go to the Kuzbass [coalfields in Siberia] to set up schools to fight illiteracy. We had to train new cadres, a new intelligentsia. I consider the present situation a complete betrayal, with total ignorance and lack of understanding of the national economy and the deliberate disintegration of the USSR.'

She reckons that, counting world wars and the civil war and the time it took to recover from them, there had been only forty-nine years to construct a socialist society between 1917 and 1985, when 'our genius' – she means Mikhail Gorbachov – came to power.

'We fools really believed he wanted *perestroika*. Of course, there were things wrong with the old system: the environment, for instance. Spending on the defence industry should have been cut and the bureaucracy thinned. But how can you carry out an experiment in a vast country like the USSR? The Chinese picked one region and introduced a free market there. We should do the same.'

After talking for several hours, Yelena Djaparidze looks as if she has the energy to make an equally long public speech on the themes of Bolshevik sacrifice and Gorbachov's treachery.

Yelena, who was awarded the Order of Lenin and twice won the Order of the Red Banner of Labour, is a product of the terrible times she lived through, able to proclaim two incompatible truths at the same time. She seems to acknowledge that polluting the environment was one of the vices of the Soviet system. Yet she is still passionately proud of what she and her generation had achieved at Magnitogorsk, an outstanding example of the giant industrial undertakings that devastated the landscape of the USSR and helped to wreck the health of millions.

'Sergo' Ordjonikidze died suddenly in 1937. Khrushchov says that he could not stand what Stalin was doing to the Party and shot himself. He was given a state funeral and the cause of his death was kept secret.

Chapter 4

# Religion

The root destruction of religion, Alexander Solzhenitsyn writes in *The Gulag Archipelago*, was one of the principal goals of the Soviet secret police throughout the Twenties and Thirties.

> Monks and nuns, whose black habits had been a distinctive feature of Old Russian life, were intensively rounded up on every hand, placed under arrest and sent into exile . . . The circles kept getting bigger, as they raked in ordinary believers as well, old people and particularly women, who were the most stubborn believers of all.

Formally, they were not being punished for their faith but for daring to pass it on to others, such as children. Sunday school was banned. The religious education of children was, under Article 58–10 of the criminal code, counter-revolutionary propaganda and a crime. 'Throughout all those years women manifested great firmness in their faith,' says Solzhenitsyn, some of them going off to the camps, while their husbands renounced their religion and stayed behind to look after the children.

The Russian Orthodox Church leadership, after initially resisting the Bolshevik assault on religion, sought survival in the long term through subservience to an atheistic regime. While churches were closed, destroyed, turned into grain stores, clubs and temples of atheism or simply allowed to rot, and while village priests, nuns and lay believers were imprisoned or shot, the Church leadership declared its loyalty to the Soviet State.

It was as if there were two, quite distinct, Orthodox Churches existing side by side. The contrast between them was shown in the harshest possible light in 1992. In late May of that year, some four hundred survivors of the Gulag gathered in Moscow for a four-day conference devoted to acts of resistance in the camps: strikes, revolts, escapes. The conference was held in the Hall of Columns in the House of Unions, earlier used for show trials and for Stalin's lying-in-state.

Among the documents to be published by the conference organisers, the Return Association, is a moving account of the quiet courage of thirty Russian nuns who deliberately chose to die for their faith. My colleague Mark Frankland told the story in a report for the *Observer*. It was originally recorded by an anonymous doctor who was also a prisoner at a camp on the Solovetsky Islands, in the White Sea, off the coast of northern Russia. The nuns came from the Shamordin convent, an important spiritual centre in tsarist times, and were imprisoned in 1929. They refused to work in the camp 'for the servants of the Antichrist'. The fact that imprisoned clergymen were already working there did not shake their resolve. They also warned the doctor that they would not agree to be declared unfit for work. 'Forgive us,' one of them said. 'We shall be obliged to say that it is not true. We are healthy. We are able to work. But we will not work for the Antichrist, even if they kill us for it.'

The doctor warned them that they would be tortured rather than killed. 'God will help us endure torture, too,' one of them replied.

Normally, the doctor reports, anyone refusing to work was severely beaten and sent to a punishment island 'from which no one came back alive.' But the nun's 'simplicity, humility and uncommon meekness' had made a deep impression on the camp's medical chief, who felt 'inexpressibly sorry for them'. It was he who suggested declaring the women unfit for work. The doctor describes them as 'staid women, calm and self-possessed, wearing habits that were patched and worn out but clean . . . All of them were handsome Russian women.'

A compromise was offered which allowed the nuns to sing psalms together while sewing quilts for the sick bay and they agreed to do this. Then a new prisoner arrived, a priest who had been confessor to some of them. They sought his views on their compromise, and he forbade them to go on working. They obeyed him.

When the camp authorities discovered what had happened, the priest was shot. The nuns responded by saying that no one now could release them from his instructions. They refused to work, were separated and were 'taken away one by one'.

When the nuns' story was told, Russian believers were still recovering from the revelation that clergymen in the highest echelons of the Orthodox hierarchy had for many years been active agents of the KGB. The security police had always kept a close watch on the Church, and it was an open secret that it had infiltrated the clergy, but chapter and verse became available when KGB files were partially opened after the failed coup of August 1991. The Russian parliamentary commission investigating the origins of the coup came across evidence that senior members of the Church leadership had acted under KGB instructions during trips abroad and at conferences in the USSR. On the commission was a former dissident priest, Father Gleb Yakunin, who paid special attention to anything in the archives about Section 4 of the KGB Fifth Department, which dealt with Church matters.

Documents were found reporting the success of agents in advancing Soviet interests inside the World Council of

Churches, which the Russian Orthodox Church joined in 1961, at meetings in Western capitals and, in 1989, during a visit to the Vatican. In these documents, the agents were identified only by code names, but a Christian investigative journalist, Alexander Nezhny, checked the KGB information against known travels by Church leaders. He published his findings in the weekly magazine, *Ogonyok*, matching ecclesiastical names with code names. He thus identifies three metropolitans (priests ranking between archibishops and the Patriarch) as KGB agents. They were: Metropolitan Filaret of Kiev, then Primate of the Orthodox Church in the Ukraine – code name 'Antonov'; Metropolitan Yuvenaly of Krutitsy, former chairman of the Church's external relations department – 'Adamant'; Metropolitan Pitirim of Volokolamsk, chairman of the Moscow Patriarchate's publishing department – 'Abbot'.

Filaret was defrocked by a conference of Russian bishops in June 1992 but had already switched allegiance to an independent Church of the now nationalistic Ukraine. Pitirim has denied committing 'illegal or immoral acts'. However, suspicions about his links with the KGB were not new. They were floated – and dismissed – in a book published in English by the Soviet Progress Publishers (see Chapter 7) in 1988 to coincide with the one thousandth anniversary of Christianity in Russia. The book, *In Search of Holy Mother Russia* by a prolific Dutch writer, Ludo van Eck, opens with an account of a long interview with Pitirim, given in September 1981.

Asked about persecution of the Church after the Revolution, Pitirim says:

> 'Some anti-Church actions did take place, but things like that are bound to happen during a revolution. It would be absolutely wrong, however, to describe them as an organised anti-Church campaign launched by the new Government. The new regime never intended to destroy the Church . . . The Church was never persecuted, with the exception of those clergymen

whose activities had nothing to do with their
ecclesiastical duties.'

Among these Pitirim places Gleb Yakunin who, he says,
was 'brought before the court not for being a devout Christian' but for 'illegally selling ikons and vestments'.

Some time later, reports van Eck (whose wife thought
Pitirim 'one of the handsomest men she had ever seen'), a
'progressive' Western Roman Catholic priest told him that
Pitirim was 'one of those KGB men who have infiltrated the
Church'. Van Eck dismissed the claim, noting that Pitirim
came from a family which had provided the Orthodox
Church with priests for three centuries.

The Bolshevik attack on the Church began the day after
the October Revolution. Under the Decree on the Land, 'all
monasterial and church lands' were handed over to local
land committees. At the end of January 1918, another decree
on the separation of Church and State nationalised all
Church-owned property and banned religious education in
schools. Lenin made his personal attitude to religion clear
beyond all doubt: 'Every religious idea, every idea of a God,
even flirting with the idea of God is unspeakable vileness
of the most dangerous kind.'

Between the two decrees, the Church struck back, con-
vened a Council and elected a patriarch for the first time
since the reign of Peter the Great over two hundred years
earlier. Patriarch Tikhon was enthroned in the Kremlin in
November 1917. The following January, he anathematised
the new godless regime and commanded Orthodox Christians to have nothing to do with the 'outcasts of the human
race'. Tikhon condemned the murder of former Tsar Nicholas and his family at Yekaterinburg in July 1918 and rejected
socialism as 'openly anti-Christian and evil'. By 1920, Tikhon
estimated that at least three hundred and twenty-two
bishops and priests had been executed since 1917. He
appeared as a witness at a trial of clergy in Moscow in the
spring of 1922 and soon afterwards was placed under house

arrest. The following year he was tried *in absentia*. Under intense pressure, he softened his attitude to the Soviet State (he signed a declaration of loyalty to the Government) and was alleged to have confessed to anti-Soviet acts. But the authenticity of the confession is disputed, and Tikhon died in 1925 amid suspicions that he had been poisoned. He was canonised in 1989.

Tikhon's successor, as *locum tenens*, was Metropolitan Sergei who, in June 1927, made a declaration of loyalty to the State, acknowledging 'the Soviet Union as our civil motherland, whose joys and successes are our joys and successes . . .'

This did not save the Church or the clergy from Stalin's Terror. Within two years, the nuns from Shamordin were dying in Solovetsky, and thousands of other members of the clergy were sent into camps or exile. By 1939, only four Orthodox bishops remained at liberty out of the one hundred and sixty-three in office in greater Russia in 1914. Of the 54,174 churches open in 1914, only some four thousand, at most, remained in 1939. Of one thousand and twenty-five monasteries, not one was still functioning.

The Church was probably saved from total destruction by the German invasion of 1941, for Stalin needed it as an ally in the Great Patriotic War. In September 1943, in the Kremlin, he met Metropolitan Sergei and agreed to a Church Council which, a few days later, elected Sergei as Patriarch. In return, the Council thanked J. V. Stalin, 'our national leader', blessed the 'works of the Government' and condemned traitors among the clergy and laity who welcomed the German invaders. All such traitors were to be excommunicated.

By 1945, there were seventy-four bishops in office and some twenty thousand churches open for services. But about ten thousand of these were closed again during the intense anti-Church campaign carried out under Nikita Khrushchov from 1959 to 1964.

Sergei's capitulation to the State in 1927 provoked a split in the Church. Some believers, clergymen and laity, chose to worship secretly as members of the so-called Church of the Catacombs and many died for it. Which policy saved the Church, allowing it to reach its millennium and benefit from the new religious freedom of the Gorbachov era, is still in dispute. There are those who insist that the Church was saved through the sacrifice of the martyrs in the Twenties and Thirties and of the dissidents, like Yakunin, who openly challenged official Church policy in the Seventies and early Eighties and spent years in the camps as a result. Others maintain that Sergei and other members of the hierarchy achieved the survival of the Church by sacrificing their personal reputations. The Church abased itself before the Kremlin, accepted the control of the Central Committee through the state Council for Religious Affairs and supported Soviet peace propaganda abroad, but there is evidence that, at the same time, bishops were quietly preparing for the future by slipping intelligent, well-educated, pious ordinands past the KGB watchdogs.

However, Solzhenitsyn is surely right to draw special attention to the stubbornness of women believers. When, under Leonid Brezhnev, the Communist authorities were still marshalling the police to keep Soviet youth away from Easter services in the onion-domed Orthodox churches, elderly women were allowed through the police lines. In their case, the State appeared to shrug its shoulders and concede defeat: the faith of the *babushka* was ineradicable. The oddity was that advancing age and infirmity never seemed to reduce the ranks of the old, headscarfed believers with figures like tree-trunks, who peopled the churches, sang the liturgy and kissed the ikons. They never died out and, without drawing attention to themselves, planted the faith in the grandchildren they helped so much to bring up.

The male hierarchy of the Church has not rewarded women with any positions within the priesthood. The Sobor

– the Council of Bishops which elects the Patriarch as head of the Church – is an all-male occasion, just like the College of Cardinals which elects the Pope in the Vatican. The Sobor is made up of three representatives from each diocese: the bishop, a priest and a lay person. All bishops and priests are male, but it is nowhere stated that the lay person must also be a man. He just always has been. This unwritten law was challenged in June 1990, when the present Patriarch, Alexei II, was elected after the death of Patriarch Pimen. The West European diocese of the Church chose as its lay representative Militza Zernova, a woman of great age and with an impeccable Orthodox background. The Church hierarchy in Moscow saw to it that she did not attend the Sobor.

In the Russian Orthodox Church, there is not even the beginning of a debate on the ordination of women of the kind which divided the Church of England. The activities of nuns are confined to the congregations in the neighbour-hood of their convents. And yet, the indestructible assertion of belief by women in Soviet times is shown not only by the sacrifices of the nuns of Shamordin but also by such loyal servants of the Soviet State as Liza, the shock worker (pp. 78 ff.), and Klavdiya, the tailor to the Politburo (pp. 193. ff.). Both belonged to the proletariat and worked hard for the regime, but both refused to join the Communist Party, because they believed in God. Liza even avoided joining the Pioneers and the Komsomol. It is a quiet strength that is also illustrated by Lena, the dissident, in the following pages.

She did not challenge the policy of the Church and she still only hints at the depth of her faith. But, when she was arrested in January 1984, at the age of twenty-four, a perceptive tribute was paid to her by Valery Fefelov, a former campaigner with her for the rights of the disabled. He had no doubt about the religious motive for her self-sacrifice. He said of her: 'Her life means service, given with the love of a deeply believing Christian, who has been led by her beliefs never to align herself with Soviet tyranny but rather to seek to preserve the dignity of man.'

# Lena

| |
|---|
| Yelena Nikitichna Sannikova |
| Writer, human rights activist |
| Born: Moscow, 1959 |
| Father: Translator |
| Mother: Theatre critic |
| Interviewed: June 1992 |

*Lena was one of the last of the dissidents and one of the last women
to be sentenced to camp and exile for 'anti-Soviet agitation and
propaganda' under Article 70 of the criminal code. Her shy, calm
diffidence conceals a will of steel and an unshakeable natural
stubbornness. You readily believe that she gave her KGB
interrogators a hard time. The poet and dissident Irina
Ratushinskaya, in her account of camp life,* Grey is the Colour
of Hope, *writes of Lena:*

> *We are of the same generation and have a similar
> understanding of Russian literary traditions. These traditions
> bind one to a certain code of behaviour – to our grief and to
> our joy . . . Yelena had no regrets that she had signed petitions
> in my defence, talked about my poetry to foreign journalists
> and retyped my poems and my biography for the* samizdat
> *collection which figured in the indictment at her trial.*

*And yet, as she tells it, Lena first found herself at odds with
the Soviet regime almost by accident. She did not set out to change
the political system. The system, rather, chose her as an
opponent.*

Lena's career in dissent began in 1980, when she was expelled from the University of Kalinin (now Tver), north-west of Moscow, on the grounds that she had failed to take part in a Communist parade. She found a job in a kinder-garten in a village near Kalinin but lost it when she revealed she was a Christian. She scratched a living as a typist and as an assistant on archeological expeditions, but otherwise found herself in Moscow with plenty of time on her hands to devote to the defence of human rights. She elected to do something practical about real social problems rather than take up grand themes like freedom of speech or fight narrow legal battles. She was attracted to a group campaigning for physically handicapped people and began helping two severely disabled organisers who were struggling to bring out a small news-sheet.

They were 'totally defenceless' but had been harassed by the KGB since the group was formed in 1978. 'Letters were confiscated, flats searched and members of the group were visited by agents or were called in to be warned that there were anti-Soviet activists in the group.' Tyres were slashed and a dacha belonging to a member of the group was burned down. Lena herself was picked up, while investigating the house-burning, and spent two weeks in a psychiatric hospital.

'There were endless conversations with the doctors about my motives for joining the group. It was an awful place.' When she was released, she was told: 'At the moment, you are not ill, but if you stay with the dissidents, you will certainly fall sick and then we'll have to bring you in for treatment.'

The KGB stopped the most innocent initiatives. 'When we tried to organise a trip for handicapped people to museums and theatres in Moscow, they jumped on that.' An attempt to branch out to the Ukraine failed, when disabled people there were persuaded to denounce the group as an anti-Soviet organisation. Lena left soon afterwards to help political prisoners. 'I was still interested in giving practical help to specific individuals.' She began to work for the Solzhenitsyn Fund, which was sending food parcels to prisoners and arranging visits to their relatives. 'It seemed the most suitable form of civil rights activity for me at that time. In order to give help, one inevitably had to collect information on prisoners, and this the KGB disliked intensely.'

She also helped produce a news-sheet called *V* (for *Vesti*, News) every two to four weeks. The *Chronicle of Current Events*, once the main underground dissident publication, was still being produced by a few survivors of the secret police crackdown of the early Seventies – but it finally died in 1983, when there was no one outside prison to bring it out.

By the early Eighties, many of those who once had the courage to sign open letters of protest and petitions had been intimidated or arrested. It was not possible to get more than eighteen or twenty signatures, compared with a thousand on a document condemning the trial of Andrei Sinyavsky and Yuli Daniel in 1966.

'We used to pay special attention to people's birthdays, and when human rights activists got together on such occasions, it was clear how our numbers were dwindling. In September 1983, I remember being at the birthday party of the human rights lawyer Sophia Kalistratova and noticing how few people were there. And they were almost all women; the men were already in prison.'

In February 1983, the flat Lena shared with her parents in Oruzheiny Lane, just off the Garden Ring Road in central Moscow, was searched.

'Masses of documents were confiscated: copies of the *Chronicle* and *V*, publications by Amnesty International, all my own notes and files and letters from prisoners in the camps. I wrote to the Procurator's Office asking for it all back, but they said it had gone to the KGB.'

Instead of being cowed by such pressure, she increased her dissident activities, collecting petitions and names of prisoners, writing letters of protest and appeals.

She was arrested on 19 January 1984 at the flat in Oruzheiny Lane, where she now lives with her mother, husband Stanislav and baby daughter Alexandra.

The flat is spacious by Moscow standards, three good-sized rooms with high ceilings. But it is run down, and plaster has come away from the ceiling in one of the rooms. We sit at a table in the sitting room where Lena produces a news-sheet about camp prisoners on a computer. She rocks Alexandra in a pram as we talk. She has a slow, deliberate manner. Her dark hair is parted in the middle and tied back. She has careful eyes and answers questions in a low voice, taking time to think about them.

'At about 7.30 in the morning, there was a ring at the door. My mother opened it and said: "They've come to see you." The corridor was full of people. I dressed and came out and the man in charge, who was involved in a lot of dissident cases, handed me a note saying I had to report to the KGB Lubyanka headquarters at 8 a.m. They said they were taking me in for questioning, but I asked to see their warrant and saw that it had "Case No. 62" written on it. So it was more like an arrest, and I asked my mother to get some things together ready for prison.'

The big briefcase her mother gave her contained books, notepaper, pens, a hair brush, a bible and a few clothes. There was no food. It made no difference: everything was taken from her. Six weeks later, the bible was returned, but nothing else.

At the Lubyanka headquarters, she met the two officers in charge of her case: Sorokin, who was aged between forty and forty-five and Gladkov, who was younger, perhaps her own age – twenty-four. Sorokin she knew had been in charge of the case of the dissident priest Father Dmitri Dudko, arrested in 1980 after he described the hierarchy of the

Russian Orthodox Church as 'the puppets of the atheists'.
Six months after his arrest he recanted on television.

Both agents struck her as nervous and uneasy. Sorokin
spoke very fast but remained polite. When Gladkov told her
she was charged under Article 70, 'his hands were shaking.
When I asked him about that, he looked embarrassed and
said it was always happening. He hid his hands.'

The same day she was transferred to the Lefortovo KGB
prison, in east Moscow.

'It was like a journey back in time. I was met and taken
to my cell by guards, exactly as described in accounts I had
read dating from the 1930s. The guards escorting me clicked
their fingers to warn others that a prisoner was being moved
and to keep out of the way. Prisoners were not supposed
to know who else was in the gaol.

'The cell was small, built in the eighteenth century for
solitary confinement. In the Soviet period, it held two or
three people. Usually I was with one other person. With
three, it was very crowded. The walls were thick and you
could scarcely hear if someone tapped on the other side.
There was a window high up opposite the door. I was lucky
because I could see sky between the bars. The window had
one pane of clear glass, instead of two opaque panes. The
walls were angled so that the entire cell could be seen
through the judas in the door.'

The guards went to great lengths to ensure that prisoners
from different cells never met by chance. The building was
on four floors and in the shape of a letter K. A man with a
flag stood at the point where all the corridors met and
'directed the traffic', as people were taken out for exercise
for one hour in twenty-four.

For five months, Lena shared her cell with a middle-aged
woman, a senior accountant in a training college who was
accused of taking bribes from would-be students. The Soviet
leader, Yuri Andropov, former head of the KGB, had
ordered a crackdown on corruption. 'It was an eye-opener

for me. I thought everyone in the country was poor. Now I learned there were millionaires and people dealing in hard currency.'

Lena was at first interrogated three times a week.

'They wanted to know everything about contacts of all kinds, what people I knew and how I met them. I was questioned about papers found during the search of my flat [on the day of her arrest]. How did the document get there? Who typed it?'

She either immediately refused to answer or first insisted that a long, involved question be typed into the record of the interrogation – and *then* refused to answer.

'I complained that my case had not been brought in accordance with the law and said I would not discuss other people on principle. Sometimes questioning went on for eight hours, and used up a lot of paper. They asked the same question over and over again. In the first month or so, they shouted at me and made threats. But that didn't work with me.'

After five months, they were begging her to sign statements. She did take pity on Gladkov, who said that his bosses were giving him hell because of her and said he wouldn't be able to go home that night unless she signed. After that she agreed to sign the record of her non-cooperation, putting her name at the bottom of each page of the account of her refusal to answer any questions.

Were you ever afraid?

'You feel afraid before you're arrested. But once you are taken in, you don't feel it. The only time I was scared was in June 1984, when they took me to the Serbsky Institute to see a psychiatrist. [The Serbsky Institute of Legal Medicine was notorious as the place where dissidents were put through psychiatric tests.] I was afraid they would say I was mentally ill. But I was lucky because at about that time the Soviet Psychiatric Association was expelled from the World Psychiatric Association. I did worry about my parents. I thought my father might lose his job at the Maurice Thorez language school, teaching English to Soviet so-called diplomats who were going to the United Nations.'

Her trial took place in October and she was sentenced to a year in a camp, to be followed by four years in exile.

'I was amazed, because I was warned to expect a heavy sentence of seven years in a camp and five in exile. They wanted to keep me in Lefortovo for the rest of the year, but I insisted on being sent to a camp. I wanted to meet people there, and I was fed up with Lefortovo.'

In December, she was transferred to Barashevo in Mordovia on the Volga, then the only political camp for women in the whole country. There were eleven women already there, sentenced under Article 70. One of them was Irina Ratushinskaya.

'We rarely saw each other in the camp. The first time I really met her was when I read her poetry after her arrest. It was religious verse and it made a deep impression on me.'

The camp was in the same compound as the central hospital serving all the camps in Mordovia.

'I was put in quarantine and kept away from the other women. I objected and said I had been sentenced to a camp not to a prison hospital. They agreed to take the lock off my cell but said I wasn't to wander around the camp. I did make contact with the other women, when they were being taken to the bath-house to wash. But I was told I was breaking the rules and was threatened with solitary till the end of my sentence. When I went into exile, I was taken from the camp punishment cells.'

Ratushinskaya explains that the KGB were determined to keep Lena away from the other women. They did not want her to go into exile armed with the latest information about conditions at Barashevo. The quarantine rule had not been enforced when the others had arrived at the camp. It was revived to isolate Lena.

Her place of exile was a village about a hundred miles north of the Siberian city of Tomsk. She arrived there, weak from a hunger strike in the camp punishment cells, and spent the first two weeks in Siberia in hospital. When she came out, she found a job as a cleaner in a workers' hostel and was given a room there. Police made life difficult for exiles. Visitors constantly had their papers checked, and locals who spoke to them were also harassed. Lena decided it was unfair to expose people to this and so avoided contact with them. Things suddenly changed in the spring of 1987, when the police stopped pestering visitors and contact became possible with local people.

'I adapted quite well to exile. I bought a house just over a mile from the village. I had two dogs and a cat. It was a beautiful place, on the bank of the River Ob and I could have lived there for a long time. I worked in the village every day, but I became very attached to my plot of land and to the forest. Except for the visits by KGB and police, it was ideal.'

She applied to Tomsk University and began a correspondence course in Russian literature there in the autumn of 1986. 'It was clear then that something had changed and the situation had eased. Prisoners were being urged to apply for a pardon. I decided not to, but on 16 December 1987 I was called to the police station and told that, under a new decree, I was being released from exile. The policeman seemed more pleased than I was. He was happy for me. I wanted either to have all charges against me dropped or to get an official apology.'

Early in 1988, she completed a term in Tomsk University and went back to Moscow for the first time in four years. 'It was a different world. There were rallies and political clubs – a lot of fuss, and I got tired of it after a couple of months. By April 1988, I was back in the house on the Ob, studying for my next exams and watching the ice crack. I spent the whole summer in Siberia and met my husband there.'

She also travelled in the vast autonomous republic of Yakutia in eastern Siberia, visiting other people in exile, till the KGB warned her off.

Today, Lena continues to produce the newsletter called *Prisoners' Page* which she founded in 1988, about prisoners of conscience in the Soviet Union from the 1960s to the present decade. In an issue in 1992, she challenges Russian President Boris Yeltsin's claim that all remaining political prisoners in Russia have been released. She points out that the infamous Article 64 remains in the Russian criminal code, though there has been talk for years of rewriting it. The Article concerns the offence of 'betrayal of the motherland'. It covers spying for, or giving secrets to, a foreign country, peddling 'anti-Soviet propaganda', defecting and attempting to defect.

'The disintegration of the USSR,' writes Lena, 'did not eliminate the machinery for suppressing the individual that was invented and built by the totalitarian regime. Letters from prisons testify to continuing arbitrariness and lawlessness.'

Lena says she faces the future 'more optimistically than I would have done in 1984 and 1985, but not as hopefully as I should like.'

# Nonna

Nonna Ivanovna Borisova

Wife of priest

Born: Moscow, 1940

Father: Chemistry teacher

Mother: Opera singer

Interviewed: May 1992

*Nonna Borisova is a Pentecostalist. She is also the wife of a Russian Orthodox priest and, with her husband, Alexander Borisov, she stood for many years with those believers who refused to go along with the Orthodox Church's policy of compromise with the atheistic State. Their immediate circle revolved around Father Alexander Men, one of the most influential clergymen to emerge in the officially Godless world of the Soviet Union.*

*Men was murdered early on the morning of 9 September 1990, on his way to his parish church in a country area north of Moscow. He was beaten about the head by unknown assailants but managed to walk back to his house. On the way, several people spoke to him and asked what had happened, but he would not describe his attackers. He collapsed outside his house and bled to death. He was fifty-five.*

*Men was not an open dissident. He kept his distance from politics, but after his death the Soviet Parliament's daily newspaper,* Izvestia, *described him as 'a spiritual pastor to many defenders of human rights, prisoners of conscience and people oppressed by the authorities'. In his quiet, undemonstrative way, he resisted the pressure of the State, as Patriarch Tikhon had done more dramatically soon after the Revolution. When the assault on religion was at its height under Khrushchov, Men gathered around him a circle of brave and dedicated young men and women like Nonna and Alexander.*

Nonna talks about Father Men, religion, her own spiritual quest and the KGB, while sitting at a table in her small flat in central Moscow, where she has lived for most of her married life. She is wearing a turquoise cardigan over a dark-blue blouse. She speaks with animation, but her eyes are serene.

The little room is lined with books: bibles, theological works in several languages, Dickens and Tolstoy. There is an ikon in a corner and, among the books, a photograph of Mother Theresa of Calcutta and another of a handsome young priest with a neat black beard, Father Alexander Men.

'He came from a Jewish family that belonged to the intelligentsia,' says Nonna, 'but his mother and aunt were members of the Church of the Catacombs [Christians who distrusted the official Orthodox Church and its links with the Communist regime and broke from it to worship secretly in small groups]. Men and his mother were baptised on the same day, when he was three [in 1938]. Most of the members of the Catacomb Church suffered in Stalin's repressions, including Men's mother and aunt and their closest friends, and many of them died.

'When I joined the Russian Orthodox Church in the early Sixties, the Khrushchov persecutions were at their peak. Then young people and the intelligentsia didn't go to church.'

But there were young people among those who gathered around Men who, at that time, lived and worked at Alabino, an hour by train south-west of Moscow. It was at Men's church there that Nonna married Alexander Borisov, a childhood friend of Men. Before he became a priest, Men studied biology and animal breeding at an institute in Irkutsk, Siberia. He went to secret lectures on genetics, a science then outlawed in the USSR. Another future priest at the same institute was Gleb Yakunin, who was to become a leading civil rights activist.

In Moscow, Nonna says, a group of young people met to

talk about philosophy. 'Many of them felt the need for religious faith and went to see Men. They were intellectuals: artists, historians, and so on. There was a kind of awakening among the intelligentsia in the late sixties. Many people came to see us in this flat. Men was the main source of information for us, and he gave us books to read, forbidden literature.

'Things became difficult when he was moved nearer Moscow, to Tarasovka, because another priest there reported on him to the KGB. We were all under constant pressure. Even when we made appointments to meet in the Metro, we were afraid we'd be followed.'

The KGB kept a close watch on the Church.

'Men was probably the first Jew from intellectual circles who was allowed to become a priest. He graduated from the theological seminary at Zagorsk. This was difficult to get into, because the KGB vetted the applicants and turned away people with higher education. The KGB didn't want intellectuals to enter the Church, because they were afraid they would exert great influence.

'In the early seventies, young people used to study the Bible in this flat, sometimes twenty to thirty people at a time, sitting around a table in this room. We did it secretly, of course, but we found out later that the KGB knew all about it. They left us alone, but they arrested Gleb Yakunin and some others who were involved in civil rights and so were considered more political.

'My husband was summoned by the KGB, not to the Lubyanka [KGB headquarters] but to the Moskva Hotel. They threatened him but also promised him all sorts of privileges, even trips abroad, if he would inform on Alexander Men. He refused. It was terrifying. We had young children [twin daughters Mariya and Vera born in 1964] and he could lose his job any minute. They told him what they already knew about him, and we felt we were living in a flat without walls. The telephone, of course, was bugged.'

Alexander Borisov entered the Zagorsk seminary in 1973, when his KGB minder from the Moskva Hotel was on holiday. At about this time, the KGB searched the Borisovs' flat. It happened after the arrival in Moscow of a foreign clergyman who had smuggled religious books past the customs at the international airport. Unwisely, the foreigner left the books in his hotel room, while he went out. The KGB, in a routine search, discovered the books and followed the visitor when he took the books in a suitcase to the Borisovs' flat. They happened to be in the country, so he left the case with Nonna's mother.

'When we got back from the country, we opened the case and saw the books. We were still looking at them when the doorbell rang. The KGB had arrived – twenty minutes after us. There was a prosecutor and witnesses. One was a woman they picked up downstairs. Alexander took them into one room, while Men and I, in the other, hid books in the piano, behind a fish tank and under the divan. We hid them all, then sat on the sofa. The foreign priest called again, while the KGB were still with us, but we managed to send him away. It sounds funny now, but then it was far from funny. They didn't search very thoroughly, perhaps because they thought we hadn't had time to hide anything. But that foreigner didn't get another Soviet visa for fifteen years.'

Nonna's mother had been a believer as a child but had abandoned her faith after she got married. She studied music and sang in opera at the Stanislavsky Theatre in Pushkin Street. The family had lived in a wooden barrack on the edge of a big wooded park in the Sokolniki district of north-east Moscow. 'We had two little rooms of eight square metres each, and we always had people staying with us.'

There was one kitchen and one lavatory for seven families, forty people. 'I remember it as a very happy time. We all celebrated everyone's birthday together. In the spring and summer, we had birthday parties in the open air, with a wind-up gramophone. We lived there before the war and again when we came back after being evacuated. Everyone shared what they had. We were very short of food and, after the war, the prices were terrible. There were lots of refugees and beggars. When you went to the market, you had to walk between rows of beggars. My mother was poor, but she gave them something. I didn't feel a constant joy, exactly, but there was a light in our lives. Now, with all we have, we feel depression. It's an atmosphere children can't properly grow up in.

'We never talked about religion. It was a forbidden subject. My mother was the only one who said anything to me about it. My father was a chemist and wrote articles proving that God couldn't exist, but he never talked about atheism to us. That question was raised later, when I met my husband. Then Father said that he did believe, deep down, but didn't go to church, because it was dangerous. Alexander Men gave me my first New Testament. At that time, people used to copy the Gospels into notebooks. I was always open about my faith. God was protecting me, and I never had any trouble because of my openness.'

It was Gorbachov's openness (*glasnost*) which put a stop to religious persecution. But long before that Nonna had felt dissatisfied with the Orthodox Church.

In the late Seventies, she was treated in hospital for a poisoned finger. The conditions in her surgical ward were bad. The patients were mainly elderly vagrant women with ugly wounds and sores. The place was overcrowded, and there were beds in the corridors.

'I spent a month in hospital with terribly unhappy people. I talked to them and lent them books. There was an old woman, covered in festering wounds, with a moustache – a creature between the sexes – who had no visitors. I began to share my food with her, but I had to make an effort to get close to her: the smell around her made me feel faint. I thought for the first time about the purpose of being a Christian. Life was getting easier. There were still persecutions, but we had our own circle. Going to church gave me spiritual protection. Now I saw a completely different world. I realised I had not only to believe in, but to serve, my God.'

She tried to enrol at the only school for nurses in Moscow, but at forty was over the age limit. She sought other ways of serving and investigated oriental religions and pagan beliefs. Finally she found what she was seeking in the Pentecostal Church. 'My husband saw the people I met and appreciated their sincerity, humility and closeness to God. But 1979 was a difficult time for Pentecostalists. Police took our names. Persecution was beginning. In 1982 our flat was searched again. It was a thorough search this time, very unpleasant.'

A Pentecostal minister was arrested and imprisoned. Nonna and other members of the Church whose flats had been searched were called as witnesses at his trial, which lasted a month. 'The general idea was that Pentecostalists were mad. We were examined by psychiatrists and they listened very carefully to us. They testified that we were sane.'

Nonna is afraid that the present religious freedom will not last. 'I think that very soon the old days will come back. That's why we still live as we used to. They don't dictate to us now, but they remember how to do it.'

Who do you think murdered Alexander Men?

'The reasons for his death are obvious. It isn't all that important to find the killer. It is clear what forces were behind it. When *perestroika* began and it was possible to talk about God openly, he sometimes spoke in public four or five times a day. He decided to take the opportunity, while it was there. He was bright, very clever and profound. And he was a Jew, in a country where anti-Semitism is widespread and, if not imposed, then encouraged by the Orthodox Church.

'While he stayed quietly in his church, he was left alone. But when he became active, he received threats from Pamyat [the extreme Right Russian nationalist movement]. KGB forces with the support of Orthodox clergymen could not stand a man that bright, and who was a Jew into the bargain. After his death, pamphlets were published calling him a heretic. Even now, his own books are banned in all the churches in Moscow – except my husband's.'

Father Alexander Borisov's church is just across the road from Moscow City Hall, where he is a councillor. There is a printing shop still installed in the church and Borisov sometimes holds services in the open air. He once conducted a funeral service in the street for a man who had died of Aids.

When Nonna met Borisov in 1960, he immediately told her he believed in God. 'In those days, it was an almost impossible thing to say, and it came as a real shock.'

Those are the dark days she fears will return.

# Kseniya

Irina Yurievna Zaitseva

Religious name: Kseniya

Mother Superior of Russian
Orthodox convent, former
journalist

Born: Shuya, Ivanovo region,
Russia, 1954

Father: Army officer

Mother: Painter

Interviewed: June 1992

*Kseniya changed her name from Irina when she took the veil, a
sign, she says, that her old secular self, with all her sins, is dead
and a new human being has been born. She became Mother
Superior of the Novo-Golutvin convent at Kolomna, seventy miles
south-east of Moscow, in 1989 – an astonishing transformation
for the child of a staunch Communist family and product of the
atheistic Soviet education system. Her story helps to explain how
faith survived the persecutions, sufferings and humiliations of the
Church under Communist rule and how monks and nuns were
found to re-open monasteries and convents, when the State's
attitude to religion changed dramatically under Gorbachov.*

Kseniya is a tall woman who combines an imposing presence, accentuated by her black habit and headdress, with a
warm, unstuffy sense of humour. She moves deliberately
and with dignity, her hands hanging loosely at her sides,

rather in the manner of a Hollywood gun-fighter, but she creates an atmosphere of jollity around her. Sisters and novices treat her with reverence, but her laughter keeps solemnity at bay.

She is rebuilding and bringing back to life a monastery that was closed in 1924, the year of Lenin's death. It was handed back to the Church in 1988 in a dilapidated state, and much of it needed major repairs. But by the summer of 1992, there were ninety sisters living, working, studying and praying in the convent. The main Trinity church – dating from 1680 – has been restored and is open to all for regular services. Below it is the St Kseniya of St Petersburg chapel, which the nuns themselves repainted and which they use daily. Another church near the main gate is under restoration.

The Mother Superior receives guests in a cool, pleasant room in a light-brown, eighteenth-century building with walls five feet thick and a corrugated iron roof.

Orthodox convents, she says, remained open, during the Communist period, in Estonia, Latvia and West Ukraine, but most of the rest were closed or used for non-religious purposes, as factories, stores, fire stations. Some were destroyed. 'Many Russian priests were exiled or died in concentration camps, but this did not destroy the people's faith in God.'

She was not brought up in the faith. Her grandparents were convinced Communists, and her parents were too busy with their careers to spend time talking to her. 'But from childhood I felt that something very important was missing.' When she left school, she first began a course in aeronautical engineering, naively supposing that a discipline connected with the heavens would somehow provide what she was seeking. She abandoned engineering and turned to the arts. She was drawn to the cinema and thought of becoming a film director. She also felt she might have a talent for painting. But it was the great writers of Russian literature, and in particular Dostoevsky, who helped her most.

'He raised questions about the meaning of life, about God and Man. These questions became central for me. That is how faith in God was born in me: through historical experience, cultural traditions, the arts and literature.'

She was baptised while a student at Moscow University, studying television in the faculty of journalism and working at television stations in different parts of Russia each summer.

'Baptism was an amazing moment of rare joy. I felt I had found something great and new in my life.'

She graduated from university, having written a diploma thesis on Dostoevsky, and went to a monastery at Pskov, near Leningrad, for a fortnight's rest.

'I couldn't leave the place and worked there for six months. I had to get up very early – services began at five thirty. I realised that the way to God was not just through books but by performing duties for Him and addressing Him in prayer. At that moment, I had no thought of becoming a nun. I didn't even know that such places existed for women as well.'

But she found her way to one in Estonia. 'In my mind, I couldn't accept that I would live in a convent; in my heart, I knew I couldn't live anywhere else.' After a year, she was unable to get permanent rights of residence in Estonia and had to return to Moscow. 'By a miracle', she learnt that a group of elderly nuns living near a ruined convent in Georgia needed an assistant and worked for them for two years. At the end of that time Metropolitan Zinovy of Tbilisi told her that her place was in the Church and that she should go back to Russia.

She wept but took his advice and found work as a choir master in a small church at Tatarintsevo, a village in the Moscow region. This led to a three-year course in church choral music and theology at the theological seminary in Zagorsk.

Taking a course in choir-training is the only way a woman can enter an Orthodox theological seminary. Some months after my meeting with Kseniya, I went to Oxford to meet Canon Michael Bourdeaux, founder and director of Keston College, which specialises in the study of religion under Communism.

'Women are the backbone of the Orthodox Church,' he says, 'but they do not have any role in it except as pew fodder.' The Church does not approve of Orthodox women studying abroad, because the Church would have no place for women with high theological qualifications.

'There is no role for women in the higher echelons of the Church. There is no equivalent of the women canons in Western Churches. Nuns are an exception but convents are separate enclaves. When Khrushchov set out to crush monasticism, whole cadres of women dedicated to the Orthodox faith set up secret convents. They kept a low profile. They couldn't be seen in the churches that remained open, but they taught in private. Now that the convents are reopening, the women who were scattered have moved back.'

Young girls, too, are looking for ways of joining them. *Moskovsky Komsomolets* responds with an article on how to become a nun:

> You can go to a convent any time, without any advance permission, talk to the Mother Superior and ask to stay for a few days. You'll be warmly welcomed, fed, taken to a sauna and prayed for.

Kseniya says she hesitated to take the veil, 'but I realised that becoming a nun was the most fruitful way forward.' She joined in an appeal to re-open the convent of Khotkovo near Zagorsk. It was finally opened in mid-1992 but, in the meantime, the Church leadership asked her to take charge of the Novo-Golutvin convent in Kolomna. She agreed and took the veil on the first Sunday after Easter in 1989.

'An important new stage in my life began. I had to learn

about architecture and how to restore everything: walls and ikons.'

The convent has a Sunday-school for children, something that was still forbidden at the beginning of the 1990s. Senior nuns also run a school for novices and young girls from many parts of Russia – including Siberia – from Ukraine and from Finland. The Mother Superior teaches ethics, and lessons include the history of the Russian Orthodox Church. The history of the Church in the Communist period does not yet appear on the course, but Kseniya indicates her position on the struggle between Church and State after the Revolution by speaking warmly and at length about Patriarch Tikhon who resisted the Communist assault on the Church in the early years of Soviet rule. 'He had a difficult life and saw pure believers being sent into exile.'

At Kolomna, Kseniya is building a self-sufficient religious community. The nuns work allotments and, ten miles from the convent, they have a farm with cows and hens. When I ask Kseniya what she thinks is in store for the Church in Russia now, I expect some expression of relief and gratitude at the ending of a period of horrendous persecution. Instead, she observes that there are 'negative processes' taking place. The first she lists is 'the great number of sects' that now exist and cites the Pentecostalists as an example of those which 'do not lead the soul to a perception of the truth'.

In this she is a true representative of Russian Orthodoxy, which joined the World Council of Churches in 1961 and formally embraced ecumenicism, but which is aghast when evangelists – with hard currency behind them – begin preaching on Russian territory.

The former television journalist thinks that television is ruining the souls of young people. 'Children have all sorts of neuroses. They learn sin at an early age, have abortions and can't become good mothers. That is why the Orthodox Church calls people to repentance and to purity in married life, to be baptised and married in church. The more people want to be faithful to God, the stronger our country will be and the longer it will survive.'

Chapter 5

# Privilege and the Ruling Class

My first glimpse of life at the top in the Soviet Union came the day after my arrival in Moscow in March 1989. The editor of the *Observer*, Donald Trelford, was recording a television interview with the former Soviet Foreign Minister, Andrei Gromyko, about his autobiography *Memories*. I went along as part of the team to Gromyko's State dacha at Zaryechie, just outside Moscow. We left the city in black official cars heading west, swung off the main road into a forest and came to a halt in front of a green gate in a high, green wooden fence. There were spotlights over the gate and it was guarded. Our credentials established, the gate opened and we drove past tall silver birches on a curving drive to the foot of a flight of steps leading up to the dacha's main entrance.

*Dacha* is an imprecise word. It can mean little more than an unheated wooden shack on a country allotment, used for a few months in the summer. Often it is a more substantial structure, one of a group of wooden bungalows or two-storey houses in a development organised by a government department or an industrial company. Top people's dachas, provided by the Soviet State at nominal rents, were much grander. They guaranteed peace and quiet in beautiful surroundings and could be used all year round.

Gromyko's official dacha was a solid country house set in woods. It was well furnished, well staffed and well supplied. You climbed the flight of stairs and entered a lobby which had a shoe-cleaning machine in one corner. There was an air of easy comfort about the place. Gromyko did his writing, in pencil, on the first floor, which was furnished with antiques. He had the manner of a country gentleman. The face that for decades had seemed set in a concrete grimace kept breaking into a smile.

Gromyko was a high-flyer. He became Stalin's ambassador in Washington in 1943, when he was only thirty-four. He was Soviet Foreign Minister from 1957 to 1985 and was the Kremlin spokesman to the world throughout most of the Cold War. He was a member of the Politburo and, for three years till he retired in 1988, chairman of the then rubber-stamp Soviet Parliament, the Supreme Soviet, and thus the figurehead Chief of State.

In the evening at the dacha, he looked on, smiling gently, as his wife Lydia, after a fine spread of *zakuski* (Russian *hors-d'oeuvre*), showed her visitors the family photo album. Andrei Gromyko died a few months later and was buried in the cemetery of the Novodyevichy monastery, a privileged final resting place.

From the early days of the Soviet period, the leaders of the Communist Party looked after themselves and their officials well. As a matter of policy, the apparatchiks toiling to build a socialist society were to be protected from petty worries about where to live, where to shop for food and where to have their clothes made. They accorded themselves privileges from birth in special maternity homes to graves in exclusive cemeteries.

Lenin set the pattern after the Revolution, and Stalin developed it into an elaborate system of privileges and rewards which served – together with Communist faith and the fear instilled by the political police – to cement together the huge, Party-controlled machine that ran the country. At the heart of the privileged class was the *nomenklatura*, the self-selecting ruling élite who operated the complex system of patronage by which sensitive jobs were filled by appointment at all levels throughout the USSR. Patronage began at the very top with the Party leader, the Politburo and the secretariat of the Central Committee. And it ran down through republics, regions, cities, towns and districts, a network of millions of jobs, whose incumbents enjoyed varying degrees of power and privilege.

A precise figure of those admitted to this magic circle has never been established, but one should not be misled by the word 'élite' into thinking of it as a narrow or tight circle. Belonging to the Communist Party of the Soviet Union – which at its peak had around nineteen million members – was not, alone, enough to gain admittance. One needed a place in the Party or administrative machine.

The Party, however, had 1,115,000 organisations across the USSR in 1987, according to Boris Yeltsin. He gives this figure in a letter to Party leader Mikhail Gorbachov, dated 12 September of that year, in which he resigned as Moscow Party Boss and as a junior member of the Politburo. Yeltsin does not break down the Party organisations figure, but he gives some idea of the numbers involved in running by proposing to cut the Party *apparat* by half.

As for the administration of the country, Gorbachov, on a trip to Murmansk in 1987, said that it employed eighteen million people. Of these 2.5 million were in 'various administrative organs' and fifteen million were running 'associations, enterprises' and other organisations. Martin McCauley of the London School of Slavonic and East European Studies calculates that if the Party, Komsomol, trade union and state farm bureaucracies are added to the eighteen million, the total could be 'as high as twenty-five to thirty million'. He goes on: 'The astonishing fact emerges that, if families are taken into account, about one-third of the population directly or indirectly runs the Soviet state.'

The sheer size of this force helps to explain why, under Gorbachov, there was such effective resistance to reforms that threatened the privileges of the apparatchiks.

The privileged circle did not end with the bureaucrats. Also included were scientists, writers, journalists, musicians, ballet dancers, cosmonauts, military officers, sports stars – anyone both distinguished and ready to toe the Party line. The number of apparatchiks who enjoyed power as well as perks was small but has been variously estimated at between half a million and a million. Real power was the ability to pick up a telephone and get a subordinate to carry out an order simply because he recognised his master's voice.

Few women reached positions in the hierarchy which gave them such power. Neither did they achieve it through marriage, though they did, of course, share privileges accorded their husbands. They were not, however, necessarily protected from the security police. Stalin had the wives of some of his closest collaborators arrested and sent to the camps and showed little warmth towards those he left at liberty. Lydia, the widow of Andrei Gromyko, declined to be interviewed, but she did provide written answers to a number of questions. She revealed, for instance, that she never joined the Communist Party herself.

She says of Stalin that she saw him five or six times at receptions. 'He spoke so quietly that, even if you stood a few steps from him, you couldn't hear anything. He never paid any attention to people like me. I spoke to him several times on the telephone, when he called Andrei. Stalin spoke very coldly. He never asked how I was.'

Before Andrei Gromyko went to Washington as ambassador, he and Lydia already had a flat in central Moscow. It was small, with just two rooms, but it was much better than ordinary Muscovites could hope for at the time.

Access to relatively comfortable accommodation in both town and country was always the most precious of the privileges accorded the ruling class. Lenin's elder sister, Anna Ulyanova-Yelizarova, lived in a five-roomed flat just outside the walls of the Kremlin and had a direct telephone link to her brother's office. In 1992, the flat was transformed into a museum in honour of the women of Russia from Princess Olga, the widow of Prince Igor, who helped to introduce Christianity in the tenth century, to Valentina Tereshkova, the cosmonaut.

Stalin had a residential complex built for his top people not far from the Kremlin, the House on the Embankment. Yelena Djaparidze, now eighty-five (see p. 137) moved into it with her mother when it opened in 1930, and was still there in 1992. Privileges, once acquired, often remained with the family. Viktor Grishin, the Moscow Party boss during the Brezhnev period, still occupied a flat in a prestige block on Alexei Tolstoy Street, when he died in the summer of 1992. Zoya Zarubina (see p. 13) has a spacious flat in another fine building in the same exclusive district which, till 1992, cost less than R.10 a month in rent.

Some of the special accommodation, long hidden from the general public by practised discretion and secrecy, became more accessible during the Gorbachov period. The Communist Party took to inviting journalists to news conferences at the Oktyabrskaya Hotel, formerly reserved for top officials, now opened to clients with hard currency. The actor Sean Connery stayed there during the shooting of *The Russia House*. The hotel is a high, brick building set back from a busy road behind a tall iron fence. It has palatial lobbies with marble-covered walls and quiet corners with potted plants. The conference room was the most comfortable in the city and its simultaneous interpreting first-rate. All major Soviet cities, if unable to match the opulence of the Oktyabrskaya, would be expected to have luxury hotels for visiting dignitaries.

Foreigners, ready to pay dollar rents, also gained access to flats once reserved for officials. What set these apart from the homes of ordinary Muscovites was not just the size of the rooms, but the generous expanse of hall and passage areas, which emphasised the feeling of spaciousness.

Under Gorbachov, Party officials and ministers began giving interviews to the media, even answering questions about their salaries. These proved to be relatively modest (R.12,000 a year for a member of the Politburo), but it was perks not pay that had always counted. Cars (from the long Zils and Chaikas to humble Volgas) were provided with drivers, and wives and children, as well as the officials themselves, were chauffered about. The special shops were not only very well stocked but their prices were low. Party workers at all levels could eat in cheap canteens. A middle-ranking official took me to lunch in an exclusive Party restaurant, where a meal with caviar cost next to nothing. Before he left, he bought a box of cakes to take home.

An army of servants looked after the creature comforts of the ruling class in Russia and the other republics: craftsmen, doctors, cleaners, cooks, maids, grocers, housekeepers, gardeners and the rest. On the whole, the rulers did not flaunt their privileges, except when their official cars swept into town from country dachas and police stopped the traffic for them, a practice that continued into the post-Communist period.

Ella Pamfilova, the one woman at the top in the Yeltsin Administration (see next page), repeatedly warned that the survival of a privileged class was a threat to reform.

# Ella

| |
|---|
| Ella Alexandrovna Pamfilova |
| Politician |
| Born: Near Tashkent, Uzbekistan, 1953 |
| Father: Chauffeur |
| Mother: Office worker |
| Interviewed: June 1992 |

*Ella Pamfilova is a whistle-blower come to power. As a member of the Soviet Parliament, she won a reputation as a scourge of the privileges the Party élite awarded themselves. Now, as Boris Yeltsin's Minister for Social Protection, she is still fighting privilege and corruption from the inside.*

Ella Pamfilova receives me in her ministerially spacious office panelled in light wood and sits across the table from me with her back to a window overlooking a quiet square, full of trees. It is the kind of view that gives a special pleasure to summer in Moscow. Pamfilova speaks precisely, sometimes with passion, but looks cool and trim. Her long blonde hair is held in a bun, with a fringe that she brushes aside as she works. She is wearing a dark-blue skirt and a knitted cotton top in black with square floral decorations woven into it in a pattern which suggests a chain of office. She occasionally breaks off to take a telephone call. One, she says, is from a pensioner to whom she has given both her office and home numbers. She has the gift of appearing to have all the time in the world. She is clearly in control.

Her Ministry is on Slavonic Square, formerly named after Nogin, an early Bolshevik. It is a short walk from the complex of buildings that till 1991 housed the huge staff of the Central Committee of the Soviet Communist Party, the heart of the vast administrative and political machine that sought to control every aspect of life in the Soviet empire. It set the pattern for the lifestyle of the Party apparatchiks in Russia and the other fourteen republics, who formed a ruling class with special access to food, drink, clothes, furniture, hospitals, schools, holiday centres, foreign currency and travel, dachas and promotion.

When I first met Ella Pamfilova in the dying days of the Soviet Union in late 1991, she was still secretary of the USSR Supreme Soviet's Privileges Standing Committee, which was about to disappear, like the Parliament itself. What worried her then was the way the old Soviet élite, the *nomenklatura*, had not only survived the suspension of the Communist Party but was luring new democratic officials into its corrupting world of privilege. They were finding offers such as better health care for their families hard to resist.

'With large-scale privatisation to come,' Pamfilova said then, 'State officials and deputies are using their positions to take the best pieces of the pie and work to the advantage of companies in which they have commercial interests. Members of the former Party *nomenklatura* are blocking reforms, because they haven't yet privatised everything to their own advantage. They are turning into capitalists in a savage form of capitalism, with monopolies for corrupt circles which keep out middle-class entrepreneurs.'

Pamfilova's work in Parliament brought her threatening telephone calls, but she had no illusions about the committee's lack of real clout. She described it as 'a cosmetic, a smokescreen'.

Now in the Russian Cabinet, she is, if anything, even

more outspoken than she was in Parliament. Just before we meet at her Ministry, she says in an interview with *Komsomolskaya Pravda*: 'I keep telling the President (and senior Ministers) about the danger of corruption and bribery, but they seem to underestimate it. You can't call on people to tighten their belts and be patient, when the authorities at the same time are building private residences and drinking toasts in champagne at public receptions. It may be legal, but it's simply not decent.'

She tells me: 'My position has not changed from last year, except that I am even more alarmed now, because we are in the process of carrying out reform. I am doing my best to ensure that the authorities don't lose the trust of the people and that reforms don't come to grief over social problems. We know that things will not improve for a long time and yet we have to work harder. But it's useless to try and *make* people work harder. They must feel the need for it themselves. They have to be direct participants, not spectators watching the results of other people's efforts.'

Some privileges have withered away, she says. Most special shops have gone, because 'if you have the money, you can buy anything. Things that used to be free – dachas and so on – now have to be paid for. But if the nature of the privileges has changed, in essence they still exist. People are trying to grab everything. Many high officials in the executive and the legislature are setting a bad example. Some of those in official positions are still simultaneously running businesses. Yeltsin signed a decree banning this, but there are camouflaged ways of doing it. Ordinary people see what is happening and they get angry.

'We have chosen the toughest kind of reforms and they are painful. It's in the nature of Russians to endure difficulties, if they know why they are suffering. They should be able to believe that we are all suffering together to rebuild the State. Unhappily, they cannot be sure of that now. Faith in reform is being undermined and people may follow demagogues, former Communists who haven't found places in the new set-up and who are ready to take advantage of painful reforms and of the Russian yearning for social justice. Public opinion could be turned round. The standard of living is falling and so is the authority of the Government.'

Pamfilova came into politics amid the sizzling excitement of 1989, when the first Congress of People's Deputies was elected in the closest the USSR had then come to free, open and contested elections. Boris Yeltsin won a landslide victory in the Moscow No. 1 constituency in which all Moscow constituents could vote, thereby coming back from the political dead and inflicting an astonishing defeat on the Communist Party, which had done everything possible to stop him.

Pamfilova, less dramatically, entered Parliament at the same time as a trade union representative of the Moscow Central Mechanical Repair Factory, where she worked as an electronics engineer. They were thrilling times for a new politician. When the Parliament assembled in the Kremlin Palace of Congresses on 25 May 1989, most of the country watched or listened to the debates that were broadcast live and in full on television and radio. Radio Moscow put the television audience alone at ninety million, a third of the entire Soviet population. Absenteeism was rampant and industrial output sank. The Congress was essentially a conservative body. The electoral rules had seen to that. But Mikhail Gorbachov, Party boss and Speaker, chaired most of the sessions, making up the rules as he went along and keeping the diehard Communist majority under control.

The debates produced no decisions of great practical importance, but they let off steam in an astonishing way. Heresies were expressed live on television that had previously been confined to family kitchens, away from telephones it was wise to assume were tapped. Georgian and Baltic deputies challenged the Kremlin's mistreatment of their small nations. The KGB was criticised. So was the

Politburo hardliner, Yegor Ligachov. One deputy even proposed removing the embalmed body of Vladimir Ilyich Lenin from the mausoleum on Red Square and giving it a decent burial. Representatives of non-Russian republics – among them Nursultan Nazarbayev, then Premier, later President of Kazakhstan – complained of the appalling damage done to their environment by the Kremlin-dictated rush to industrialise. Green politics had arrived and Pamfilova became part of it as a member of the Ecology Committee of the Supreme Soviet, the standing parliament.

Yet, within a year, Andrei Sakharov, the great, brave dissident and reformer who spoke fearlessly from a seat just below Gorbachov, was dead and hopes aroused by the new Parliament had evaporated. What went wrong?

'We put off reforms for a long time. The more we delayed, the worse the situation became. Many people were ready to roll up their sleeves and get down to work. Now it's more difficult to solve the crisis. This afternoon [at a Cabinet meeting], we have been discussing the Government's reform programme. I think it should be written down in such a way that every citizen will understand it. If we explain now, in plain words, what is in it for everyone, then we shall overcome passivity and excite and interest people again. But we are very short of time. We are the damaged products of our system and our time. We can't expect new, perfect, honest people suddenly to come to power now. Where could we find them? We have to grow them ourselves.'

Are you confident, I ask, that the reforms will work?

'I don't have any doubt about it. But what the cost and the sacrifices will be and how long it will take are different questions. One illusion I don't have is that it will be quick. It will take decades, at best, and will need very hard work. This is what we should be telling the people. Only our own heads and hands can save us. Other countries may help, of course, but the main burden will be ours. Unfortunately, not everyone understands this yet, but more and more are beginning to. If real life beats you over the head every day, you are bound to understand in the long run.'

How does Pamfilova combine running a ministry with her duties as wife and mother?

Her fifteen-year-old daughter Tatyana, she says, does much of the housework. As for her husband, he has forbidden her to mention his name in interviews and stays away from government receptions (rumour has it that he is a military man).

Pamfilova was brought up in Uzbekistan because her family were evacuated there during the war. Both her parents were Russian. Her father ran away to join the army, when he was sixteen. He died in 1990. Her mother is retired. Pamfilova herself won a gold medal at school.

As Minister for Social Protection, does she believe there is social justice for women in Russia?

'In other countries, women are fighting for equal rights at work. Here we have enough of such rights and obligations. But we do have a difficult problem, because women carry a bigger burden at work and in everyday life. Yet there are very few women in public life, and I find that unjust. Now would be a good time to have more of them. Women are more even-tempered than men and could help to solve acute problems such as inter-ethnic disputes. These occur mostly outside Russia, but they concern Russia. When grown-up men behave like hot-blooded teenagers and when ambitions collide, women could contribute wisdom and thoughtfulness and help to settle contradictions.

'I admire the women in this country. Despite all the difficulties, they manage to look attractive, find something to wear and have their hair done. Thanks to them, I hope Russia will survive and flourish.'

How do her Cabinet colleagues treat her?

She laughs: 'On the whole, very well. But sometimes I surprise them by my decisive, courageous, man-like

behaviour – even more masculine than they dare to be themselves.'

She laughs again, to underline that she is just joking, but
it is not difficult to believe that this is a pretty accurate
description of her performance in Cabinet.

# Klavdiya

Klavdiya Fyodorovna
Lyubeshkina

Seamstress and tailor

Born: Soimonovo, near
Serpukhov, Moscow region,
1928

Father: Department head in
Moscow greengrocer's

Mother: Textile factory worker

Interviewed: May 1992

*Klavdiya spent a quarter of a century making clothes for top
Communist Party officials, before she retired in 1985. Her
customers included members of the ruling Politburo, Party bosses
of the Soviet republics and retired officials and officers – and their
families. She made suits for General Secretaries of the Party from
Nikita Khrushchov to Mikhail Gorbachov and embroidered stars and
laurel leaves with gold thread on the marshals' uniforms of Soviet
Defence Ministers. Every eighteen months, she made a new suit
for the embalmed body of Vladimir Ilyich Lenin.*

Klavdiya belonged to a team of sixty tailors, cutters and
assistants who laboured long hours under armed guard at
No.5 Kutuzov Avenue, opposite the Gothic skyscraper of
the Ukraine Hotel, to keep the Kremlin bosses well dressed
in suits made from the best imported cloth at only nominal
cost to themselves. The secret workshop had two official

names: Military Unit No. 11–64 and Third Section of the Tenth Bureau of the Ninth Department of the KGB. The Ninth Department was responsible for the security and all other services for the members of the Politburo. It supplied them with bodyguards. It is not, therefore, surprising that security was tight around the KGB-controlled workshop where the Kremlin leaders had their clothes made, from hats and overcoats to underpants, and where their wives ordered their dresses and fur coats.

No one was allowed out alone during working hours except with special permission of the workshop's director. For meals, KGB guards took the staff by coach to the Kremlin canteen. They could receive and make telephone calls only through the workshop operator. At the end of a shift, the garment each was working on was locked away in a safe till next day.

Klavdiya worked at the big GUM department store and at the Ministry of Defence tailors' shop before she and a cutter with whom she teamed up joined the KGB workshop. 'I was thoroughly checked out; so were my parents and sisters,' she says.

Although retired seven years ago, she still cannot forget the old rule forbidding Soviet citizens to speak to foreigners. She refuses to meet me and I put my questions to her through a Russian newspaperman, Sergei Pluzhnikov.

Klavdiya tells him that the workshop was started in 1938 by Joseph Stalin's personal tailor, Legner – a former secret police officer and designer of the dictator's grey, buttoned-up tunics – who recruited Moscow's best tailors, cutters and seamstresses. The workshop was first located in the centre of the city, then moved across the Moskva River to Kutuzov Avenue.

The top people rarely went there. They were measured and had their fittings in the Kremlin, where cutters were admitted with special passes. Stalin and Khrushchov refused to have fittings, and their clothes were made on tailors' dummies.

Klavdiya says she made suits for Yuri Andropov for sixteen years. He was the head of the KGB, then Party General Secretary from November 1982 till his death in February 1984. Though reputed to be an austere man, he appreciated well-made clothes, she says. 'He regarded me as his personal tailor. When I wasn't available, he waited for me.'

She liked Khrushchov, too: 'a nice, kind-hearted man', who sent round cakes and chocolates on the eve of public holidays and who refused to allow a tailor to be reprimanded for burning a hole in one of his new jackets. She did not like Mikhail Suslov, the 'grey cardinal' responsible for ideology in the Brezhnev Politburo. He was 'an ill-tempered man who used to throw a suit on the floor, if he didn't like it.' Brezhnev himself, for a time, had his clothes made at the Ministry of Defence tailoring department, a rival enterprise, until he concluded that his Politburo colleagues were better dressed than he was.

The fine woollen cloth used for suits was imported, often from England, Scotland and Austria. The workshop director went abroad to place the orders – accompanied by a representative of the KGB Ninth Department. Some customers brought back cloth themselves from foreign trips. 'I made one suit for Gorbachov, before I retired. But he used to buy very good, ready-made clothes abroad and have them restyled in Moscow.' Foreign Minister Andrei Gromyko was thrifty: he preferred to have old suits repaired rather than order new ones.

Access to the services of Military Unit 11–64 was not limited to the immediate families of the élite. One retired Red Army Marshal, a hero of the Civil War, once ordered a new uniform for himself and a smaller version of it for his six-year-old grandson.

By far the most prestigious customer was Lenin, whose

body lay in the pink marble mausoleum on Red Square. Every eighteen months, Klavdiya made him a new suit of dark-grey cloth. 'The jacket had a special cut, because he lies with his arms folded on his chest. Someone gave us the measurements: a small size.' Another woman in the team made Lenin's underclothes and shirts.

In the early 1980s, Klavdiya's salary was only R.190 a month but she, too, enjoyed perks, which trickled down from the senior Party officials to those who served them. By far the most important perk Klavdiya ever had was the flat she was allocated soon after making a suit for the then Prime Minister, Alexei Kosygin. It was not a luxurious place, but it did have two rooms, kitchen and bathroom – spacious by Moscow standards – and she did not have to wait decades for it. Later, in 1978, she and her husband got a one-room flat in a big modern block in south-west Moscow after moving to the top of the normal waiting list. They then transferred the two-room flat to their son and his family.

Like the rest of the staff, Klavdiya had a month's annual holiday, instead of the normal eighteen days, because they put in a lot of overtime. Every year, she had the right to a winter coat and two dresses – paying only the cost of the materials. Occasionally, they were able to buy food at a special canteen-cum-commissariat reserved for top officials in Granovsky Street, a short walk from the Kremlin and next door to the 'Fourth Department' polyclinic – another top people's perk.

Klavdiya says she was invited several times to join the Communist Party, but refused. 'I didn't want to waste time at meetings. Besides, I believed in God and didn't hide the fact.'

When she retired in 1985, she drew a pension of R.120 a month. Sergei Pluzhnikov describes her as a lively, friendly, plump little woman who is appalled by the new prices and the rate of inflation. Her pension, in May 1992, went up to

R.1,192 but she says: 'I don't know how the Government thinks we can live on this. In a village, at least there are cows to provide milk, but in a city people are still having to live on their stocks.'

For her, the perks had come to an end.

Chapter 6

# Education

Not many Soviet girls had Stalin to advise them personally on their choice of higher education, as Yelena Djaparidze did (see pp. 137 ff.). But her experience nevertheless illustrates the way the Soviet Union quickly and effectively set about educating its people and pulling itself up by its own bootstraps. In 1917, about three-quarters of the population were illiterate. Now the Russians must be among the world's most voracious readers. The education explosion of the Soviet period did not simply teach everyone the three Rs; it created a highly educated society, and women benefited as much as men in the rapid growth of secondary and higher education. This sexual equality in learning began early, as both Yelena and Kseniya testify.

In those days, higher education was directly linked with the country's enormous needs for technicians and engineers, and people were given great responsibility at an early age. It must have been a time of heady excitement for these young builders of a new society and economy, and it is hardly surprising if some of those who lived through it should still be under its spell. Yelena was already an experienced electrical engineer at the age of twenty-five.

Early Soviet educationalists stressed the importance of practical labour as a means of teaching and some of them acknowledged a debt to Western – especially American – progressive ideas on 'learning-by-doing' in education. This led to an enthusiasm for vocational education which was disowned by the Central Committee in 1931 in favour of more traditional and academic educational values. The Party rejoiced in the success of its decision of a year earlier to introduce universal primary education and claimed that in twelve months the number of pupils in primary and secondary schools had soared from 13.5 million to 20 million. Even so, 'the Soviet school is still far from meeting the tremendous demands which are placed upon it in the present stage of socialist construction.' The 'project method' of teaching was out and more traditional methods were in. The objective, the committee said, was to turn out literate people, 'all-round builders of socialism', who have mastered the basic subjects of scholarship, physics, chemistry, mathematics, geography and the native language.

However, one of the central purposes of education in creating a 'new Soviet man' was unchanged. It was to 'develop collectivist traits' in children. The effect of decades of Soviet schooling on spontaneity and individual initiative was graphically described in 1988 by Gennady Yagodin, then head of the Soviet State Education Committee. Too many teachers, he told a news conference in Moscow, treated their charges like nails. If one stood out, it was hammered on the head until it was on a level with all the others. Yagodin announced that Soviet schools would henceforth give more attention to the child as an individual and not as the member of the collective.

This may have happened in some schools, but six-year-olds who started primary school in Moscow in September 1991 quickly learnt that it was still not a good idea to stand out or 'show off'. Their mothers, too, were often in awe of teachers who insisted that new pupils should come to school equipped with materials, then almost impossible to find in

Russian shops, for making cut-out letters of the Cyrillic alphabet.

The importance of the collective and of strict discipline owe much to the ideas of Anton Makarenko, the ideologist of education in the pre-war Stalinist period. His fame and influence rested on his work in creating colonies for orphans and juvenile delinquents in the 1920s. He believed that children should be subjected to a strong, almost military form of discipline (they were required to salute their teachers) but he also taught that the children should practise collectivism through a kind of classroom and group self-government. Makarenko set out his ideas in *Road to Life*, his account of the building of his colonies, and they became fashionable among Western theorists. He died in 1939, but long afterwards Soviet schools continued to foster collectivist values and suppressed individualism.

In some ways, however, schools did respond to the Gorbachov reforms. When the policy of *glasnost* was lighting up formerly hidden corners of Soviet history, the teaching of history in schools had to change. Exams in history were cancelled in Soviet secondary schools in 1988. Textbooks were 'full of lies', as *Izvestia*, the daily newspaper of the Supreme Soviet, put it bluntly. The books were certainly offering a very different picture of Soviet history from the newspapers and magazines of the time. Some teachers began to use newspaper cuttings instead of the out-of-date schoolbooks. Others kept to the old practices. Lyuba Vinogradova (pp. 230 ff.) reveals that in the 1990s she was still being taught the old-style propaganda version of history by a convinced Communist teacher. It is significant, too, that her boyfriend taxes her with 'showing off', something Soviet education sought to discourage.

A greater surprise to me was the hostile reaction of Anna Broido (pp. 202 ff.) to her school's emphasis on the interests of the collective. It is unexpected in such a keen former member of the Komsomol. What is more depressing is that it must also spring from a belief that educational reforms will fail and that the old ideology will continue to shape young Russian minds.

# Anna

| |
|---|
| Anna Ilinichna Broido |
| Journalist |
| Born: Moscow, 1964 |
| Father: Artist, Jewish |
| Mother: Theatre costume designer and housewife, Russian |
| Interviewed: June 1992 |

*Anna, at twenty-eight, says she is about to emigrate. Her mind is made up. She is not leaving because the Russian economy is in chaos or to escape widespread anti-Semitism. As she analyses her motives, she gives a vivid account of an individualist's struggle with a system designed to indoctrinate its citizens to serve the 'collective' at the expense of their own self-interest. She describes the stages of her conversion from keen, full-time member of the Komsomol, the Young Communist League, to anti-Communist emigrant.*

Anna has what at first sounds a simple, single motive for leaving Russia: 'I feel I am ready to have children but don't believe I have the right to bring them into this country. I don't expect anything much for myself out of emigrating. It will be hard starting life all over again. I don't think I'll get rid of the pain I feel inside me, when I'm in Israel. And I shall lose many things I like here. I don't think people communicate very easily abroad. Russians get their greatest pleasure from talking to each other about their troubles.'

The motive may sound simple, but the reasoning behind it is more complex. She begins with the Soviet education system she has always loathed: 'School taught me nothing and for ten years tried to break me.' Her mother was once called in to see the headmistress who told her: 'Your daughter is insane and should see a psychiatrist. Normal children don't argue with their teachers.'

Anna readily concedes that she antagonised her teachers by standing up and telling them where they were going wrong. 'As a decent Komsomol member,' she laughs, 'I felt obliged to correct teachers who were betraying Communist ideals.' Not surprisingly, she felt that 'they disliked me more than they did the most backward pupils in the class.' She looks for an explanation for her own behaviour in her family background.

It is racially mixed. The Soviet description would be 'international', a word on which the Kremlin built the myth of the Soviet empire as one big happy family of more than a hundred nationalities. Inter-marriage is common and was accepted in the Soviet period as proof that the 'national problem' no longer existed. Citizens had their nationality recorded in their internal passports (Jewish was a nationality). But the USSR claimed to protect and foster national cultures, while abhorring divisive nationalism.

The new Russian Government promised to scrap the internal passport system in due course, but it continued to play an important part in the life of everyone.

Anna describes her father, who is Jewish, as 'kind and tender-hearted'. He is an artist and makes mosaics and stained glass. Her mother is Russian. She trained as a theatrical costume designer but gave up work to bring up Anna and her four brothers, a very large family by modern Moscow standards. She keeps the family together with what Anna, half-jokingly, calls 'totalitarian' strength and discipline. She believes she takes mostly after her father but also has some of her mother's 'totalitarian' attributes.

'From an early age, I felt I had to protect my individuality.' She wanted to 'belong to the collective' but rebelled 'when the collective started to suppress me'.

Her clashes with teachers were probably inevitable. The Soviet education system set out to indoctrinate children in the belief that their purpose in life was to serve the 'collective', to fit in, not to try to advance their own self-interest. Individualism and attempts to be different from other children were firmly discouraged. Anna could, of course, have learnt to keep quiet, but that has never been her way. She comes from a creative, intelligent family, and grew up in a home full of books. Her parents taught her to read and to think for herself. She is a fast reader and used to get through the books on the school curriculum a year ahead of her class. She is glad she did, she says, because school, otherwise, would have taught her to hate literature.

There is a strong combative streak in Anna which perhaps has something to do with growing up with four brothers. She says she has heard that Israeli children, when they are little, are taught in school to 'protect their own dignity from the teachers'. If this is true, she says, it would be enough to attract her to Israel. Otherwise, she is not intent on emigrating to any particular country; 'I am leaving a particular country.' Given a free choice, she would prefer France or Spain. In practical terms, the choice is confined to Israel, because her father is a Jew, or Germany, because one of her brothers is already living in Cologne.

Apart from schools, she wants her children to escape the dilemma of choosing between honesty and happiness in a society as corrupt as Russia has become. 'Honest people are always unhappy here. If I don't emigrate, I just won't have children.'

Street wisdom, exploiting *blat* (connections, influence, pull), knowing whom to bribe and when to give 'presents', are skills as essential to survival in post-Communist Moscow as they were in the Soviet years. They have long been needed to 'acquire' anything in short supply: tickets to the Bolshoi, a refrigerator, a bicycle, a pair of shoes. If anything, the scope for corruption has expanded with the move towards private property in a country where almost every-thing used to belong to the State.

Over everything, in Anna's view, hangs an impene-trable uncertainty. 'The whole history of the country testi-fies to the fact that you can't be sure what will happen: when the Government will change. This is why business-men are trying to grab as much as possible, while they can.'

Another reason Anna gives for leaving is her father's sense of guilt at having so many children in Russia. 'He is sixty now and gets terribly depressed when he thinks of his death and of leaving us in a country where conditions are getting worse every day.'

Is anti-Semitism another reason for leaving?

Anna pauses. 'That is a difficult question, but I shall try to answer it.' She takes time to think through her response, as she does throughout our conversation. 'I believe,' she says, 'that many Soviet Jews exaggerate anti-Semitism. But we live in a country where Russian is the only nationality that isn't cursed. You can criticise an Armenian or a Jew, but never a Russian. I think the Russian minorities in other republics are suffering now because of this kind of attitude in the past.'

She believes that in recent years anti-Semitism in Moscow has been overtaken by 'anti-Caucasian' attitudes (racism directed at people from the southern republics of the former USSR). Anti-Semitism was encouraged by the Soviet State. The Orthodox Church, Anna notes, also fosters a 'primitive' kind of anti-Semitism which, in her view, is of little impor-tance since the Church has not played a major role in every-day life. Then there is a crude 'kitchen' anti-Semitism based on myth, such as the story that babies' blood is an essential ingredient of unleavened bread.

'It's impossible to have a discussion with people who use illogical arguments. They make the same impression on me as when someone who isn't blind says I'm tall.'

Anna is conscious of being short – about five foot two inches. She has fair hair, fashionably cut. Her eyes, which she narrows to emphasise a point, are made up. She is wearing a dark-blue top and close-fitting, striped jeans, which emphasise her trim figure.

When she was sixteen and applied for her internal Soviet passport, her father begged her not to register her nationality as Jewish. She reluctantly agreed to take her mother's Russian nationality, as children of mixed marriages commonly do. It is humiliating for the Jewish parent, but it saves the child from a lifetime of writing the word 'Jew' in answer to the inevitable question about nationality on any official form.

Partly because she took this defensive measure and partly because of her looks, Anna says she has not suffered very much personally from anti-Semitism. She feels it most keenly when it upsets her father.

'I never try to hide my Jewish background, but Russian friends who don't know about it sometimes come out with their opinions about Jews in front of me. When I tell them I am Jewish, they apologise and say they didn't mean to insult me.'

Anna pulls at the silver chain round her neck and holds up an enamel Star of David pendant. 'There are two people inside me. I had a good Russian upbringing and always considered myself a Russian. Anti-Semitism helped me to acquire Jewish national consciousness.'

It did not help her to acquire religious beliefs. 'I couldn't do that, though it would make my life easier if I could.' Communist atheism may have deprived her of any hope of religious faith, but she has no regrets about joining the

Communist Youth movement. Like most Soviet children, she became a Little Octobrist at the age of seven on 7 November, Revolution Day, a Pioneer at nine and a member of Komsomol at fourteen. The rituals, the pin with an image of Lenin as a child, the red scarf, were all part of the indoctrination process, but to children they were stages in growing up.

'In the Pioneers' charter,' Anna says, 'there is nothing bad except the promise to love the Communist Party. You learnt to love nature and animals and to help old people. I never thought much about ideology. On paper, Communist ideals are not very different from Christianity. But I would sacrifice my own interests to those of the collective only if I wanted to, not because someone made me. My quarrel with ideology was at that level.'

Her parents were anti-Stalinist *Shestidiesyatniki* (Sixtyists), having come of political age in the 1960s after Nikita Khrushchov's 'secret speech' denouncing Stalin's crimes. But they still believed in Lenin. So did Anna. 'There were no books around to stop you being a Leninist. Some children didn't even have access to anti-Stalinist books.'

Now, she says, young people claim they can't understand how one could sincerely believe in Communism or how soldiers could go to Afghanistan convinced they were fighting for the truth. 'Some boast that they never joined the Komsomol. I ask them when they were fourteen and they say 1988. Well, I was fourteen in 1978. I think our generation is luckier, because we did believe in something once. They are nihilistic; they have no faith in anything. We were taught to struggle, that a happy future and hope depended on us. We are stronger anti-Communists than they are, because we worked it out for ourselves.'

Anna's most active period in the Komsomol came after she left school. After a marriage to a student, which lasted only a year, she got a job in a Moscow college – there were no jobs to be had in her narrow speciality, designing ballroom dresses. A college Komsomol leader organising a summer working camp was looking for a commissar, a second-in-command theoretically responsible for political education.

As Anna describes the job, she was an entertainments officer rather than an ideologist. 'The idea is to build a group and get together as a collective after work. I had to keep them amused and lead them in the right direction. In their free time, they were in no mood for political lectures. If I had tried to give any, they would have told me to go to hell. The best ideology is a good disco.'

Anna enjoyed herself and acted as commissar again the following year to a fifty-strong student group working in northern Russia. Gorbachov was in power, and she thought it was 'wonderful' that the Communist Party could launch the *perestroika* reforms. She was sure things would improve. When in late 1987 she was offered a full-time job as a Komsomol deputy-secretary, the lowest rung on the ladder, she gladly accepted. 'I was in charge of ideology,' she says with a sharp laugh. She left when friends told her it was wrong to persuade people to believe in the Komsomol, and when she found that some of the movement's officials were setting themselves up in business using Komsomol funds. She got a job as a trainee journalist on the college newspaper and from there progressed to the post of parliamentary correspondent with the small independent IMA news agency.

On the way, she studied law part-time and became involved in 'informal' – independent – student organisations, including the Moscow Students' Club, where she helped organise support for the Chinese students in 1989. She was attracted by the philosophy of the anarcho-syndicalists but thought it was too early to try to put their ideas about self-government into practice in Russia.

Anna feels she has left Communism behind, but she is clearly marked by her experience of it. Like many Russians, she still has some of the vocabulary and attitudes of her Soviet past. She is unable to believe in God, yet finds it unsettling not to have a strong commitment to some higher ideal or goal. She seems older than her years in her criticism of Russians younger than herself. She is worried by the fact that so few young people these days are taking an active part in the life of the country.

'The only moment when youth showed itself was during the coup [in August 1991]. Even then it wasn't really a conscious defence of democracy but more a longing for adventure.'

Anna herself was on holiday in southern Russia at the time, renting a room from an old woman who woke her up early saying: 'That dreadful Gorbachov has been toppled at last.'

In her quest for something to believe in, she says she is now closer to existentialism than anything else. She has read Jean-Paul Sartre on the subject and came across *The Plague* by Albert Camus, after working with students in Leninakan, one of the Armenian towns wrecked by an earthquake, with great loss of life, in December 1988. She was amazed to find conversations in *The Plague* that she heard in Leninakan. 'He almost forecast what I saw there.'

But her search for a new philosophy is far less urgent than the desire to have children. She is no feminist. According to her account of her brief marriage, her husband was a weak, idle man of twenty, under his mother's thumb, who behaved more like a child than a man – a common complaint of over-worked Russian wives. Now, Anna says, she is attracted to men over forty. She is sure that the man should be the head of the family, and the mother its soul.

Reporting on Russia's Parliament and Government, as a journalist, has left her without illusions. 'It's an unpredictable country. Things may be very good or very bad. But if very good, it won't be soon, and I'll be past child-bearing age. That's why I am emigrating.'

# Lyubov

Lyubov Kuzminichna
Balyasnaya

Educationalist and politician

Born: Vesyoloye, near
Zaporozhye, Ukraine, 1929

Father: Railway locomotive
driver, Ukrainian

Mother: Housewife,
Ukrainian

Interviewed: June 1992

*Lyubov Balyasnaya is intensely proud of the Soviet education
system, which Anna Broido hates so much, for she had a hand in
developing it. Born into a poor family of peasant stock, she was
a star pupil at school and came to the notice of the Communist
Party Central Committee in Moscow after rising, in the Ukraine,
through the ranks of the Komsomol youth movement, the
conventional route for political advancement. In 1964, at the age
of thirty-five, she was appointed Deputy Minister of Education of
the giant Russian Federation and held the job for twenty-three
years. She is now witnessing what she regards as the destruction
of much that the State educational system created.*

---

Balyasnaya establishes her political position from the out-
set.

'My life is typical of millions of Soviet people, and it is
with a great feeling of dignity and pride that I use the word
"Soviet". It is fashionable now to denounce what the State

has done in bringing up children. That's why, at first, I didn't want to meet you. I absolutely disagree with totally negative attitudes to past education policies. I don't like many of the things being done now. It's a constant worry.'

From this I understand that Balyasnaya's initial refusal to be interviewed stems from a suspicion that she will not get a fair hearing. As it happens, I am anxious to hear an authoritative defence of the Soviet education system, after listening to Anna's assault on it.

We meet on a cold, wet summer's day. As agreed, I collect her outside the Exhibition of Economic Achievements of the USSR, where she has been attending a meeting, and drive her to my flat for our talk. After decades of having an official limousine at her disposal, she now gets about by Metro, bus and trolleybus. She is a handsome woman with features set in an expression of genteel but by no means soft benevolence. Her fair, now greying, hair is swept up. She is wearing a dark-purple dress, buttoned up on the left. She has silver earrings and – unexpectedly – bright red shoes. She speaks in a quiet, carefully modulated voice, which hardens when she wants to emphasise a point. As we talk, Margaret Thatcher's voice and interview technique come to mind.

Lyubov was born into a large family: parents, grandmother and six children. Both parents had been married before and had three children from their first partners. Lyubov was one of two children born of the second marriage. The sixth child was adopted.

Her parents had only three year's education in a village church school. They left their village, after Lyubov was born, and moved to a construction site on the Dnieper River, where 'people of all nationalities from all over the country were helping, with great enthusiasm, to build the first and biggest hydroelectric power station in the USSR.' Her father's first job was delivering water in barrels with a horse and cart. Then he became a railwayman, first as a fireman, then as a driver.

Their housing on the Dnieper was primitive at first. They lived in what Balyasnaya now describes as 'a hole in the ground, with walls made of clay and a window at ground level'. It was roofed over and the ground was covered with grass in summer and straw in winter. From there they progressed to a separate flat, with two windows in a barrack. 'There was no central heating, but it was warm and light. We had a stove and there was running water in the yard.'

During the war, the family was evacuated to the Urals. Lyubov's father was called up, became a tank driver and survived. One of her sisters joined up as a sniper and killed 'sixty-nine fascists' in Latvia, before being killed in action herself. Balyasnaya recalls the wartime slogan *'Everything for the Front, for victory'*.

'Women and children formed the bulk of the labour force at most enterprises, and many young people gave up school altogether. I didn't, but I worked an allotment, growing potatoes. I collected firewood for the kindergarten and learnt everything about harvesting grain.' The second slogan she remembers of the period was *'Give everyone an education'*.

'Before the Revolution, eighty per cent of the population were illiterate. First, education was made compulsory up to standard four to age eleven, then up to standard seven to age fourteen. We needed scientists and, beginning in the 1930s, children received secondary education. There was a special programme for the construction of a thousand schools. My secondary school was a big spacious place that was built in a year. It had ten grades, chemistry and physics laboratories and a big gymnasium.'

Zaporozhye grew up around the power station and became a major industrial centre. By the time the war began, it had a population of three hundred thousand. Most of the Ukraine was occupied by the Germans and schools were evacuated. Lyubov's went to the Chelyabinsk region of the Urals. The children had classes in the evening, so that they could work in the daytime. When Zaporozhye was liberated in 1944, Lyubov and her family went back to find it almost entirely destroyed. People lived in dugouts again, while the place was rebuilt. Despite all the upsets of the war, Lyubov graduated from secondary school in 1945, the equivalent of an American 'straight-A student' with a gold medal to prove it, won in the first year the medals were awarded. She went to Dnepropetrovsk University and graduated in 1949 with a degree in mathematics.

She was invited to stay on at university to teach maths, but instead became a full-time Komsomol official. She rose to the position of first secretary of the Zaporozhye Regional Committee, then went higher still to join the Komsomol Committee of the Ukraine. From there she went to Moscow to specialise in out-of-school activities for members of the Pioneers and the Komsomol. This remained one of her main interests as Deputy Education Minister of Russia.

'The whole of my life has been spent on the upbringing of children; all my troubles and joys are connected with it. Soviet pre-school education and after-school activities were unique in the world. I can now look back at what we achieved with great satisfaction. But this makes it even more painful to see that this achievement is not only being criticised but is being destroyed. It is impossible to organise free time without the participation of the State and of society.'

Teachers were paid extra to give voluntary lessons after school hours. They also helped organise clubs of every kind. Local plants and offices helped by adopting schools. There was a slogan that said: *'Bringing up children is a task for the whole State, the whole Party and for all organisations.'*

'I remember hundreds of directors of factories, orchestras, collective farms and so on, who did so much. They talked about "our schools", "our children", "our teachers". They helped with equipment, hobby groups and handicrafts. Colleges used to help too. It was all unselfish. Now the non-Russian word "sponsor" is used.

'There was a huge network of premises for out-of-school activities: Pioneer camps and centres, art studios, places for young hikers and nature lovers, miniature railways with stations run by children, sports centres. In the 1970s, we revived the Lenin *subbotniks* [unpaid work sessions] and raised millions of roubles to build Pioneer centres. There wasn't a single scholar, scientist, actor or chessplayer who didn't start in a Pioneer centre. That's how Yak, the aircraft designer, started. Most children went to Pioneer camps in the summer free of charge. Others paid thirty per cent of the cost. Now they cost between R.4,000 and R.8,000 a month. Even Artek [the showpiece youth holiday centre opened in the Crimea in 1925] is the subject of speculation. It's so expensive, it's almost impossible for children to go there. I have no savings and, on my pension, can't even buy a Pioneer trip for my grandson. At the end of May, we used to have a general inspection of all premises for children. Today, children are abandoned. No one seems interested in them. They are the main victims of the reforms.'

Juvenile delinquency, says Balyasnaya, has always been caused by three factors: bad upbringing, poor relationships within the family and idle hours after school. 'All three factors have now reached crisis level and juvenile delinquency is terrifying.'

She praises the work of the Soviet educationalist Anton Makarenko, who, in the early 1920s, set up 'colonies' to rehabilitate young delinquents and save Civil War waifs and strays from drifting into crime by giving them a 'collective upbringing' and teaching them a sense of responsibility. 'They were in the collective, for the collective, with the help of the collective,' says Balyasnaya.

In the same vein, she quotes Lenin's widow Nadezhda Krupskaya: '"I or we, which is more important?" We were strong because we were "we". A song says: "First think about the motherland, then about yourself." Now this is mocked on every page of the democratic press. But it is the highest morality to put yourself second. My main concern with my son was to bring him up to be a good friend, to put the interests of others above his own, to subject self-interest to the collective interest.'

Balyasnaya is grateful to as well as proud of the Soviet system of pre-school education.

'We are the only country with such a mighty system. Every plant director, every television head would try to make sure that every mother working for him would have a nursery or kindergarten available. Today, people claim that children were levelled down at kindergarten. But I don't know how I would have managed with my son without his. Now pre-school education is under threat. What is most important for State and society, justice for every child or ultra-large incomes for a limited circle of people? Our system of education was very just and very democratic. It gave every child the right, regardless of nationality, whether in a big town or a village and no matter who his parents were, to a secondary education and the right to go on to higher education. World practice shows that only three to five per cent of children will go to private schools. So the main concern must be with mass education. The people's education must be financed by the State. No troubles in moving to a market economy should jeopardise that.'

Balyasnaya speaks as if the children of the Soviet ruling class never had privileged access to education, to the finest kindergartens, to the best secondary schools. But there is much in her argument in favour of State education that is persuasive.

She does regret the 'feminisation' of child-rearing and of the education system. 'There are no exemplary relationships between men and women either at school or at home. Women have to carry full responsibility in the family and at work. As a result, there are few happy women, and Anton Makarenko said that it was a real art to bring up a happy person: it could be done only by a happy person. The trouble is that our schools never really prepared children for married life.'

She invites me to go with her to see the Makarenko Museum, which is run, she says, by a divinely talented Jewish former headmistress, who lost many members of her family in Stalin's repressions, and whose husband was arrested in 1953 at the time of the purge of the Kremlin doctors, most of them Jewish.

As I drive Balyasnaya to the nearest Metro station, after the interview, she nods at a group of youths with long hair chatting in the children's playground outside my block of flats. Such idleness, clearly, would not have been tolerated in the old days.

A few days later, we visit the Makarenko Museum, in a Pioneer centre off Kutuzov Avenue. We meet the director, Ronni Mikhailovna Beskina, a woman in her sixties whose hair appears to be dyed dark-blue and is tied in a severe bun.

She shows us round the exhibits, mostly photographs of the pupils of Makarenko's colonies, some of whom went on to have distinguished careers in the armed forces and industry. One colony was named after Felix Dzerzhinsky, Lenin's chief of secret police. Here, Balyasnaya tells me, an ultra-modern camera factory was built and produced very good cameras.

As we walk round the museum, Balyasnaya frequently interrupts and corrects Ronni Beskina with a quiet but emphatic authority. Afterwards, while we are drinking tea, the conversation turns to nationalism and the conflict between Armenia and Azerbaijan, which the museum director regrets. Balyasnaya breaks in to observe that there were a hundred and thirty-one nationalities in the Soviet Union but that Stalin declared in his 1936 Constitution that 'we had settled the national problem.'

Ronni Beskina is clearly expected to confirm this, and she

says: 'We lived and grew up in an international country. No one cared what nationality you were.'

Balyasnaya says: 'In general, the national problem *was* solved, because all nations were equal, but problems of inter-ethnic relations still exist, just as you have the Irish problem. We have a hundred and two nationalities in Daghestan [in the North Caucasus] alone.'

Ronni Beskina says: 'It is, of course, a serious problem, though I personally could never say that it interfered with my work.'

# Tanya

| |
|---|
| Tatyana Alexeyevna Petrenko |
| Film director |
| Born: Samarkand, Uzbekistan, 1956 |
| Father: Aircraft mechanic turned driver |
| Mother: Schoolteacher |
| Interviewed: June 1992 |

*The Soviet education system suited Tanya. She shone at school, at university and at VGIC, the Moscow State Institute of Cinematography. Like Lyubov Balyasnaya, she won a gold medal at school. Unlike Anna Broido, she has decided to bring up her children in Russia and has dropped the idea of emigrating, although her husband is a Jew and she finds anti-Semitism far more widespread and upsetting than Anna does.*

Tanya is small, slim and usually dresses in tight jeans and pastel-coloured tops. When it is very cold, she wears a long fur coat. Her waist-length fair hair is usually tied in a bun, but she lets it down when she and her husband Lyonya (the film editor Leonid Melman) entertain friends at home in their tiny flat near the Garden Ring in north-central Moscow. They have two rooms, kitchen, bathroom and separate lavatory – twenty square metres in all. Their bedroom also serves as study, library, music and television room. The other room has bunk beds and a climbing frame for Pavel, aged eight, and Alexei, aged five, whom they call Paul and Alex. When they ask friends in, there is space for six adults round the table they put up in the children's room.

Tanya has fine features and a high forehead. When she jokes, she drops her voice to a husky, low register. If only because of the jokes and her air of unshakeable calm, Tanya is not at all the harassed worker-mother who rushes through her many duties feeling she is a failure at all of them. The most famous such figure is Olga, heroine of a story by Natalya Baranskaya, published in the monthly *Novy Mir* in 1969. 'A Week Like Any Other', one of the most frequently quoted pieces about Soviet women ever written, records Olga's struggle to hold down a job in a Moscow research laboratory, feed her family and bring up her two young children. She gets through the week at a gallop, except for the hours wasted in long queues, and ends it exhausted and frustrated.

It was a bold cry of female anguish to print in 1969, and it is still taken as a pretty accurate description of the life of many a well-educated worker-mother in Moscow today. Tanya and Olga are both unusual in having two children, and Tanya describes how only by using taxis could she combine child care with her cinema studies, when her first son was a baby and she was a student.

But now, she never seems to be in a hurry, despite a tight schedule managed on foot or by public transport, picking up the boys from different schools and taking them to different after-school activities. 'This year Paul goes swimming and Alex to acrobatics three times a week. While Paul is in the pool, I run to the kindergarden for Alex, pick up Paul, take Alex to acrobatics, take Paul home, then collect Alex.'

Western mothers are familiar with the routine, but Tanya, like most Russians, has no car. Shopping is done on foot and food carried in bags, on foot. Tanya places great importance on finding the right schools for her children. In September 1992, her schedule became very much tighter when she placed Paul in a private, progressive school on the other side of the city.

Tanya differs from Olga in one important respect: she does not have a nine-to-six job in a country where getting to work on time is usually judged more important than the quality of performance in the workplace. Tanya, as a film director, works in bursts. When she is shooting a film or rewriting a script, she is heavily dependent on help from her husband – which he, untypically for a Russian spouse, provides. The slump in the Russian film industry now makes it easier for Tanya to cope with her family duties, but the resulting drop in income, at a time of sky-rocketing prices, brings new, unpleasant pressures and anxieties. By October 1992, her salary is R.3,000 a month, 'but it's not enough to buy Paul a decent pair of boots.'

In Soviet terms, Tanya made a highly successful start in life. She has vivid memories of winning a gold medal at school (awarded for fives – excellent marks – in all subjects in her last two years) and of winning at both Samarkand University and at VGIC, the Moscow Cinema Institute, a red diploma, instead of the usual blue one, again for straight grade fives. She recalls teachers at the institute with affection and respect and clearly enjoyed her time there, although both her children were born while she was a student. Equally clearly, she sees her academic success as a victory over a corrupt system.

She says she had two incentives for winning a gold medal at school. First, her mother agreed that, if she succeeded, she could have her hair cut short. Second, in a serious talk one day, her mother told her there was no money to pay bribes to get her into university. The first 'high goal' was achieved: the day she came home with her medal, she put it on the kitchen table and went straight to the hairdresser's.

Tanya wanted to be a ballet dancer, but her mother, who brought her up (she and her younger sister Natasha saw little of their father), forbade it.

'She thought it indecent. My father is Russian and my mother of mixed Slav blood, but strict Uzbek rules somehow penetrate Russian families. By the time I left Samarkand I was twenty-four, but I had only been to a restaurant once – with a university group – because decent girls didn't go to such places. I find something of that attitude in myself even now. But when my mother said no to ballet school, I thought my life was ruined. I might not have been a gifted ballerina, but I could perhaps have become a good ballet director. So, as a girl from special English language School No. 37, my destiny was the foreign languages department of Samarkand State University. My school was a good one – all the teachers were Russian – but there was intense competition to get into the university. There was a quota system and a list of those who could be admitted. It wasn't a contest about knowledge but a game to find out whose parents had most influence.'

Tanya's gold medal meant she had to take only one entrance exam instead of four. She also needed a respectable record in the Komsomol and a final school report (*kharakteristika*) 'which was almost as important as your marks'. Even so, her mother paid for her to have private coaching by a university teacher, before the entrance exam.

'This allowed me to become known to the examiners. I don't know whether this was honest or not. But of the ten people in my group reading English at university, seven didn't know a word of English. They were Uzbeks and Tartars from the villages. So for two years I did almost nothing. Then our parents rebelled and a new group was formed. This time, seven of the ten were from my school, and university became more interesting.'

Teachers, students and recent graduates put on plays in English: *Pygmalion* and *The Importance of Being Ernest*.

At nineteen, Tanya got married – 'out of curiosity, I suppose; it didn't last long' – to a young graduate from the architectural college, who was to become a successful engineer.

'He had a flat, a car and good furniture and he was a loving husband. But I found it very, very boring. There is no cultural life in Samarkand. There are just two cinemas in the centre that are more or less safe for a woman to go to, but I never went alone. You could never go out in the evenings without an escort, usually one on each side of you. So I spent my holidays outside Samarkand, usually in Leningrad. But once I went to Moscow and realised it was my city.'

A friend of the family who worked on the Moscow City Komsomol Central Committee advised her to get divorced, which she did, and found her a part-time job, although she had no Moscow residence qualifications.

'She told me I would forget everything – marriage, divorce, and so on – in six months. She was wrong; I forgot it all in less than a week.'

But she was shocked at the sexual behaviour of young Muscovites.

'I was very earnest and I really thought that you couldn't have a serious relationship with a man before marriage, though I'd had lots of absolutely platonic love affairs in Samarkand.

'In Moscow, it was thought ridiculous for any girl to be a virgin at nineteen. Perhaps that's the usual thing in a capital city. I saw myself as very old-fashioned and was ashamed of my puritanism. So I tried to slip out of my old skin and told myself to behave like everyone else and not take everything so much to heart.'

She had met Lyonya by chance in Uzbekistan and they became friends in Moscow, on close enough terms to confide in each other about their love affairs. Lyonya undertook to find her a husband, in order to solve her residence problems. Now they are married to each other, Tanya says, all her old attitudes to sex have returned.

'I know many families in which the husband and wife lead separate lives. My family is the only thing in my life.

I am faithful to my husband and I am absolutely sure he is to me – though even my mother says you can never be that sure about men. In our difficult times, when everything outside seems to be mad, the only thing you can rely on to keep you sane and sometimes even happy is your relationship with your husband. I don't think I know another family that's like this, at least to the same extent, among my close friends. Sometimes we have terrible quarrels, of course, but there is something between us that makes this of little importance. We had a long talk about this the other night, when our sons were asleep, and Lyonya thought it was because of the children. I don't agree that the success of a family depends on children. Lots of families have children.'

Tanya became a film director because Lyonya one day had a brilliant idea for solving her residence problem. If she got a place in a college, she would get temporary residence rights in Moscow for five years – and anything could happen in that time.

'He couldn't think of anything easier than VGIC. There were more than two hundred and fifty applicants for each place, and I still can't understand how I got in. Out of all those who won places, only one boy and I were not the children of famous people in the cinema.'

She almost fell at the last hurdle. She was placed seventh and there were only seven places. Then a girl candidate from Tajikistan produced a telegram from a film studio in Dushanbe to say it was nominating her. This gave her the right to go to the top of the list, pushing Tanya down to eighth place.

'So I was not accepted. Lyonya was nailed to the wall of the corridor in shock. I said let's go, but we couldn't move.'

She heard an elderly examiner call out her name. He told her he was writing a long letter to the Rector begging him to find her a place. A month later she went reluctantly, with Lyonya's knee in her back, she says, to call on the Rector.

'I was very shy. He was a big man and he didn't look at

me. He said there was no letter about me. I felt a real fool, but I couldn't leave because the door was locked. Then he looked through some papers and seemed very impressed by my gold medal and the red diploma and took me in.'

She entered VGIC in 1982. Paul was born in April 1984, when Tanya was twenty-nine, and Alex in August 1987, just after she completed her course. Through contacts she found a bed for both confinements in a 'good, clean' maternity clinic. 'There was a bribe, of course, but it wasn't expensive in those days: just a good bottle of cognac.' But even with special attention in a good clinic, she did not see Paul or Alex until they were four days old.

In her ninth month of pregnancy with Alex, Tanya took her last oral exam at VGIC and got a five and another red diploma. This gave her the right to enter a studio as film director, third category (class), instead of having to work on five films as assistant director. And having a job gave her the right to two years' paid maternity leave.

She shows me the diploma, which lists all the subjects studied, the total classroom hours spent on each and the marks earned. The list begins like this:

| | | |
|---|---|---|
| 1. History of the Soviet Communist Party | 120 hours | excellent |
| 2. Marxist–Leninist Philosophy | 140 hours | ,, |
| 3. Political Economy | 100 hours | ,, |
| 4. Scientific Communism | 80 hours | ,, |
| 5. Essentials of Scientific Atheism | 24 hours | ,, |
| 6. Marxist–Leninist Aesthetics | 70 hours | ,, |

Tanya had worked her way through all these subjects at Samarkand University and so did not need to spend much time on them at the institute. She says that she spent some of the lessons sitting at the back of the lecture hall with a Bulgarian student reading the *Kama Sutra*.

'It was enjoyable studying at VGIC. For the first time in my life, I was treated as an individual. We saw good films every day, and for someone from Central Asia who had never heard of good foreign films, it was like opening the Bible for the first time.'

She and Lyonya had a flat a long way from the institute. The taxi fare was two roubles each way, 'quite a sum out of my grant of R.56 a month'. But using taxis was the only way she could keep up with her studies and breastfeed Paul, who was looked after during the day by a neighbour, a single mother, 'a most loyal friend and the nicest person I've ever met.' Lyonya was earning R.150 a month as a film editor, but a quarter of this went on alimony to his first wife. They were helped by his father, who paid the rent, and her mother, who sent them R.50 a month.

After graduating, Tanya decided to spend her maternity leave at home with her young children – drawing R.50 a month – but when Alex was ten months old she was tempted back to work. A young director was wanted to make a thirty-minute television film on the history of Russian choral music, a much more exciting proposition than the popular science documentaries beginners usually started with. ('We called them screws-in-tomato-juice pictures.')

She spent three months at the Lenin Library (now called the Russian State Library) reading everything about choral singing since the eighteenth century and studying ikons and church architecture. She re-wrote the script and shot exteriors – landscapes and churches – in the beautiful, old cities of Suzdal and Vladimir. She came to know the distinguished choir director Valery Polyansky. He persuaded her that the film should be a full-length fifty minutes and she completed it in six months, instead of the year she was entitled to spend on it under studio rules.

In addition to her salary of R.160 a month, she received a bonus of R.3,000 ('a great sum'). It led to another film, seventy-eight minutes long, with Polyansky. For this she received R.6,000 as scriptwriter and R.6,000 as director – R.9,050 after tax. She spent R.3,000 on the fur coat she still has. Before the fur, she faced winters with three sweaters under a thin woollen coat.

Tanya now has the rank of director, second category, and with inflation her salary, in June 1992, is R.1,020 a month before tax, while Lyonya's staff salary is R.3,000 a month. But very few films are being shot and bonuses are rare. Mosfilm studios in Moscow worked on 400 films in 1991, but only 25 in 1992.

'People who run the cinemas now prefer to show silly American films that bring in more money. Even if a Russian film is made, it isn't shown. We can't see our colleagues' work. And our financial position has changed. We used to be a wealthy family, meaning we could afford to buy anything we wanted in the farmer's market. We never spent much on clothes, furniture or the flat. A month ago I went to the Central Market – it's the most expensive but it's the closest – and for the first time came out without buying anything. They were selling cherries and bananas outside the Metro, but Alex looked at them and said: "They are too expensive, aren't they?"

'Everything's changed completely with all those new prices, and I don't think there's a way out. I don't think the country or the film industry will come through. Most of my friends are abroad and I've been thinking about leaving too, of course. There are material reasons and there's also the attitude to Jews in this country. I could easily have given my children a Russian surname, but I couldn't offend Lyonya. Alex and Paul have his name, Melman. It's a Jewish name and when it is called out at a children's clinic, I feel the reaction. Maybe I'm too sensitive, but I don't think I'm exaggerating. In Paul's school [which he has now left], there's a big picture on a wall over the stairs and someone has carved a famous inscription in the frame: "Beat the Jews and Save Russia". It wasn't like this in Samarkand. Jews were well regarded there for their high professional standards. But here, one of my neighbours, who is a Jew, was shouted at in the queue at the bakery: "When are you Jews going to stop eating our Russian bread?"

'Once when I was taking Paul somewhere, I met an old man who was complaining about how hard it was living on a pension. I felt sorry for him and tried to comfort him, but then he said: "It's because of the Jews; they've ruined everything." It was like a knife in my heart. This is why almost all parents in mixed marriages give their children non-Jewish names. I know only one other family which hasn't done that. And the wife even took her husband's family name, herself. She's much braver than me.'

Tanya is a practising Christian. Her parents were not believers, but her grandmother gave her a Bible when she was ten. At fifteen, she wanted to become a nun, 'but all my boyfriends laughed and said I was too sinful for that. I never went to church in Samarkand. If anyone had seen me, it would have been the end of my career. There were only a few churchgoers, mostly pensioners. But when I got to Moscow, no one knew me and I was free to go to church.'

She now feels strong anti-Semitism in the Russian Orthodox Church. Her film on choral music was shown at a religious film festival and she was surrounded by a hostile crowd, because she had included a work by the contemporary Russian composer Alfred Schnittke. They called him a 'Jewish scoundrel' and said Tanya should 'make films about groceries, not destroy our culture.'

'I was crying. Schnittke is a Catholic, but that doesn't matter to them. He may be half or quarter Jewish. I was very upset and went to see a friend who is a priest. He told me that those people weren't true Christians, but somehow that didn't help. I feel this attitude very often. But I think we shall stay here. It's very difficult to emigrate to Western Europe. Lyonya doesn't want to go to Israel. Australia is a very long way from Europe and I don't think I could live so far from our culture and our history. So I think we shall stay here.

'After all the events in the Caucasus and in Central Asia, I've been expecting shooting and barricades in Moscow. Once it starts here, it will never end. And then they will remember all the Jews.'

Who will?

'The Russian chauvinists.'

# Lyuba

Lyubov Vladimirovna
Vinogradova

Ecology student

Born: Moscow, 1973

Father: Space engineer,
retired

Mother: Chemist and lecturer
in fine arts

Interviewed: July 1992

*Lyuba is the granddaughter of Kseniya Godina (see chapter 2) and shares her grandmother's concern for the environment. She is studying soil science and ecology in order to do something about it herself. She grew up during Gorbachov's* perestroika *period. She was in school as faith in Communist ideology withered and died. She is studying for the future amid all the uncertainties of a country in transition from one system to another.*

Lyuba is a beautiful young woman with black hair, bright eyes and the kind of personality that lifts the spirits of those around her. She speaks good, though hesitant, English, and came to see me with her mother, Galina, who helped her with vocabulary and sometimes joined in the conversation. Their relationship is clearly based on mutual trust and respect.

Lyuba left school two years ago and entered an agricultural institute to learn about soil pollution and, incidentally, farming machinery. She arrived, preoccupied with the exam she was taking on machinery next day. She said she had dreamt about my interview during the night and, in the dream, I questioned her exclusively about tractors and combine harvesters.

What kind of machines does she have to study?

'I can show you my textbook. I always have it with me, like an ikon. People look at me in the Metro as if to ask why a nice girl is reading a book full of awful pictures of big, complicated machines. I quarrelled with my boyfriend over it. We went on holiday to Lithuania and I pointed out the machines in the fields and told people what they were for. And I asked people what plants they were growing. My boyfriend told me I was just showing off. I was so insulted, I wanted to beat him black and blue. Some time in the future I'll take all these machines seriously, but not now.'

Lyuba's boyfriend is an ex-student. He was expelled from his institute after failing some exams and went into business, buying and selling. She is not sure exactly what he does, but he assures her that it is a 'serious' business.

'He's like many of our young people, who are leaving their institutes to earn money. It's a serious problem. It changes people so much. And it's not just students. I know good teachers and doctors who can't live on their salaries and are giving up their jobs to go into trade. I'll never do that.'

Lyuba left school No. 199, a special biology school, and entered her institute in 1990, when she was seventeen. The school is in south Moscow, a long way from her parents' flat in a dreary northern suburb of the city, composed of dozens of near-identical blocks of flats. She travelled two hours a day by bus, Metro and trolleybus, but she thought it was a 'wonderful school'. She especially enjoyed her history lessons there, and her history teacher became a friend of the family.

This surprises me, because history became increasingly

difficult to teach in a country which was almost daily changing its views about its past.

'The woman history teacher at school told us the truth, I
think. She collected information on the real situation in
Russia before, during and after the Revolution and about
the terrible years of Lenin and Stalin. She gave us what she
found in books, magazines and newspapers. She taught us
to understand what history was about. She was a great
teacher. We used to have to learn the political economy of
socialism. Now we have no socialism, so we have no political economy lessons. They didn't know what to teach us.
Marxism–Leninism isn't taught now: I haven't even read
*Das Kapital*. We used to have a textbook called *Social and
political history of the twentieth century*, but it was really the
history of the Communist Party.'

When she entered her agricultural institute, she was
shocked to find history being taught by a man who was a
Communist true believer.

'He told us lies. I can only compare what he did with
prostitution. He told us awful things about how everything
is bought and sold in foreign countries and went on about
the socialist and communist aims of our life. He was saying
the same old things, when we knew the truth. And that
was only a year ago. He took us to the Revolution Museum
and made us put flowers in front of a bust of Lenin. We all
laughed. But when he did it a second time, we were angry.
He's changed his position this year. After the putsch
[August 1991], he told us he would have liked to defend
the White House [Parliament building] but unfortunately
was out of Moscow at the time. He said nice things about
the new Russian Government. We studied philosophy for
one year, but now we don't study the humanities at all.'

She thinks her ecology course can lead her towards two
kinds of job: doing research in a laboratory and doing practical fieldwork, travelling round the country analysing soil
and water, perhaps fining companies that are causing

pollution. She hasn't yet given much thought to what she wants to do but is clear that the main task is to put a stop to pollution.

Lyuba's mother Galina intervenes: 'Scientists have to work on the problem now. As a chemist, I see a terrible situation but scientists aren't thinking about ecological problems at all. Nothing is being done. Science should be prepared to play its part. We can't wait for it.'

Lyuba picks up the theme and says the figures about soil and water pollution and the damage to the ozone layer do not bear thinking about. 'I don't see any way out at all, not just for my country, but for the planet. I have decided that the best thing for me is not to worry about politics and ecology, but to live a free life.'

What does that mean?

'For me it means not having exams about agricultural machinery.' She laughs out loud and disperses the air of gloom that has settled on us.

Galina is optimistic about the Yeltsin reform programme and believes it is going to work. Lyuba is more cautious.

'It's sad that young people are indifferent to what is happening in the country. A year or two ago our parents were going to demonstrations. I went two or three times but didn't see any young people at them.'

Galina: 'There were young people around the White House during the coup.'

Lyuba: 'Of course, the coup changed a lot of attitudes because it was a decisive, crucial moment. But now everything seems to have gone back to where it was, and the young try not to think about the problems.'

What do her friends say about the reforms?

'They say they don't believe in anything, but in the bottom of our hearts I think there is some hope that things will get better. But many people of my age don't want to live in this country. They are trying to get out of here. Many of our acquaintances are in the United States or Israel. It's strange:

they pity us and we pity them. In my family, we have decided we don't want to leave the country as long as our lives are not in danger.'

I ask her what has happened to the girls in her class at school. She says that most of those in the special biology school have gone on to study in scientific institutes and medical schools or Moscow University. Only one is married. It is quite different for the girls in her class in the neighbourhood school she went to in the north Moscow suburb. Half of them are already married and none has gone into higher education.

What do she and her friends do in their spare time?

Lyuba says that in summer she enjoys boating on a small lake at VDNKh, the Exhibition of Economic Achievements. She likes dancing and swimming and plays a little tennis. In winter, there's ice-skating, but not much skiing, now that the Moscow winters have become so mild. (Since 1989, winter temperatures have hovered around freezing, instead of plunging to between minus fifteen and minus twenty degrees Celsius.) She rarely goes to the theatre or to concerts, preferring the cinema. But she says it is hard to find good Russian films. 'Our good actors appear in silly films. The best Russian films are not distributed.'

What gives her most pleasure is amateur archeology and helping to restore old churches. She has been working in her spare time at the Andronikov monastery in east Moscow, where the great ikon painter Andrei Rublyov was a monk in the fourteenth century.

'We are going to take up the floor of one of the cathedrals and see what is underneath. The monastery is said to have been built on the site of a pagan temple. There are more women than men helping there. They are devoted to the work. I'm glad I found their company. They are clever and nice. It's hard work for older women, but not for me: I'm young and strong.'

She is about to join a group restoring churches and old

houses at Byelozersk, a town on a lake near Vologda, some two hundred and sixty miles north of Moscow.

'There are thirty-five of us and we shall be going for three weeks at our own expense. When I wake up in the morning worrying about agricultural machinery, just thinking about this expedition puts me in a good mood. It's wonderful. Yesterday, we were shown slides of Byelozersk. There are so many churches in a critical condition there that have to be saved. No, I am not a believer. Many of my friends have been baptised in the past two years. It's a very serious step and I'm not ready for it. I have to say that I can't accept the religion all those old women believe in. It's too naive. I know people who got baptised because they are looking for support in a difficult period of their lives. I don't feel the need for this. But I do want to work for our culture.'

Chapter 7

# The Arts

Suddenly, in the summer of 1992, a 'commercial shop' opens on the august premises of the Moscow Art Theatre, whose co-founder was the great actor-director Konstantin Stanislavsky. It charges high prices for what, to Western eyes, is a typically dispiriting collection of clothes, jewellery, shoes and cosmetics. The appearance of such a place at the theatre, just off the former Gorky Street, where Anton Chekhov's most famous plays were first produced, is a clear signal that the arts, too, are suffering in the general economic crisis. The prices of tickets at the Art Theatre quadrupled in the first half of 1992.

For decades, the Soviet authorities poured subsidies into the performing arts. Dancers, musicians, circus artists and army choirs were allowed to perform abroad, and they reflected glory on the Soviet system which produced them. At home, the prices of theatre tickets were nominal and theoretically within the reach of all, though getting in to see the great stars required ingenuity, influence and something to barter, as was the case with everything in short supply. Books, newspapers and magazines were also cheap. The price paid for the subsidies was a heavy one: the stifling control the Communist Party exercised over writers, actors, directors, playwrights, composers and painters, lavishing privileges on those in favour in the Kremlin and banning or harassing those who were not.

Ways were found around this. Forbidden books were smuggled out to be published abroad and were copied and passed around in *samizdat* editions at home. Political comments were slipped past the censors by theatre and film directors. The restrictions were gradually removed under *glasnost*. Boris Pasternak's *Doctor Zhivago* was published, as was Vasily Grossman's wartime epic, *Life and Fate*. Even Solzhenitsyn's *Gulag Archipelago* came out at last. The State-run record company, Melodiya, posthumously released recordings of Vladimir Vysotsky, the actor–poet–singer whose huge popularity in his lifetime rested largely on the circulation of amateur *samizdat* tapes of his songs. Later, the State-run television screened films by Andrei Tarkovsky, the director who struggled with Soviet censors for twenty years and died an exile in the West.

Under Gorbachov, the limits of what was permitted to be read and seen steadily expanded and contributed to the excitement that his reforms at first generated. After his fall, it quickly became clear that the new freedom also brought problems. In the theatre, political innuendo was no longer interesting, when old taboos were broken daily in newspapers and on television, even in Parliament. By the autumn of 1992, Moscow theatres, while still staging the classics, were striving to satisfy public demand for lighter entertainment: comedies, melodramas, cabaret and musicals. And where Moscow led, provincial theatres were expected to follow. Playwright Grigori Gorin forecast that a third of Russia's theatres would close, another third would go on foreign tours, while the rest would provide 'carefree entertainment' for the well-off. He gloomily said to *Literaturnaya Gazeta*: 'I used to consider myself a free artist in an unfree country. Now I am bought.' But the immediate problems were financial rather than artistic. Theatre seats which a year before cost less than five roubles now cost up to R.150.

Newspapers, as Katya explains in chapter 1, found costs outstripping income and could no longer look to the Party to keep them and their big staffs afloat.

At the Bolshoi, a new production of Faust was delayed, because suppliers of costumes and sets held up delivery until they could legally charge higher prices. The director of the Bolshoi, Vladimir Kokonin, complained to the weekly *We* in mid-1992 that the Government of the Ukraine was still generously supporting the Kiev opera which could pay soloists four times more than the Moscow company. The Bolshoi ballet had been in trouble for years, its leadership increasingly authoritarian, and had lost its best-known dancers. In this chapter, Yekaterina Maximova and Olga Lepeshinskaya describe two different worlds. Lepeshinskaya's talent was instantly recognised and her intense patriotism and belief in Communism made her a favourite in the Stalin Kremlin. She contributed beauty and glamour to official receptions and met all the important foreign visitors. She was one of the first winners of the Stalin prize and the huge financial reward that went with it. While still looking more like a schoolgirl than an adult, she had a seat on the Moscow City Council.

But the State reserved the right to hold the brightest stars behind the Iron Curtain. Khrushchov, in his memoirs, gives an example of this 'disgraceful heritage of the closed border which lies like a chain on the consciousness of the Soviet State.' Prima ballerina Maya Plisetskaya, whom he calls 'the best in the whole world', was never allowed to travel abroad with the Bolshoi. The authorities refused to run the risk of a spectacular and embarrassing defection. The dancer was not only denied the highly prized privileges of foreign currency and access to Western shops but also lost the chance to see modern Western ballet and exchange ideas with foreign dancers.

She appealed directly to Khrushchov as Party chief. She wrote that she was a patriot and was hurt and insulted at being so distrusted. Khrushchov had never met her, but put her request to the Central Committee and recommended that she be allowed to go with the company on its next foreign tour.

Khrushchov writes in his memoirs:

> Maya Plisetskaya went on the tour, and I was
> rewarded many times over by her brilliant performances
> abroad. She enhanced the fame of Soviet ballet and
> Soviet culture. And she came back. This was our reward
> for the labour invested in building a Socialist society
> of which Plisetskaya was proud to be a citizen.

She is no longer with the Bolshoi and now lives in Spain. Maximova, too, spends much of her time abroad. The border is open, but with the end of State control, the arts have also lost the patronage of a huge, powerful State. They will take time to adjust to the new freedoms and the new economic constraints. The theatres have a special problem, for not only are they being obliged to put up ticket prices sharply, but also their potential audiences seem, at least temporarily, to have lost interest in what they have to say. Russian writers seem better placed to benefit from the end of the old regime, and Natalya Perova displays a refreshing confidence in the quality of new Russian writing by men and women.

# Olga

| |
|---|
| Olga Vasilyevna Lepeshinskaya |
| Prima ballerina |
| Born: Kiev, 1916 |
| Father: Engineer |
| Mother: Housewife |
| Interviewed: May 1992 |

*Stalin's secretary Poskrebyshev once said to the Bolshoi star Olga Lepeshinskaya: 'You are a product of the times. You always dance optimistic, cheerful roles. Ulanova belongs to the world and to all time; you belong to Moscow and the Soviet system.'*

*Her loyalty to the system, though shaken when her first husband was arrested in 1951, remained firm. She was an enthusiastic member of the Komsomol and the Party and gave up a comfortable life in Munich to return to Moscow in the late 1980s to help Russian ballet through hard times.*

Lepeshinskaya is small and her hair is now white, but the eyes are as wide and bright as in the photographs of her in the files of the Bolshoi Theatre museum. There is one of her in *Don Quixote*, high above the stage in a great, joyous leap, her right hand flung back holding a folded fan. She stopped dancing thirty years ago but still works tirelessly for the ballet. She makes speeches of welcome when foreign companies come to Moscow. She travels round the country encouraging young companies, as President of the Russian

Choreographic Association, and brings young stars to perform in Moscow. She is a senior member of the cultural
establishment.

She lives in a corner block on Tver Street, near the Byelorussian railway station. The building is now surmounted by
a huge red and yellow neon sign, advertising computers
built by the South Korean Goldstar company. Her flat, spacious by normal Moscow standards, is crammed with
antique furniture and china, the walls covered with paintings – portraits and landscapes. Among the books is Raisa
Gorbachov's autobiography *I Hope*. There are no photographs of Lepeshinskaya herself.

We are greeted at the door by Susie, a tiny Yorkshire
terrier with a high, sharp bark. Lepeshinskaya obliquely
establishes her place among international stars by remarking
that Liz Taylor has four Yorkshire terriers to her one. She
is wearing black slacks, a black blouse with small pink dots
and a big pink bow round her neck. She serves tea in fine
bone-china cups.

'My parents were Russians of noble origin – I can say that
now. My father was an engineer, a bridge-builder. But for
the October Revolution I would never have become a ballerina, because children of the nobility were not allowed to go
on the stage. When, at the Kremlin, I was awarded the
Order of the October Revolution, I was honestly able to say
thank you to the Revolution.'

Her idea of becoming a dancer dates back to the 1920s,
when the family used to spend their summers in the
Crimea.

'We stayed in a doctor's house and the children had a
room overlooking the summer garden, where an orchestra
played in the evening. When my parents went out to play
bridge, I used to dance to the music, on the balcony. A
painter with the Bolshoi and his wife, who was a dancer,
were staying in the same house one summer. She saw me
dancing and told my mother I should learn ballet.'

Olga applied to the Moscow Choreographic Vocational School. 'It was pure luck whether you were accepted or not. I was put on the waiting list and got a place only because one of the girls who had been accepted had appendicitis and didn't turn up after the operation. I was eight then – my mother said I was nine – and I graduated when I was seventeen. I went straight into the Bolshoi and immediately became a soloist. I was never in the corps de ballet.'

In her book *Soviet Ballet*, Iris Morley says that in fact Lepeshinskaya was the first pupil in a hundred and twenty years to graduate from the Moscow school with the title of prima ballerina. Morley describes her at the age of twenty-eight as 'a virtuoso dancer and accomplished actress . . . very small, dark-haired with blue eyes and a decisive and capable chin . . . She is thoroughly Komsomol.'

Lepeshinskaya thinks back to the early Thirties: 'In my last two years at the school, we had some outstanding teachers from Leningrad, which was then the home of the classical ballet, while Moscow was more experimental, always in search of something new. In those years the Bolshoi began to take the lead. A young generation came in to the company and gave it fresh energy. By the time I joined in 1933, a new school was emerging that combined tradition with new ideas.'

Lepeshinskaya danced at the Bolshoi for thirty years, till 1963. Ballets were created for her, among them Prokofiev's *Cinderella*, and the State showered honours upon her. She won four USSR State Prizes and the Order of Lenin and was made a People's Artist of the USSR. With Galina Ulanova and Marina Semyonova, she was among the winners of the Stalin Prize, when it was awarded for the first time in 1941. With the honour came R.100,000 – 'a huge sum'. She spent R.12,000 on furniture for her mother. Then the war broke out and she donated the rest of the money to the national defence fund.

She says she was 'active' in the Bolshoi Komsomol and

counts her years in it as 'amazingly creative'. She was also
a member of the Moscow City Council (Mossoviet) when
she was only twenty and, while in the Komsomol, won
a 'Badge of Honour', which brought no money but great
prestige. She joined the Party proper in 1943.

The arts, she says, flourished in the Soviet Union in the
1930s. 'Stalin loved the Bolshoi, and the Government had
to do the same – perhaps they really did like it. Stalin used
to come whenever he had time, perhaps for an act of *The
Queen of Spades* or of *Eugene Onegin*. He liked the ballet
*The Flames of Paris*, with music by Boris Asafiev [in which
Lepeshinskaya starred] and saw it nine times. Life for
musicians and artists was good. We began to get high salaries. We had our own sanatorium at Serebryany Bor, on
the banks of the Moskva river, and another for children on
the Black Sea.'

She was invited to receptions in the Kremlin for foreign
leaders, such as Churchill and de Gaulle, and met top Soviet
officials. 'Yuri Andropov [head of the KGB and later Party
boss] knew a lot about the arts. But at one reception I
couldn't swallow any food because, out of the corner of my
eye, I saw Lavrenty Beria [Stalin's chief of secret police]. He
had a handsome face but, when he frowned, a deep line
appeared in his forehead and it gave me a very unpleasant
feeling.'

She danced at all the concerts in the Kremlin from 1934
to 1952 – the year before Stalin died. The performance that
sticks in her mind is of *Red Poppy*, which she calls 'a patriotic
spectacle' and ballet historians say is the first Soviet
ballet. With music by Reinhold Glière, it tells the story of
a Soviet ship's captain who takes a cargo of rice to the
hungry Chinese. It was first staged at the Bolshoi in
1927 and revived in 1949. Then, in 1951, Lepeshinskaya
danced in a gala performance of the ballet on Revolution
Day (7 November) attended by Stalin and the entire
Politburo.

'That's when I broke my leg on stage. I couldn't go off, because the ballet had reached its climax. I had to wait for the ship's captain to give me the red poppy, the symbol of Revolution and freedom. When the act ended, I fainted with pain and was taken in an ambulance to the Kremlin hospital. The X-rays showed four fractures. I realised it was serious, when I saw the nurse and doctor getting ready to give me an injection. I was still in my Chinese make-up, and the nurse crossed herself when she saw me.' She recovered quickly, was rehearsing within weeks and danced for another ten years.

The accident happened about six weeks after her first husband, Leonid Reichman, was arrested – she did not know why – and taken to the Butyrskaya prison in Moscow. She had been unable to sleep and was exhausted by Revolution Day and thinks that's what caused her accident. She hated the visits to her husband in prison.

'As I went in, the doors clanged shut behind me. It was a terrible experience and after that my ideas about the October Revolution changed somewhat.'

Whatever her reservations, she never openly rebelled against the regime. She divorced Reichman when he was released in 1955 and married a senior army officer, General Alexei Antonov. When he died in 1962, he was buried in the Kremlin wall, and the Soviet leadership lined up in his honour on the top of Lenin's mausoleum. Lepeshinskaya went into shock and says she lost her sight for thirteen days. 'The last thing I saw was Leonid Brezhnev [the future Party boss] wiping his tears with a handkerchief.' It was then, at the age of forty-six, that she decided to give up dancing.

Looking back, she concedes that 'Stalin did bad things'. She did not like censorship or the treatment of Shostakovich, whose ballet *The Clear Stream* was banned by the Ministry of Culture. 'But Stalin knew that the arts were necessary in every country and that if you killed the arts, you would kill humankind. Despite all the terrible things that happened to artists, really talented people were better off than the rest of the population. Artists did not suffer the same difficulties as the ordinary people.'

She burned with patriotism during the war. She says she threw her ballet shoes 'behind the wardrobe' and volunteered to fight the German invaders, having qualified in the Komsomol as a 'Voroshilov' crack shot (from the name of the former Defence Commissar). She was turned down, but Stalin agreed to let her perform for the troops. On one occasion, the Front was near Mozhaisk, only three hours by car from the centre of Moscow. On another, near Kharkov, she met Nikita Khrushchov, another future Soviet leader. After the war, she toured the USSR raising money to reconstruct destroyed cities. Dancing *Swan Lake* on one unfamiliar stage, her partner, who was carrying her, walked backwards and fell into the pit. She avoided landing on him but damaged her ankle. The appeal for a doctor in the house produced a vet.

'I saw a big red-haired man with broad shoulders and a red moustache. His sleeves were rolled up and I could see the red hairs on his arms. He took hold of my leg and jerked it. I yelled and he said '"woah", the way you shout to stop a horse. I was crying, but I was very grateful to him, because he put my ankle back and a month later I was dancing again.'

She hints that it was also patriotism that made her give up a well-paid teaching job and flat in Munich and come back to Moscow in the late 1980s, after many years in the West. 'I felt I was in the wrong place. I am not abnormally patriotic. I just felt I should be here. So I came back. It was probably because of the conscientiousness I learned in my Komsomol years. This is a hard time for the arts. There are great, urgent financial problems. And we have lost a generation to discos and hard rock.'

Now she wants to teach fifteen-year-olds and is looking

for young talent in the Urals, Siberia and the Far East of Russia – still at seventy-six and in the post-Communist era as 'thoroughly Komsomol' as she appeared to Iris Morley half a century ago.

# Yekaterina

| |
|---|
| Yekaterina Sergeyevna Maximova |
| Prima ballerina |
| Born: Moscow, 1939 |
| Father: Engineer |
| Mother: Journalist |
| Interviewed: June 1992 |

*Maximova belongs to the post-Stalin generation of dancers at the Bolshoi Ballet. In 1959 – two years before Lepeshinskaya ended her stage career – Maximova and her husband Vladimir Vasiliev danced the leads in Prokofiev's* The Stone Flower. *They had graduated from the Moscow ballet school only the year before, but they were immediately accepted as the company's star partnership. And so they remained until the long-simmering quarrel between dancers and the chief choreographer, Yuri Grigorovich, led to the departure of most of the mature lead dancers, including themselves and the legendary Maya Plisetskaya.*

'We were simply thrown out,' says Maximova. 'Suddenly, we were told we weren't needed.' She now gives only seven performances a year at the Bolshoi, all of them in January, in order to leave the rest of the year clear for other work, mostly foreign tours.

When we meet, she has just been rehearsing and is wearing a loose floral smock over her tights, her dark hair tied back. She is tanned and has sharp eyes, but her smile warms her whole expression. We are sitting in the ill-lit, cavernous staff canteen at the Bolshoi Theatre. A stainless-steel samovar rattles on the counter, at the far end. There are two waitresses visible and both are seated at the only table near a window, drinking tea. At another table in the gloomy centre of the room, Vladimir Vasiliev, his blond head emerging from a thirty-year-old dressing-gown of many colours, is giving an interview to a radio journalist.

He has long been on the record as one of the leading in-house critics of Grigorovich's authoritarian ways. What is the couple's relationship with the chief choreographer now?

'We don't have one,' says Maximova. 'I don't know what his attitude to us is: we haven't spoken for years.'

But she is generous in her praise of the impact Grigorovich made on ballet in Moscow, when he left Leningrad to join the Bolshoi in 1964 at the age of thirty-seven.

'He is a very talented choreographer. When he came to us, he started a new epoch. He created a great deal and opened a new page in the history of the ballet. He was a symbol, a leader and we believed in him.

'It's a great pity to see what is happening now. He has changed so much. In the early years, art was his life, not promotion, intrigues or career-building. Now he is not interested in the ballet itself. If he can't stage new ballets himself, then he should let someone else do it. As chief choreographer, he is responsible for the fate of so many people.'

But surely, in the new economic climate, it is exceptionally difficult to put on new productions of anything. The Russian press is reporting that the Bolshoi is free to raise salaries but doesn't have the money to do it.

Maximova dismisses the economic argument.

'It is very difficult, but it's possible [to do new work]. I was a child of the war. I remember dancing without ballet shoes. We made costumes out of nothing. Things are always difficult, but people manage.'

She worries about the loss to the country of great dancers who should be teaching new generations. Plisetskaya, for instance, who has settled in Spain.

'It's a crime. When I entered the Moscow ballet school [in 1949, at the age of ten], it was attached to the Bolshoi, and it was a close connection. Students took part in performances. Girls of thirteen and fourteen had the roles of animals – rabbits, foxes, birds and so on. In *Don Quixote*, there is a little cupid, who was always danced by a girl. Your life in the theatre began when you went to the school.

'We studied ordinary secondary school subjects as well as ballet, the history of music, art and theatre in the daytime. After school, we had rehearsals and then performances, sometimes three or four a week. We went to bed at midnight and had to be up ready for school next morning. In the summer, when we were at Pioneer camp, we were brought back to Moscow for performances.'

The students were taught by outstanding dancers. Maximova herself was a pupil of Yelizaveta Gerdt and was coached in her classical roles by Galina Ulanova.

'From an early age, you knew everyone in the Bolshoi and they knew us. It was like being brought up as a child in a family. There's a special spirit you can't learn from lectures or books. That tradition has been lost and it's a pity. The school is now independent from the Bolshoi; it's just an academy. There are some advantages in that, but pupils do not often take part in performances now. When they graduate and come to the Bolshoi, they are strangers.'

I ask how she knew she wanted to be a dancer.

'When they are seven, ninety per cent of girls want to be dancers. There was a ballerina living in my block and when her daughter went to ballet school, I asked my mother if I could do the same.'

Her mother divorced when Maximova was small and lost her job in journalism after her father was arrested in 1935.

'What happened to the whole intelligentsia happened to

my grandfather,' Maximova says in a matter-of-fact tone. 'He was teaching philosophy at Moscow University. He may have translated the wrong people. I don't know exactly what happened. He was executed in 1937, in Tomsk [Siberia]. After *perestroika* started, Memorial [the civil rights organisation] helped us get some information about him.'

Maximova gives some classes herself at the State Academy of Fine Arts, but the teaching must be sporadic, to judge from her programme for the coming six months. It includes trips to Canada, the United States, Japan (twice) and Paris, where she will dance the lead in *Cinderella* – costumes by Nina Ricci.

Vasiliev, who has finished his radio interview, joins us and explains that he cannot bring himself to throw away his tattered dressing-gown, which he has had since he began his career. He is now fifty-two and is working increasingly as a choreographer, at the Stanislavsky Theatre, at the Palace of Congresses in the Kremlin and for foreign tours.

Maximova jokes about the character parts he dances these days.

'In *Anyuta*, he is my father; in *Cinderella*, my stepmother. If he offers me Juliet, will he be the Nurse?'

Vasiliev takes the joke well. He is no longer the god-like, athletic dancer who could leap higher and further than any of his contemporaries, an outstanding Spartacus (in the part choreographed for him by Grigorovich in the late Sixties). But he still has an immensely strong presence on stage, and he is a successful choreographer. He put on a brilliant, exciting *Romeo and Juliet* in 1990, using the young dancers of the Stanislavsky Theatre.

He leaves us, and I ask Maximova if she would step outside to be photographed. She opens the stage door into Petrovka Street and immediately pulls back. 'Ah, the market,' she gasps.

The pavement is jammed with amateur and semi-professional traders, who moved downhill to the Bolshoi after the local authorities banned the improvised street market in and around the Dyetsky Mir (Children's World) department store.

The new market economics, which have transformed the once secure financial structure of the Bolshoi, have also changed the look of the street it stands on.

We climb the stairs and find a big empty room, where Maximova sits, smiling, behind a window that looks across a garden towards Red Square.

# Margarita

Margarita Borisovna
Terekhova

Actress

Born: Urals, 1942

Father: Actor, Russian

Mother: Actress, Polish

Interviewed: June 1992

*Terekhova worked with the great Soviet film director Andrei Tarkovsky both on the screen and in the theatre. She starred in* The Mirror, *one of the handful of films he made in the USSR, and played Gertrude in his stage version of* Hamlet. *Neither she nor Tarkovsky was a dissident, but she suffered from her association with a genius whose gifts and stubbornness frightened his Communist masters. She believes that her career was saved by the existence of other republics in the USSR, which meant that she could work in films and television outside Russia. She therefore has a strong personal reason for regretting the rise of nationalism that helped to break up the Soviet Federation.*

In the summer of 1992, Terekhova herself arranged for her latest film, *Only for Lunatics*, made in Estonia, to be shown one evening at the Moscow Cinema Centre, near the Russian Parliament building. It won a prize, for her fine performance, at the San Remo film festival in 1991 but had never been released in the Russian capital. She managed to borrow a copy of the version shot in both Russian and

Estonian with Russian subtitles. In it, she plays a psychiatrist who is destroyed by an act of impulsive generosity. She is on duty at night in a hospital ward where a young man is strapped to a bed, after an attempt to commit suicide in despair over his sexual impotence. He wakes, frees himself, tears the bandages off his wrists and tries to jump out of the window. The Russian woman takes him to her room and spends the night with him. He recovers. Her reward is the contempt of her daughter and neighbours and a violent death at the hands of the boy's father-in-law. The screenplay is based on the true story of a woman who once worked at a Moscow hospital.

'Estonian women said such a thing could never happen in their country,' says Terekhova. 'The director [Arvo Iho] began shooting with an Estonian actress, but she refused to act in the nude. So he dropped her and made a lot of enemies, but everyone said the role was typically Russian. In every nation there are holy fools, unselfish women who help people regardless of the consequences, who never worry about themselves and see their reflections in the people around them. In Russia, this is much more obvious than elsewhere. In Dostoevsky, there is Sonya in *Crime and Punishment*, and Lizavyeta in *The Brothers Karamazov*.

'Then there is the Blessed Kseniya, who lived in the time of Catherine the Great and was canonised as a saint. She was a normal woman from a good family, but at the age of thirty she lost her beloved husband and gave all her property away, keeping nothing for herself. Her relatives took her to court over this, claiming she was mad, but the court found her perfectly sane. She walked about barefoot in the street and people poured abuse on her. But then it was noticed that everyone who did this met with trouble of some kind. Everyone knows that you mustn't harm a holy fool. That's why the Estonians were so cross with me over this film, after the tanks went in. [Early in 1991, Soviet troops and riot police killed Lithuanians in Vilnius and Latvians in Riga. The Estonians expected to be attacked next.] They thought the film was saying Estonians killed a blessed woman and that this would be bad for their whole country. A film director living in Latvia said he thought the film was about Estonians killing Russia. Before the tanks, such an interpretation would not have occurred to them.'

Terekhova brings to the part a warmth and mature *insoucience* that makes the story credible. These are not recently acquired qualities for, when she was thirty-four, Tarkovsky cast her as Gertrude in his mid-Seventies production of *Hamlet* at the Lenin Komsomol Theatre in Moscow. She demonstrated her versatility by switching roles to play Ophelia on the last night. In Tarkovsky's autobiographical film *The Mirror*, she also plays two parts, as the mother – old-fashioned, feminine but strong – and as the emancipated, modern wife. It was her extraordinary qualities as an actress that led Tarkovsky to introduce the second character, when the shooting of the film, as written, was nearly finished.

In his book *Sculpting in Time* he says: 'We liked Margarita Terekhova as the mother but felt all the time that the role allotted to her in the original script was not sufficient to bring out, or make use of, her tremendous potential.' So he added the episodes with her as the wife and reshaped the whole film. Terekhova makes no such claim. But she says, with some pride, that Tarkovsky, who listened to and trusted his actors, made three practical changes she suggested, while the film was being shot.

Terekhova did not know at the time how Tarkovsky was shaping the picture. He did not let the actors see the complete script and relied on improvisation. His parents were on the set during filming, and his mother Mariya was available to Terekhova with advice and photos of Andrei as a boy. Terekhova was virtually unknown when she got the part. Among those who tested for it was Marina Vlady, the

French actress and wife of the Russian poet–actor–singer Vladimir Vysotsky.

Terekhova says that, like everyone else, she 'worshipped' Tarkovsky even before she worked for him. In October 1992, she told the weekly *Ogonyok*: 'I am sure that, if he wanted it, a log would act for him, simply out of love for him.' He once said to her that Italy had everything except Russian actors. He complained that when Western women talked to him, they had dollar signs in their eyes, as they tried to work out what he was worth. He felt that Western actors were going the same way.

Terekhova now wants to direct herself and make a picture of Chekhov's *The Cherry Orchard*, which she describes as written for the cinema in 1903, before the cinema existed.

'It reads like a prophesy about our new businessmen, who are springing up like mushrooms in a world where everything is done for money. The characters are cutting down the trees and the roots, not only of the old classes but under themselves as well. This is what's happening today. It wouldn't be in modern dress, because we don't have any such estates left now. I want to show an atmosphere of happiness in places which no longer exist. My idea is to shoot the whole film in the open air, in the orchard; the characters would only look into the house through the windows.'

She says she has backers ready to put up R.4 million, but the new prices have pushed the cost up to R.15 million, 'and all those who have many millions feel as if they are sitting on a smouldering powder-keg.'

What she means by this is the disorder in the former USSR, the nationalism and bloody conflicts in places like Georgia and Moldova and the warnings from Russian leaders such as Vice President Alexander Rutskoi and the Parliament Speaker Ruslan Kasbulatov that Russia might intervene in such conflicts.

'This is a nightmare. A journalist says he saw friends on

opposite sides in Georgia who didn't know whether they were shooting at Georgian or Ossetian villages. [In 1992, South Ossetia, which was part of Georgia, was seeking union with North Ossetia on the other side of the Caucasus mountains in southern Russia.] How can they secede from one another, when they are so mixed? No one knows how to calm things down. Russian troops are everywhere [in the former USSR], and if they get officially involved, that will be the end. That's why I say that this is not a time for the arts. Of course, people can still travel from one republic to another, but the conditions are not right for creating master-pieces. It's possible to do something interesting, if you have the money, but there are no big enterprises to help you. I have never cared about money, but now money is what I need.'

A few days later, Terekhova is handed a thick envelope, stuffed with R.50,000, by a South Korean businessman who has promised to finance annual cash awards for the best film director and the best actress in Russia. Terekhova has won the best actress award for 1992 and will serve on the jury in later years.

I undertake to drive her to the awards ceremony and collect her, on a hot, sunny afternoon outside her flat in a big, luxury block, solidly built of red brick on Bolshaya Gruzinskaya Street, central Moscow. She has arranged to pick up a friend, a young photographer, on the way. She spots him, as I pause at traffic lights not far from the old circus on Tsvetnoi Boulevard. She opens her door and calls 'Seryozha' (a familiar form of Sergei), in a voice of concentrated power, perfectly produced with no apparent effort. It is distinctly audible to Sergei a hundred yards away. He skips through the traffic and jumps into the car, just before the lights turn green.

Terekhova, off-stage and off-screen, has high nervous energy. She talk in bursts, often through laughter, running her hands through her shoulder-length fair hair.

Her mother, she says, was a Polish actress, 'red-haired and beautiful', who was working in the Crimea when the Second World War War came to the USSR in 1941. Her husband, a Siberian actor, was called up and she was evacuated to the Urals. She was with a travelling repertory company when Margarita was born in April 1942. Terekhova has two children. Anna, also an actress, was born in 1967. Her father is a Bulgarian actor who appeared with Terekhova in a Soviet–Bulgarian joint production. Her son Alexander, now eleven, has a different father whom she prefers not to identify.

She is critical of conditions both past and present. She talks about 'the complete degradation of the Russian theatre' today and the troubles Tarkovsky had with officials in the film industry in Brezhnev's time.

'Every theatre has been turned into a bastion of commercialism and is trying to negotiate contracts for foreign tours. It's small companies which don't have their own premises, like the one my daughter is in, which can survive.'

She criticizes the Mossoviet Theatre, off Mayakovsky Square, where she has worked for many years, but where, she now complains, a group of actors in alliance with the administrators 'imagine they have the power to make decisions for others – it's the worst thing that can happen in a theatre.'

Terekhova is clearly an actress with a great instinctive talent, honed by experience. But she is acutely sensitive to the social context she is living in and seems unable to make sense of the chaos of post-Communist Russia. Perhaps she needs a genius like Tarkovsky, in whom she has complete trust, to do her best work. Now, when she does make a film, she does not even know where it is being shown. She is also afraid for herself and for her children. Burglars recently broke into her flat and made a mess of it. And she was horrified in the summer of 1991, when several children staying at an élite holiday centre in the mountains, where she had sent her son, were killed in a car crash. She holds the director of the centre responsible, 'but this year that man is still looking after children on holiday. The country is in complete disorder – anyone can do anything.'

The anguish she projects, you feel, is a reflection of the state of her country, but her mood is not dark for long. She still savours the way Tarkovsky could occasionally make fools of his old enemies in Goskino, the State cinema organisation.

'He was awarded the Golden Lion [at the Venice film festival in the early Sixties] for his first film [*Ivan's Childhood*], but he had great difficulty making every other picture. He was supertalented, but he was always robbed. In twenty years, he made only five films in the Soviet Union. Almost everyone betrayed him in the end.'

The officialdom wanted to destroy *The Mirror*, on the grounds that no one would understand it and no one needed it.

'They tried to get him to change it. He edited it several times the way he wanted to do it and finally left the officials totally confused. A cameraman, at the time, said: "I think we have just shown them the first version, and they've passed it."' She laughs at the memory.

Terekhova, despite her personal regret at the passing of the USSR, has nothing of the Communist diehard about her. Like many other Russians, she is appalled by the bloody struggle between Armenians and Azerbaijanis. She is upset about the ethnic conflict between Russians and Romanian speakers in Moldova, for she made three films there, at a time when her own studio, Mosfilm, was offering her parts only in films that were never shot.

She is instinctively – and because of her experience of censorship in the Soviet cinema – on the side of the Russian democrats. During the attempted coup in August 1991, she immediately decided to oppose the plotters and walked from her flat to help protect Boris Yeltsin's White House.

She was a popular figure there and, when the coup collapsed, her fellow demonstrators gave her an affectionate testimonial that quoted from the title of Mihail Bulgakov's novel *The Master and Margarita*.

'To Margarita,' it reads, 'from the Masters of the Barricades.'

# Natasha

| |
|---|
| Natalya Alexeyevna Perova |
| Translator and publisher |
| Born: Moscow, 1941 |
| Father: Refrigeration engineer |
| Mother: Design engineer and housewife |
| Interviewed: June 1992 |

*Natasha (Natalya) thinks of herself as a woman with a mission. When her twin daughters were babies, the mission was to get Dr Benjamin Spock's* The Common Sense Book of Baby and Child Care *published in Russian in the Soviet Union, which she did. Now her children are aged twenty-five and her new mission is to translate the best of new Russian writing and introduce it to readers in the West. Her chosen instrument is* Glas, *a literary magazine in English, which has been warmly welcomed by Western critics.* Glas 3, *which appeared in autumn 1992, is a selection of prose and poetry by Russian women writers.*

Natasha talks about Dr Spock over lunch in her unusually spacious flat at Matveyevskoye, a pleasant suburban development on a hill south-west of Moscow. She is an energetic woman, who speaks English quickly and well. She recalls how reassured and relieved she was when she came across the Spock book, as the wife of a young Soviet diplomat in Pakistan. Her twins, Mariya and Anastasia, were seven months old, and she had no relatives to turn to.

'I learnt this book by heart. When you read it, you feel as if a very kind, wise old man is trying to help you. I read all the Soviet books on bringing up children I could find, too. They tell you they should smile at one month, raise their heads at two months, and they know precisely at what age they should walk. But when the babies are born, nothing happens as they predict, and you think your children are abnormal. I was going through torture because of this. I read Spock when my daughters were seven months old (the American children's doctor in Karachi gave me a copy), and I cried because I had worried unnecessarily. Spock says: "Listen to your child's individuality." I fell in love with his book and promised that, when I got back to the USSR, I would tell everyone about it.'

Three days after returning to Moscow, at the end of her husband's five-year tour of duty in Pakistan, she began going the rounds of Soviet publishing houses.

'I told them how the book had saved me, but no one wanted to listen to this Western propaganda. But one day Dr Spock made a speech protesting against the war in Vietnam. I got a contract and the book came out, just one edition and not very big. Then I think Spock said something nasty about the Soviet Union, and they didn't dare print a second edition. The black market made a lot of money from it. When *perestroika* began, pirated editions appeared. They use my translation, but nobody pays me – except the Communists. Pravda, the former Central Committee's publishers, paid quite handsomely.'

Natasha defends Spock against the charge that his permissiveness ruined an American generation, though she concedes that this view used to be widely held in the Soviet Union.

'He does say it is okay to spank your child and that you don't have to force yourself to act against your instincts. But his ideas were certainly at odds with the education system in this country. With *perestroika*, people said it was time to stop training our children like future soldiers and to bring them up as human beings. But I can't say my children were raised by the Dr Spock system. The schools spoiled all my efforts. When they went to kindergarten in Moscow, they were broken. They became different people. They were shut in cupboards as a punishment. They were frightened and humiliated. They became quiet and subdued. They changed visibly. They are different from each other, though. They are not identical. One is blonde, one is dark; one has brown eyes, one has blue. Masha (Mariya) is a guide with Intourist. She is very conscientious and responsible. Anastasia is more self-centred. She is unemployed. She graduated as an economist but had to study the Soviet economy at college, and that knowledge is useless now. She is waiting for a friend to start up a private business and give her a job.

'My daughters are nice people, but they are not very strong personalities, and in the younger generation, it's the strong who have been least affected by ideological pressure. Some young people have got carried away by business opportunities; they are greedy, even. Others have given up and become sceptical about everything. They see the same absurdities, only now these are called democratic. So they are quite passive. But there are some who are bright, enterprising and honest. It will probably take several generations before we have a different breed of people who will start an effective economy.'

Natasha was twelve when Stalin died in 1953. No one in her family was arrested and she did not personally know anyone who had been in prison. In this, her family was unusually fortunate. She says it came as a shock to learn from Solzhenitsyn and other writers what went on in the camps of the Gulag. But, even as a child, she was conscious of a heavy, oppressive atmosphere. Her father told her that he could never reach the top as an engineer, because he was not a member of the Communist Party.

'I was apolitical and outspoken and people would hush

me up. I grew up with the feeling of a huge, awesome power hanging over us, invisible but threatening. While Khrushchov was Party leader [1953–64], there was a short period of relaxation, exhilaration and freedom, but somehow it seemed phoney. A revolution from above is always phoney. They allow you as much freedom as is good for them, not for you. But when I was at university in Moscow, there were recitals of poetry unthinkable before, concerts of new music, new trends in literature and the arts, new exhibitions. Books were circulating. It was a wonderful time in a way.'

When she was nineteen and a student, Natasha ran into the KGB. She was arrested on holiday in the Caucasus for associating with a group of American students, who had formed a choir and were singing old Russian folk songs in the streets – tsarist hymns, her interrogator alleged. She was released after a couple of days, but for six months was openly followed and harassed in a variety of ways in Moscow.

'They poisoned my life. But I was young and pretty and in love, I was enjoying university and had a lot to do. And everybody had an oasis where he could breathe. It was said that kitchens weren't bugged, so people gathered in their kitchens and talked into the night, not just about politics but about the meaning of life, the arts, their loves, their friends.'

Natasha had to find her oases in other people's kitchens, because her family lived in a communal flat: one room in an old mansion which had been partitioned off into thirty rooms. Their room was in what had been a big hall. The ceiling was six metres high, and all the rooms shared the same flooring.

'When I came back from a date in the early hours of the morning, I used to take my high-heels off but, however careful I was, the floor creaked, and it creaked under all those cubicles in the hall. All hell broke loose and everyone would start shouting. I was very unpopular in that place.

When I got married at twenty-one, the main reason was to get away from there. There was only one toilet and no piped hot water. There were no gas stoves. We used Primuses and people used to cook big saucepans of soup, enough for three days. An old lady, a descendant of the former owner of the mansion, lived there and was very inventive in the way she took her revenge on us. I think she was mad. Sometimes she put a dead rat in a pan of soup. Or she cut a clothesline, so that it broke when you touched it and the washing fell on the floor.'

When she returned from Pakistan, Natasha went back to communal living, with her husband and two children in a single room of ten square metres and sharing kitchen and bathroom. But they had only one neighbour, and the place at first seemed 'like paradise'. This did not last: the neighbour did not take to the twins.

Dr Spock came to the rescue again. The fee for Natasha's translation of *Baby and Child Care* was enough to buy a flat in the development being built at Matveyevskoye, in what was then the countryside near Stalin's old dacha. The flats in a cooperative block were privately owned and luxurious compared with normal State housing. Natasha's has three bedrooms as well as a large living room – sixty square metres in all, including the kitchen and bathroom. Matveyevskoye is handy for Moscow University on Lenin Hills and many of the neighbours are academics. Natasha, who married twice and divorced twice, shares the flat with her daughters. They thus have twenty square metres per person, instead of the State-housing norm of nine square metres.

When she finished the Spock translation, Natasha got a job as proof reader with the Progress publishing house, which specialised in foreign-language books.

'It was started by the Comintern, and some of the old enthusiasts were still alive when I started. But they were disillusioned. Progress was full of good intentions to speak about Russia to the outside world, but they didn't do it properly. The Central Committee wanted to make a profit and to control it ideologically and in every other way. They put their own people in, and the ideological pressure was terrible. The company didn't have much money – the Central Committee was very stingy – and they didn't use the best translators. The general level went down and down.'

Natasha climbed the ladder and eventually became head of the English language section at *Soviet Literature* magazine. She says that she and other translators naively tried to get good books published but failed.

'Translations were literal, often just gobbledegook. A lot of quite useless books were translated and that was called Soviet propaganda. At meetings, I used to say it was anti-Soviet propaganda. I made myself unpopular with the authorities, but I think they decided at some point to let a few *enfants terribles* say what they liked but made it clear that no one need take them seriously.'

In her new mission, Natasha is seeking out the best new writing in Russian, and her team then undertake to produce high-quality translations. When she was setting up *Glas*, her first partner was the distinguished English translator Michael Glenny, a man of huge energy and appetite for life. He died suddenly in Moscow in the summer of 1990.

Her new partners are Arch Tait and Andrew Bromfield, and they intend to combine the efforts of Russian and English native speakers to produce translations that are both accurate and readable. Natasha argues that the twentieth century, which is nearly over, has produced Russian writers as great as those of the nineteenth.

'Tolstoy didn't become internationally famous till the end of his life. When his great novels were already written, it was obvious to very few people that he was a writer of genius and belonged to world literature. I think the same is happening now. At least ten Russian writers of this century are worthy of world attention. It will take time to translate them properly and before they register in people's minds as great writers.

'Many potentially great writers were destroyed in the camps. But however carefully the regime tried to exterminate Russian culture, new shoots of genius are still coming up. There are people I am convinced will last: Alexander Terekhov and Vladimir Sorokin, for instance. If they go on as they are, they will be classics of the twenty-first century.'

Both appear in the second issue of *Glas*, devoted to the 'Soviet Grotesque'. Sorokin is represented by what Natasha describes as 'a harsh, cruel story', an exerpt from his novel *Four Stout Hearts*, which opens in Moscow on New Year's Eve 1991. It is violent in language and imagery and contains passages of explicit homosexuality. Its selection caused uproar among the publishers of *Glas*, but Natasha is unrepentant.

'The writing is for those with strong nerves or who can read it as if it has nothing to do with their own lives. But his description of Russia today is very accurate. It's a sensitive person's reaction to what is happening here, especially if he has had contact with all the different mafias. People prefer not to know the truth. This captures something that's hidden from ordinary people, but they can sense the horrible force that is capable of anything, of torture and murder. Sorokin gets the tortures he describes from court cases. He hasn't invented a single detail, except for the group of people who are pursuing a certain, unspecified aim, that has to be fulfilled. It's a metaphor for the Communist era. The writer describes a hell that exists – sometimes you get glimpses of it.'

Here Natasha interrupts herself to tell a very Russian joke. It is familiar but revealing of the way Russians laugh at themselves. 'A dead soul arrives in the other world and finds two doors marked "Communist Hell" and "Capitalist Hell". The soul bribes a doorman and asks which is the better place. "The Communist Hell is much better," says the doorman. "The heating is always out of order. Sometimes there's a shortage of coal or the stoker is drunk. The Capitalist Hell is much more efficient. Everything works there, and you will burn."'

Natasha emits a long, musical laugh.

'In this world, of course, the Communist Hell is very efficient. Even today you can feel a kind of organised, repressive force. You are still not safe. The trade mafia is linked with the KGB mafia and the former Communist mafia. They haven't laid down their arms. They are still there. They will never get back to power, unless it's for a very short while. But they are not defeated. You can still feel their presence.'

I ask Natasha to name some of the writers she expects to represent Russia eventually in the list of twentieth-century greats. From the first part of the century, she selects the following: Andrei Platonov, novelist; Varlam Shalamov, poet and novelist who spent many years in the camps; Yevgeny Zamyatin, novelist; Isaac Babel, novelist and playwright; Mikhail Zoshchenko, satirist; Mikhail Bulgakov, novelist; Ivan Bunin, Nobel Prize winner; Boris Pasternak, poet and novelist; Alexander Blok, poet; Osip Mandelstam, poet; Anna Akhmatova, poet; Marina Tsvetaeva, poet. To these she adds: Alexander Solzhenitsyn, novelist and chronicler of the Gulag; Vasily Grossman, novelist; Yuri Dombrovsky, novelist.

Natasha later sends me a more considered and longer list. On this, writers from the second half of the century include Andrei Sinyavsky and Tatyana Tolstaya, Victor Pelevin and Zufar Garayev who are featured in *Glas 4*, and two women whose work appears in *Glas 3*. Nina Sadur, poet, novelist and playwright, grew up in Novosibirsk, Siberia, and makes her living as a cleaner in a theatre. She is represented by mysterious, powerful short stories from a collection called *Witch's Tears*. Marina Palei is thirty-seven and lives in

St Petersburg. She graduated from medical school but, while writing, has in her time worked as cleaner, stoker and model. Her harrowing description of a 'women's ward' in a provincial hospital appears in *Glas 3*.

I ask Natasha what the main differences are between the new male and female writers. She finds the question perplexing and puts it to friends and colleagues, before concluding: 'There is no real distinction. Women are still trying to emulate men. The problem is that the feminist movement in Russia is very weak. Protest is not natural.'

*Glas 3*, however, does contain a poem which vividly describes what it is like to be a harassed Russian wife and does it, moreover, with wit and humour. It is by Nina Iskrenko, aged forty-one, a physics graduate who helps to bring out an occasional literary newspaper, *The Law-abiding Centaur*, which jokingly calls itself an 'organ of aesthetic intercourse'. Her poem 'The Other Woman', translated by Andrew Bromfield, is addressed to a husband and attempts to visualise his image of the perfect woman. It begins on a day:

> when I confuse the kids
> with dinosaurs
> and take the favourable disposition of the heavens
> for mere politeness
> when at seven forty-five it's time to
>   and at eight forty-five it's time to
>     and at ten forty-five it's time to and the radio's
> telling me all sorts of awful things
> when the telephone's turned off because it can't take
>                               any more
> and the conjectural lump of butter won't spread
>   on the imaginary slice of bread and what's
> more
> in the middle
> of the night
> in the dark
> I stumble over the bicycle
> in the hall

I hear the drowsy half-irked crackle of a match
　and smoke creeps under the door. It's you
　　starting to nag me about the other woman

　　　The other woman in your place
　　　The other woman in your position
　　　The other woman at our level of civilisation
　　　she wouldn't make a fuss over those trifles
　　　every month she wouldn't
　　　make a fuss she wouldn't

My forehead bursts with the strain of imagining
the other woman's sexy seductive capacity to cope
　　　　　　　with our level of civilisation
and when I finally crack it
I smile the trustful-disdainful smile of a cheshire cat
or Julio Cortazar
gladly allowing the other woman into my place
at the stove
and in dream-time
　as well as each and every one of
　　my horizontal-vertical-trigonometric
　　　ear-kneed cold-nosed spiral-eyed positions
and while she gets to grips with them
　　paying no attention to me
I sneak over to the door
groping for my shoes with my feet
　thinking only about
not getting snagged on the bicycle
in the hall
The door-bell
I open up
The other woman
　in a plaintive leaping-out-of-her-dress voice asks me
　　to call the cops her husband's drunk
　　　　　she smacked him with
　　　　　　　a skillet full of cutlets

Chapter 8

# Business

It was the opening of cooperative restaurants in Moscow that gave the impression that Gorbachov's *perestroika* reforms were bringing real changes. Some charged hard currency, but in return they offered good food, a welcoming atmosphere and attentive service. After the surliness of waiters in State-run eating places, which always declared themselves full, the co-ops were revolutionary. Other kinds of small businesses sprang up quickly and by mid-1989 there were about 133,000 of them employing three million people. They were mainly offering services, but there were small manufacturing companies, too, looking to satisfy demands the big State enterprises could not or did not bother to meet. Further fast growth became inhibited by public resentment at high cooperative prices and by the Government's fear of breaking the Communist commandment against 'the exploitation of man by man'. Co-ops suddenly found new obstacles thrown in their paths and thousands of them went out of business.

Farmers' markets continued to flourish, although their prices, too, were high because, theoretically, the young men selling fruit and vegetables and Russian women selling eggs, pickles, cottage cheese and flowers were marketing goods from their own plots of land. In some cases this was true, but very often the food was brought to market by middle-

men, and resentment grew against the dark-skinned 'speculators' from the now-independent southern republics.

Then suddenly, after the price reforms of January 1992,
the streets of Moscow were filled with crowds of men and
women with something to sell. The signal for the street
trading that changed the face of the city was a decree signed
by the Russian President, Boris Yeltsin, on 29 January.
Intended to give a lift to market economics, it granted firms
and individuals the right to trade freely without special
licences (except for firearms, explosives and other dangerous articles). Almost overnight, a street market materialised
around the big Dyetsky Mir (Children's World) department
store.

Traders, most of them women of all ages, stood in lines
outside the store holding up their wares and staring with
glazed, stoical expressions at the prospective buyers of
clothes, toys, footware and cosmetics, who shuffled between the human hedges. Some of the new entrepreneurs
were, perhaps, selling off family treasures in order to buy
food at the new prices. But in most cases the goods were
new, often sold in their original, rough cardboard boxes,
stamped with an old official price which the street dealers
multiplied by a hundred or so. Some of the traders were
cashing in on hours spent queuing to buy, at subsidised
prices, the T-shirts, door-locks, lipsticks, shampoos,
trainers, talking dolls and Columbus anniversary alarm
clocks they now held up for re-sale at huge profits. Others
no doubt had access to goods at the old price with the help
of insiders at factories or in the distribution network. Either
way, what was going on was 'speculation', a form of private
enterprise once punished as a heinous crime.

The speculating was being done openly on Lubyanka
Square, which Dyetsky Mir shares with three buildings that
used to house the Soviet secret police, the KGB. A shorn-off
column in the centre of the square used to support a statue
to Felix Dzerzhinsky, the Polish Bolshevik who founded

Lenin's secret police, the Cheka. The cast-iron statue was removed by the Moscow city authorities after the abortive coup in August 1991, out of fear that anti-Communist crowds would otherwise topple it into the road and perhaps send it crashing into the Metro beneath.

It was still illegal for individuals to sell their goods *inside* a State-owned store like Children's World, but hundreds did just that on cold days. One middle-aged woman, I noted, had on offer a blanket for a child's cot. She was standing just outside the store's blanket department and was undercutting its own new price.

A policeman with a megaphone tried to expel the invaders. Two girls with pink folding umbrellas for sale ignored him and went on licking their ice-creams. He did no better with a well-built young woman who had a green, remote-controlled toy truck for sale at the equivalent of a third of the then average monthly Moscow salary. She laughed in his face, and other illegal traders joined in the merriment. He complained to me that he and his two fellow officers were 'unprotected'. In that crush, 'anyone can insult us and we can't do anything about it'. Minutes later, I saw him again. With rare resilience, he was trying out another remote-controlled toy offered for sale by a black-bearded man in jeans.

It took another Government order to stop the street trading in and around Dyetsky Mir, but the dealers simply moved down the hill and swarmed around the Bolshoi Theatre. Lock-up kiosks mushroomed all over the city, selling imported liqueurs and cigarettes, shampoos, condoms, sex manuals and other items, some never on open sale for roubles before the great price rise.

One centre of the new commerce was the Byelorussian railway station, already the site of the biggest flower market in a city where flower-giving is one of the few respected common courtesies. Flower-sellers spread around the front of the old pastel-green building. Pavements were crowded with vendors of beer, soft drinks, eggs and (displayed unappetisingly on wooden packing cases) shiny smoked fish. One salesman specialised in plumbing parts, pipes, screws, taps and washers, articles once available only on the black market. There were trestle tables covered with books and badly printed soft-porn magazines. Street traders even began selling bananas, previously available only in hard currency stores.

The item most obviously subject to street-market forces of supply and demand was vodka. Some kiosks sold nothing else and the price of a half-litre bottle fluctuated daily, as competition began to operate. When winter began, vodka had to be queued for at State wine shops, but it was cheap. By spring, there were crates of it on offer in private kiosks, but a half-litre cost more than the old average weekly wage. Even at the new rates of pay, it represented about two days' average earnings.

It nevertheless sold well, and its effects were visible. In the streets around the station, the sight of an inebriated male, gently supported by two friends, became commonplace. Some drunks lay sleeping where they fell, in doorways or on patches of dusty grass, their heads bloodied. It was by no means drunkenness on a massive scale, but it was a sharp reminder of the stereotype of the hard-drinking Russian male.

The extraordinary street scenes strengthened the impression that Russia was collapsing in chaos. Talk of privatisation had so far failed to create new industrial structures to replace the dying dinosaurs of the command economy, and the Yeltsin Government's scheme to give everyone a stake in the privatisation game was viewed with instinctive suspicion. Where were the new entrepreneurs to come from? Looking for an answer, I spent a day with businesswoman Zoya Gavrilova. She looks the part and puts on a powerful show. She simultaneously answers my questions, signs papers, issues intructions to her staff, takes telephone calls and thinks up new money-making ideas.

She tells me she is taking over the distribution of an American brand of fruit drink. She imports fashion clothes from Europe and the US. She manufactures little painted boxes and colourful, electrically operated samovars. She has a share in a restaurant, and proposes to open a second with a strip club attached. She has plans to raise chickens and open a 'high class' sex shop.

She is not a practising Christian but says she contributes to charities and helps restore churches and monasteries. An idea comes to her: 'Perhaps monks could raise the chickens.'

We abruptly leave her office at Granovsky Street (where the élite used to go for food and special health care) and speed across town in a white Mercedes to a mid-afternoon lunch in her restaurant on the Boulevard Ring. Then it's back to Granovsky Street to make a few more million.

Zoya says there are not many women in business in Russia yet, but those who have emerged are 'very gifted, more honest and hard-working than men; and the female mind is more flexible'. Many of these women, she says, come from the performing arts. She herself trained as a ballet dancer and was at the Bolshoi for a while before she joined the State circus, where she stayed for twenty years.

She clearly has phenomenal energy, but her circus background contributes to the feeling I have that Zoya is giving a performance, albeit a persuasive one, as a business-woman. This may be unfair to her, but the image matches that of a whole country trying to learn unfamiliar roles in a play that is still being written: the millionaire, the stockbroker, the street vendor. The activity looks frenetic and seems to consist of making money fast, while there is a chance.

'When privatisation comes,' says Zoya, 'beautiful people will rise to the surface.'

But will any of them want to run Russia's big, obsolete,

industrial plants or take over land from the overmanned collective farms?

In fact, there are individuals already setting themselves up as independent farmers, but they have a fight on their hands, as I discover during a day in the country.

# Nadya

Nadyezhda Ivanovna
Myesenko

Farmer

Born: Bashkiriya, the Urals,
1962

Parents: State-farm workers

Interviewed: June 1992

*The future of Russia depends very much on the courage and success
of men and women like Nadya Myesenko. Without a thriving
network of independent farmers like her, the country will never
be able to feed itself, despite its vast size and immense natural
resources. The collective farm system, forced on the country with
great cruelty and loss of life, has failed. It is hopelessly inefficient
and wasteful of both labour and produce. Overmanning is a way
of life, and some thirty per cent of the food which is harvested spoils
before it reaches any market or shop. The failure is a national
humiliation. But the State and collective farms (distinguished by
whether the State or the farm collective formally owns the land)
remain bastions of Communist habits and methods. The independent
farmer has to be patient, resilient and strong-willed.*

At first sight, Nadya is miscast. She is thirty, blonde and
pretty. Her hair is light brown and she wears a grey, low-cut
top with large black spots, above a black skirt. But there is
an air of tough self-confidence about her. Her eyes are
shrewd: no one is likely to pull wool over them. She has a
determined chin.

She has two children, a boy of ten and a girl of nine. Her husband drives lorries for a cooperative firm based in Moscow, about forty miles away from the Leninsky Luch (Lenin Sunray) collective farm in the Krasnogorsk district, where Nadya till recently ran the central boiler-house. She still rents a two-storey cottage belonging to the farm, and her neighbours are part of its workforce of one thousand five hundred, cultivating some six thousand acres.

Nadya's years of work at Leninsky Luch entitle her to 3.7 acres of land, as her share of the commonly owned property. Under Russian law, she does not have to buy it or pay ground rent for a lease. Theoretically it is hers by right, although she will not be allowed to sell it for ten years. She will eventually have to pay tax on it, but the tax is waived for the first five years.

Exercising the right is proving difficult in practice. The first two obstacles were quickly overcome. She first approached the board of the collective farm which owns the land. Within a week, it gave its consent. Then she had to apply in writing for the approval of the village soviet (council) and they confirmed in a matter of days that they did not object to the farm board's decision. The difficulties began at stage three: seeking the agreement of the Krasnogorsk district executive committee. This, she was told, was controlled by 'democrats' and she would have no trouble from them. Nine months later, she is still making weekly visits to the committee, seeking title to her land. She has met with an endless variety of delaying tactics and is now convinced that the new regional authorities are 'the old *nomenklatura* – Party appointees – under new names'.

First the committee whittled down her entitlement from 3.7 to 2.64 acres. It objected to the first field she chose, because there were plans to build dachas on it. She picked a second field, but the committee allocated this to another family. Her third choice was also approved by the collective farm and village council. She had all the documents, except the 'State Act' which only the regional executive committee can give. But the planting season was upon her, so she had the field ploughed. A surveyor measured and marked out the land. He was promptly followed by the chief agronomist, who removed the surveyor's markers and divided the field up into small allotments. Nadya threatened to sue him and was then offered field number four. This she has now had ploughed and planted with three tons of seed potatoes, which she hopes will yield twenty tons in the autumn, but she is conscious that she has taken a great risk in going ahead with planting before the paperwork is done. But, as a sign of confidence, she has given the farm a name and called it Anna, after her mother.

Nadya knows her costs by heart. She paid R.30,000 for the seed potatoes and bought six two-month-old piglets for R.180 each, before the January price increases (now, she reckons, they would cost up to R.1,500 each). She also has four sows and some hens. 'I'd love to have a cow, but they're too expensive.' She and her husband are building a brick storehouse, with a cellar where she plans to keep her potatoes.

'We have bought four thousand bricks at four roubles each. I don't know if that will be enough. We can't afford to pay a builder, so my husband and I are doing the job ourselves. To dig the cellar, we hired an excavator at R.3,000 a day. We can also hire equipment from the regional authorities, but the fees are high, because we are considered "kulaks". People don't call us this to our faces, but they expect us to be rich one day.'

Her husband, who is keeping his driving job while helping his wife, has never been keen on farming himself, and Nadya says she had to teach him how to use a spade. He is incensed by the suspicion and jealousy they have to put up with from neighbours.

'They know how hard we work,' she explains, 'and he

sees them sitting around drinking and playing cards, while we don't have a minute to ourselves.'

Her husband's nephew is also an independent farmer. He already has his plot of land, so they are sharing machinery with him. A new tractor now costs about R.250,000, far more than they can afford. They bought an old, broken-down machine for R.300, before the price increases, and coaxed it back to life. Her husband and nephew drive it. They intend to pay friends to help them harvest the potatoes, and beet for the pigs. One day they hope to own their own truck. Meanwhile, they will have to hire or borrow one.

The brick storehouse will be important, because 'we'll be able to sell gradually on the market through the winter, when the prices are high. Some people try to sell wholesale. Some do deals with circuses and factory canteens that have storage facilties. This is all very new for us. We've never sold anything before.'

It is clearly uncomfortable living cheek by jowl with collective farm workers who disapprove of what she is doing. Their two-storey, semi-detached cottages are built in lines, separated by gardens that abut each other. There are no hedges, no fences, just strips of wire to mark the boundaries. They are under the eyes of the neighbours all day long.

'Older people, who have been working on the farm for thirty or forty years, look on the land as theirs. They are against giving away property that used to belong to everybody.' She knows that one of her neighbours, a retired dairymaid, has loudly objected at collective farm meetings to letting her take land. The woman is entitled to more than seven acres herself, if she wants to take it, but asks: 'Who would work it?' Her son, aged thirty, is not interested.

Another hostile group comprises administrators and the agronomists, economists and other experts the farm employs full-time, instead of calling in consultants when needed. 'If all the land goes, they will be out of a job.'

Nadya says that uncertainty is the biggest disincentive to independent farming. On the collective farm, there are regular pay packets and you are not expected to work from morning till night, but the real problem is not knowing what is going to happen in the country as a whole. She follows Moscow politics closely these days, although she feels the politicians do not know what they are doing. 'They say one thing and do another and have no idea what's happening in reality.'

A neighbour tells her that at a recent meeting of the collective farm board someone said that the land would be taken back from independent farmers 'when they get rid of Boris Yeltsin'. It is this kind of general, all-enveloping uncertainty that worries her and her husband, not simply the uneasy feeling that they may be denied legal title to the land they are already working and investing in.

Despite her low regard for politicians, Nadya looks on President Yeltsin for now 'as a kind of guarantee'.

# Natasha

Natalya Artyomovna Averina

Police officer

Born: Tbilisi, Georgia, 1955

Father: Factory worker, Armenian

Mother: Medical worker, Russian

Interviewed: January 1992

*Natasha is a police captain. She teaches criminology at a senior police college. In the early 1980s, her career seemed doomed. She denounced fellow policemen for corruption, and was under investigation herself for almost two years before finally being cleared of stealing secret documents. She is now an honoured member of the force and president of the newly formed Russian Policewomen's Association. But now she is planning a new career, as a businesswoman.*

There is a striking quality of repose about Captain Natalya Averina. She speaks quietly, smiles often and is totally sure of herself. There is a hard-won peace of mind behind the soft, gentle looks.

She is a beautiful woman in the Ava Gardner mould, born of an Armenian father and Russian mother in Tbilisi, the capital of Georgia. She has long black hair and, when I first met her in Moscow, she was wearing a grey and turquoise sweater, black skirt, boots and tights and her nails were varnished bright red. Now, at home in her small two-room flat in north Moscow, with its pink floral wallpaper, shelves of books, a bluish painting of birch trees, Dutch television set and Japanese radio cassette player, she is casually dressed in jeans and grey sweater. On official occasions, such as the gala inauguration of the Policewomen's Association which she founded and heads, she is neatly turned out in a simple grey uniform dress with her captain's stars on her epaulettes.

Top male policemen and bureaucrats in dark suits, who welcome the new association in the grand ballroon of the Moscow Palace of Youth, make faintly patronising speeches and embrace the new president. At least they try to, for, like many Russian women, Natasha has not yet learnt to offer a cheek in greeting, but dips her head and meets puckered lips awkwardly with her brow.

But with the Moscow police chief in attendance, Natasha looks at ease in front of the television cameras – the darling of the force, it seems. Less than ten years before, the force came close to ending her career and sending her to gaol.

She came to Moscow in 1973, when she was eighteen, to go to medical school and worked for a while, after graduation, as a court pathology expert. She met detectives and thought they had a romantic, interesting job, but she did not immediately join them. She went to law school first.

Then in 1980, she was offered a job with a sixty-strong police team operating at the Cosmos Hotel, the curved, twenty-five storey, 3,600-bed home for foreign tourists built for the 1980 Olympic Games. The police team's general brief at the Cosmos was to protect foreigners from the Soviet criminal classes. Natasha was to pay particular attention to prostitutes. It was the start of a specialisation she later continued as one of eleven experts on a Soviet commission looking for ways of dealing with an ancient profession which theoretically did not exist under Communism.

At the Cosmos, she found that prostitutes sailed through

the police and other protective barriers that humiliatingly excluded innocent Muscovites from what they believed to be the glittering luxury of the hotel. Corruption was everywhere. Waiters carefully sat girls next to rich foreigners at restaurant tables. Chambermaids signalled the room numbers of unattached males and failed to report the women who spent the night with them.

Natasha watched all this and one day, at a meeting of the Cosmos police unit, denounced her fellow officers for various forms of corrupt behaviour, especially of taking bribes. Her persecution began the same night, an investigation into *her* alleged crimes that lasted twenty months. She endured eighty-five interrogations and three trials. At the end of 1986 she was cleared of the charges against her: abuse of authority, theft of secret documents (proved to have been planted on her). In October 1987, *Pravda* itself finally told her story and set the seal on her rehabilitation.

She got her job back and was paid compensation, but the personal cost was enormous. Her marriage broke up when her battle began, and she had a toddler son, Artyom, born in 1984 just before the ordeal began, to look after. Two months after forged 'evidence' was found in her parents' flat, her father had a heart attack and died. Natasha was sacked for bringing discredit on the police force and was out of a job for two years.

Some of her persecutors were later sacked in their turn, but some are still in the force, and Natasha's rare courage and resolve seem to have changed little in practice. A distinguished Russian woman writer, invited to breakfast at another tourist hotel in central Moscow, has to be met in the street and escorted past the door guards, while prostitutes find their way in without apparent difficulty. When I last stayed at the Cosmos – some years after Natasha's epic whistle-blowing – I was quickly targeted as a single male. Someone calling herself 'Ludmilla Gorbachov' rang my room and asked about my plans for the evening. The Cosmos was back to its sleazy normal.

Natasha is realistic about the enormous difficulty of stopping the spread of prostitution because, as the economy collapses, access to hard currency becomes ever more enticing.

'It's a joke,' says Natasha, 'trying to talk a girl into changing her profession, when what she is doing is so profitable.' What worries her most is the growing number of teenagers 'on the game' in Moscow, some of them only thirteen.

'A few years ago, it was unusual to see a prostitute under eighteen, but in a recent study of two hundred and fifty girls, fifty or sixty of them were teenagers.'

A Moscow newspaper once reported a conversation, which it presented as fact, with a prostitute who hailed from a good academic family. 'What is a girl like you, whose parents are both university professors, doing in a profession like this?' 'I was just lucky, I guess,' the girl is alleged to have replied. True or not, the anecdote does reflect the fact that prostitution and easy money look glamorous to young girls yearning for pretty clothes and access to 'smart' hotels.

Natasha believes that the way to stop this is to strike hard at those who recruit teenage girls, not just the professional pimps, but the 'stepfathers, sports coaches, teachers, who do it. There is not a single case of an adult being charged for this.'

She suggests there should also be penalties under the criminal code for anyone convicted of profiting from prostitution: taxi-drivers, hotel workers and the rest. But she is opposed to gaoling prostitutes themselves. She favours persuasion with the help of social workers, doctors, lawyers, even economists. Still the quiet troublemaker, she did not hesitate to stand up in public and contradict a superior officer who advocated ten years' imprisonment for convicted prostitutes. But she recognises that there will not be much hope of progress without 'radical changes in the economy'.

On a more modest level, she wants improvements in the way women, in general, are treated in the Soviet Union, for instance making it easier for mothers to work part-time. She has arrived at these conclusions pragmatically in the course of her work, not because she has adopted feminist or political views ready-made from others.

Where do the Moscow prostitutes come from?

'From all social strata. I couldn't say there are more from working families than from the intelligentsia.'

She describes different classes of prostitutes: 'street girls', 'railway station girls' – often not professionals but 'degraded women' trying to make money – but in her work she has encountered mainly the hard-currency specialists, 'and this group has increased considerably in recent years. When you compare their standard of living with that of a policewoman like me, I don't think the comparison is in my favour. I am a single mother of a seven-year-old boy and do my own shopping. But I am sorry for them. I have come to understand that feelings such as love and friendship are unknown to them. And in my experience they don't change. Even those who get married and appear devoted wives and mothers still can't give up prostitution.'

Natasha chose police work instead of making a career in medicine, the law or the arts, as she might have done. She studied music and painting as a child and dreamt of becoming a film actress. She did appear in a BBC television documentary film called *Prostitutki*, shown in Britain in 1989, and through it became 'famous'. She was invited to the US and was photographed with the Governor of Minnesota.

Natasha left active policing to teach criminology – mainly to men – at a senior police college. She takes her son to school, and his grandmother looks after him when he comes out and until Natasha finishes work. She finds it difficult to live on a rouble salary.

She remembers the birth of her child without pleasure. But she typically does not talk about the pain or discomfort.

She discovered that a new drug was being tested on her newborn child. She made a huge fuss, she recalls, then discharged herself from hospital and took Artyom home out of reach of the experimenters.

Her Caucasian blood, she says, taught her to treat a man 'as a wall I can lean on', but Soviet men have been a disappointment and she says she does not intend to marry again. 'I had to change a lot, to fight for my son, and I became independent. I found such strength that I can't submit to anyone.' Her hopes of fulfilment, she says, now lie in a quite different direction: business.

She is trying to make the Policewomen's Association pay its way and has been experimenting with ways of making money. She is confident she can already tell a real businessman from a phoney.

One idea she has is to get women prisoners at a gaol in Mozhaisk, a small, pretty town west of Moscow, to turn out good quality fashion clothes. She wants to provide them with modern sewing machines and is looking for Western partners to help with investment and sales outlets. Profits would be shared between the Association, the Western partners and the prison inmates.

The idea grew out of the need to improve conditions for women who work for nothing and are treated 'like slaves'. Policewomen work as warders in a place where the atmosphere is 'so bad that people are turned into hardened criminals.'

In the autumn of 1992, I ask Natasha how many policewomen there are in Russia. The answer comes back: 69,409 out of the total strength of the Russian Ministry of the Interior which she gives as a staggering 7,065,668. Can that figure possibly be accurate? Natasha explains that it includes 'interior troops', the special forces used to deal with inter-ethnic violence, and everyone else working for the Ministry.

The Soviet Union, one must remember, was a heavily

policed state, and police in Russia still do a wide range of jobs which their Western counterparts do not have to cope with. They are responsible for managing the system of internal passports and registered accommodation, they issue car plates and inspect motor vehicles and they staff the prisons. Western policemen have a difficult time coming up with reliable figures with which to compare Russian forces with those in the West.

One recent visitor tells me that he helped to count the Moscow police and arrived at the figure of 120,000 men and women. If police are as thick on the ground in the rest of Russia as they are in the capital, then their total is of the order of two million. The London Metropolitan police force, by comparison, is only 28,000 strong and the numbers for the whole of England and Wales are 110,136 men and 15,257 women, 125,395 in all. Women account for just over twelve per cent of the total. In Russia, the percentage is between one and 3.5, depending on which figure one accepts for the national total.

Natasha's personal experience promises to lead her away from police work, if market economics take root in Russia. She is becoming an entrepreneur in the hope of improving conditions in prisons both for the women inmates and for the members of her association, who are the warders.

'If I succeed with one project,' she says, 'I'll go on in the same way. I find business thrilling.'

# Chronology

The new calendar is used, which puts dates thirteen days ahead of the old. For instance, the October Revolution 1917, when the Bolsheviks seized power, took place on 25 October: 7 November, according to the new calendar.

| | |
|---|---|
| March 1881 | Reforming Tsar Alexander II assassinated in St Petersburg by members of People's Will Party, including Sofia Perovskaya, who is hanged. |
| November 1894 | Tsar Nicholas II succeeds Alexander III. He is crowned in Moscow, May 1896. |
| March 1898 | Founding Congress in Minsk of the Russian Social Democratic Labour Party, forerunner of the Communist Party. |
| July–August 1903 | Second Congress of RSDLP in Brussels and London. Party splits into Bolsheviks (Majority) and Mensheviks (Minority), with Lenin leading the Bolsheviks. |
| 1904–05 | Series of Russian defeats in war with Japan, culminating in destruction of Russian fleet at Tsushima. |
| 22 January 1905 | 'Bloody Sunday' in St Petersburg. Troops fire on crowds marching to the Winter Palace to present petition to Tsar Nicholas. |
| June 1905 | In Odessa, crew of the battleship Potemkin murder officers and join Revolution. |

| | |
|---|---|
| October–December 1905 | Workers' Soviet, in which Leon Trotsky plays leading role, formed by St Petersburg strikers. |
| December 1905 | Trotsky and other leaders of Soviet arrested. At Bolshevik conference in Finland, Lenin and Stalin meet for the first time. Stalin, then known as Koba, is an underground Bolshevik leader in the Caucasus. |
| April 1912 | Troops fire on strikers in Lena goldfields, Siberia. |
| August 1914 | Russia enters First World War against Germany and suffers heavy casualties. St Petersburg is renamed Petrograd. |
| 8 March 1917 (23 February) | International Women's Day. Petrograd women textile workers strike against food shortages. Strikes spread. |
| 12 March | Troops mutiny. |
| 15 March | Nicholas II abdicates. |
| 7 November (25 October) | Bolsheviks seize power in Petrograd and arrest all members of Provisional Government, except Prime Minister Alexander Kerensky, who escapes. |
| 8 November | New Government formed under Lenin: Council of People's Commissars. Feminist Alexandra Kollontai is Commissar for Social Welfare. |
| 20 December | Government decree founds the Cheka secret police, forerunner of the KGB. |
| 3 March 1918 | Russia accepts harsh German peace terms and signs Treaty of Brest-Litovsk. Russian empire loses 1.25 million square miles of territory. |
| 16 July | Ex-Tsar Nicholas and family murdered at Yekaterinburg. |
| 1918–21 | Civil War. Allies assist White forces, French in Black Sea area, British at Murmansk, the Baltic, Baku and Turkestan, Central Asia. Baltic States gain independence. Millions die of hunger on Volga and elsewhere. Lenin reintroduces market forces with New Economic Policy. |

| | |
|---|---|
| 13 January 1924 | First Constitution of USSR ratified by Congress of Soviets. Federation consists of Russia, Ukraine, Byelorussia, Azerbaijan, Armenia and Georgia. |
| 21 January 1924 | Lenin dies. The Stalinist era begins. |
| 1928–29 | Trotsky exiled to Kazakhstan, then deported from USSR. Stalin launches First Five-Year Plan, orders forced collectivisation and 'liquidation of kulaks [so-called rich peasants] as a class'. |
| 1930–33 | Many millions of peasants die in or en route to exile, in camps and in the man-made famines in the Ukraine and parts of Russia and Central Asia. |
| December 1934 | Sergei Kirov, Party boss in Leningrad, assassinated, probably on orders of Stalin, who uses killing as pretext for purge of Party, the 'Great Terror' of 1937–38. |
| March 1938 | Show trials in Moscow reach climax with the conviction and prompt execution of Nikolai Bukharin, the early Bolshevik used by Stalin to eliminate the Trotskyist Left. |
| August 1939 | Hitler–Stalin non-aggression pact signed, with secret protocols giving Kremlin free hand to occupy Baltic States, western Ukraine and part of Romania (incorporated into USSR as Republic of Moldavia). |
| 21 August 1940 | Trotsky assassinated in Mexico. |
| 22 June 1941 | German invasion of Soviet Union. |
| 9 May 1945 | Soviet Victory Day. The Great Patriotic War against Germany has cost the USSR an estimated 27 million dead. |
| 5 March 1953 | Stalin dies aged 73. |
| February 1956 | The new Party leader Nikita Khrushchov denounces Stalin's cult of personality and crimes in 'secret speech' to Twentieth Party Congress. |
| October 1964 | Khrushchov overthrown and replaced by Leonid Brezhnev, who remains in power till 1982. |

| | |
|---|---|
| 1982–85 | Yuri Andropov is head of Party for sixteen months, succeeded by Konstantin Chernenko for thirteen months. |
| 11 March 1985 | Mikhail Gorbachov elected Party leader. |
| 26 April 1986 | Fire at Chernobyl nuclear power station in Ukraine. |
| December | Human rights campaigner Andrei Sakharov released from exile. |
| March 1989 | Partially contested elections to new Parliament. Boris Yeltsin wins Moscow seat by landslide. |
| 9 April | Troops kill twenty-one demonstrators (sixteen of them women) in Tbilisi, Georgia. |
| July | Soviet miners strike. |
| December | Sakharov dies. |
| January 1990 | Tanks crush nationalists in Baku, Azerbaijan. |
| March | Lithuania declares independence. |
| 1 May | Gorbachov booed at May Day parade in Red Square. |
| May | Panic-buying sweeps USSR in advance of planned price reform. |
| July | Yeltsin quits Communist Party. |
| December 1990 | Foreign Minister Eduard Shevarnadze resigns; warns of impending dictatorship. |
| 13 January 1991 | Soviet troops kill 13 Lithuanians in assault on Vilnius television tower. |
| 20 January | Massive demonstration in Moscow against Vilnius killings. |
| 12 June | Boris Yeltsin directly elected President of Russia. |
| 18–21 August | Coup against Gorbachov fails. Conservative coup leaders arrested. One, Boris Pugo, the Interior Minister, commits suicide. |
| 24 August | Gorbachov resigns as Party boss; urges Party to dissolve itself. Remains USSR President. Ukraine is among the Soviet republics declaring independence. |
| 7 December | Leaders of Russia, Ukraine and Belarus, formerly Byelorussia, meet near Minsk and declare that USSR has ceased to exist. |

| | |
|---|---|
| 21 December | Eleven former Soviet republics sign agreement setting up Commonwealth of Independent States. |
| 25 December | On television Gorbachov announces resignation as President. Red Flag ceases to fly over Kremlin. |
| 2 January 1992 | Russia frees most prices, which rapidly rise. For most Russians 1992 is a year of hardship: rapidly rising prices, growing unemployment, falling production. By December, inflation is running at about 25 per cent a month. Over the year, retail prices increase by 2,000 per cent and wages by 1,200 per cent. The rouble falls to 420 to the US dollar. It is also a year of political and constitutional confusion, as Yeltsin's personal popularity wanes, and opposition to him grows. The political crisis reaches a climax at the end of the year. |
| 1 December | The upper Parliament, the 1,040-strong Congress of People's Deputies, elected in March 1990, meets in Moscow despite Yeltsin's attempts to delay the session till the spring of 1993. The speaker of the Parliament, Ruslan Khasbulatov, once a close Yeltsin supporter, is now a leading opponent. |
| 10 December | Yeltsin calls for a referendum to decide whether Congress or Parliament will rule Russia. Vice-President Alexander Rutskoi opposes the move and becomes more obviously a potential rival for the presidency. |
| 14 December | Yeltsin, having, for the moment, dropped the referendum idea, also loses his reformist acting Prime Minister, Yegor Gaidar. Congress elects Viktor Chernomyrdin, a conservative former apparatchik, as the new premier. He promises continued reforms, but with closer attention to the 'social factor', i.e. living standards. |

| | |
|---|---|
| 17 December | Gaidar rejoins the presidential team as Yeltsin's economic adviser. |
| 19 December | Yeltsin cuts short a visit to China stating that 'the master must return to restore order' in Moscow. |
| 23 December | Key reformers are reappointed to the new cabinet under Chernomyrdin, but Yeltsin faces a continuous struggle to keep them there. |
| 3 January 1993 | Yeltsin and George Bush sign a new arms control treaty, Start 2, under which US and Russian nuclear arsenals will be cut by a third by the year 2003. But Russians, preoccupied by daily battle to make ends meet, show little immediate interest in what Yeltsin calls 'the treaty of hope'. |
| February | The rouble falls in value to R.600 to the dollar. |

# Select bibliography

Alliluyeva, Svetlana, *20 Letters To A Friend*, Hutchinson 1967.
Atkinson, Dorothy; Dallin, Alexander; Lapidus, Gail
  Warshofsky, *Women in Russia*, Stanford University Press
  1977.
Bourdeaux, Michael, *Gorbachov, Glasnost & The Gospel*, Hodder
  & Stoughton 1990.
Bourdeaux, Michael, *Risen Indeed, Lessons in Faith from the USSR*,
  Darton, Longman and Todd 1983.
Browning, Genia K., *Women & Politics in the USSR*, Wheatsheaf
  Books 1987.
Clark, Ronald W., *Lenin*, Faber 1989.
Conquest, Robert, *The Great Terror, A Reassessment*, Pimlico 1992.
Conquest, Robert, *The Harvest of Sorrow*, Arrow 1988.
Crankshaw, Edward, *Putting Up With the Russians*, Macmillan
  1984.
Crawshaw, Steve, *Goodbye to the USSR*, Bloomsbury 1992.
Custine, Marquis de, *Journey For Our Time, Russia – 1839*, George
  Prior 1980.
Daniels, Robert V., *A Documentary History of Communism*, I.B.
  Tauris 1987.
Deutscher, Isaac, *Stalin*, Penguin 1986.
Eck, Ludo van, *In Search of Holy Mother Russia*, Progress 1988.
Ellis, Jane, *The Russian Orthodox Church, A Contemporary History*,
  Croom Helm 1986.
Feshbach, Murray and Friendly, Alfred, *Ecocide in the USSR*,
  Basic Books 1992.
Fishlock, Trevor, *Out of Red Darkness*, J. Murray 1992.

Fletcher, Giles, *Of the Russe Commonwealth 1591*, facsimile edition edited by Richard Pipes and John Pine, Cambridge 1966.

Frankland, Mark, *The Sixth Continent*, Hamish Hamilton 1987.

Gorbachov, Mikhail, *Perestroika*, Fontana 1988.

Gorbachov, Raisa, *I Hope*, HarperCollins 1991.

Gray, Francine du Plessix, *Soviet Women*, Doubleday 1990.

Grossman, Vasily, *Forever Flowing*, Collins Harvill 1988.

Heitlinger, Alena, *Women and State Socialism*, Macmillan 1979.

Hill, Ronald J.; Frank, Peter, *The Soviet Communist Party*, Allen & Unwin 1986.

Hosking, Geoffrey, *The Awakening of the Soviet Union*, Heinemann 1990.

*Khrushchov Remembers*, Little, Brown 1970.

Leggett, George, *The Cheka, Lenin's Political Police*, Clarendon Press 1986.

Lewin, Moshe, *The Gorbachov Phenomenon*, Radius 1988.

Maclean, Fitzroy, *Portrait of the Soviet Union*, Weidenfeld and Nicolson 1988.

Maclean, Fitzroy, *Eastern Approaches*, Papermac 1982.

Moss, Vladimir, *The Imperishable Word, True Orthodox Christianity in the Twentieth Century*, Gresham Books, Unwin Brothers 1980.

McCauley, Martin, *Gorbachov and Perestroika*, Macmillan 1990.

O'Clery, Conor, *Melting Snow*, Appletree Press 1991.

Parker, Tony, *Russian Voices*, Cape 1991.

Porter, Cathy, *Fathers & Daughters, Russian Women in Revolution*, Virago 1976.

Porter, Cathy, *Women in Revolutionary Russia*, Cambridge University Press 1987.

Ratushinskaya, Irina, *Grey is the Colour of Hope*, Hodder and Stoughton 1988.

Reed, John, *Ten Days That Shook The World*, Penguin 1988.

Richards, Susan, *Epics of Everyday Life*, Penguin 1991.

Roxburgh, Angus, *The Second Russian Revolution*, BBC 1991.

Schapiro, Leonard, *The Communist Party of the Soviet Union*, Methuen 1970.

Solzhenitsyn, Alexander, *The Gulag Archipelago 1918–1956*, Fontana 1982.

Smith, Hedrick, *The Russians*, Sphere 1976.

Smith, Hedrick, *The New Russians*, Vintage 1991.

Stern, Dr Mikhail & Dr August, *Sex in the Soviet Union*, W.H. Allen 1981.

Szamuely, Tibor, *The Russian Tradition*, Fontana 1988.

Teague-Jones, Reginald, *The Spy Who Disappeared*, Victor Gollancz 1990.

Voznesenskaya, Julia, *The Women's Decameron*, Mandarin Paperbacks 1990.

Walker, Martin, *The Waking Giant*, Sphere 1987.

Wilson, Andrew and Bachkatov, Nina, *Living With Glasnost*, Penguin 1988.

Yeltsin, Boris, *Against the Grain*, Jonathan Cape 1990.